Sidney M. Moon
EDITOR

SOCIAL/EMOTIONAL ISSUES, UNDERACHIEVEMENT, AND COUNSELING OF GIFTED AND TALENTED STUDENTS

A Joint Publication of Corwin Press and the National Association for Gifted Children

ESSENTIAL READINGS IN GIFTED EDUCATION
Sally M. Reis, SERIES EDITOR

CORWIN PRESS
A Sage Publications Company
Thousand Oaks, California

For information:

Corwin Press
A Sage Publications Company
2455 Teller Road
Thousand Oaks, California 91320
www.corwinpress.com

Sage Publications Ltd
1 Oliver's Yard
55 City Road
London EC1Y 1SP
United Kingdom

Sage Publications India Pvt. Ltd.
B-42, Panchsheel Enclave
Post Box 4109
New Delhi 110 017 India

Printed in the United States of America

Library of Congress Cataloging-in-Publication Data

Social/emotional issues, underachievement, and counseling of gifted and talented students/ Sidney M. Moon, editor.
        p. cm.—(Essential readings in gifted education; 8)
"A joint publication of Corwin Press and the National Association for Gifted Children."
Includes bibliographical references and index.
ISBN 1-4129-0433-1 (pbk.)
    1. Gifted children—Education—United States. 2. Gifted children—Counseling of—United States. 3. Underachievement—United States. I. Moon, Sidney M. II. National Association for Gifted Children (U.S.) III. Series.
LC3993.9.S63 2004
371.95—dc22

                                    2004001207

This book is printed on acid-free paper.

                07   08   10   9   8   7   6   5   4   3   2

Acquisitions Editor:	Kylee Liegl
Editorial Assistant:	Jaime Cuvier
Production Editor:	Sanford Robinson
Typesetter:	C&M Digitals (P) Ltd.
Cover Designer:	Tracy E. Miller
NAGC Publications Coordinator:	Jane Clarenbach

Social/Emotional Issues, Underachievement, and Counseling of Gifted and Talented Students

ESSENTIAL READINGS IN GIFTED EDUCATION

SERIES EDITOR

SALLY M. REIS

Contents

About the Editors

Sally M. Reis is a professor and the department head of the Educational Psychology Department at the University of Connecticut where she also serves as principal investigator of the National Research Center on the Gifted and Talented. She was a teacher for 15 years, 11 of which were spent working with gifted students on the elementary, junior high, and high school levels. She has authored more than 130 articles, 9 books, 40 book chapters, and numerous monographs and technical reports.

Her research interests are related to special populations of gifted and talented students, including: students with learning disabilities, gifted females and diverse groups of talented students. She is also interested in extensions of the Schoolwide Enrichment Model for both gifted and talented students and as a way to expand offerings and provide general enrichment to identify talents and potentials in students who have not been previously identified as gifted.

She has traveled extensively conducting workshops and providing professional development for school districts on gifted education, enrichment programs, and talent development programs. She is co-author of *The Schoolwide Enrichment Model*, *The Secondary Triad Model*, *Dilemmas in Talent Development in the Middle Years*, and a book published in 1998 about women's talent development titled *Work Left Undone: Choices and Compromises of Talented Females*. Sally serves on several editorial boards, including the *Gifted Child Quarterly*, and is a past president of the National Association for Gifted Children.

Sidney M. Moon is a professor of Gifted Education and director of the Gifted Education Resource Institute at Purdue University. She has been active in the field of gifted education for more than 25 years as a parent, counselor, teacher, administrator, and researcher. In that time, she has contributed more than 60 books, articles, and chapters to the field. Her most recent book is a co-edited volume, *The Social and Emotional Development of Gifted Children: What Do We*

Know? Sidney is active in the National Association for Gifted Children where she currently serves on the board of directors, the publications committee, and the affective curriculum task force. Her research interests include talent development in the STEM disciplines (science, technology, engineering, and mathematics) and personal talent development.

Series Introduction

Sally M. Reis

The accomplishments of the last 50 years in the education of gifted students should not be underestimated: the field of education of the gifted and talented has emerged as strong and visible. In many states, a policy or position statement from the state board of education supports the education of the gifted and talented, and specific legislation generally recognizes the special needs of this group. Growth in our field has not been constant, however, and researchers and scholars have discussed the various high and low points of national interest and commitment to educating the gifted and talented (Gallagher, 1979; Renzulli, 1980; Tannenbaum, 1983). Gallagher described the struggle between support and apathy for special programs for gifted and talented students as having roots in historical tradition—the battle between an aristocratic elite and our concomitant belief in egalitarianism. Tannenbaum suggested the existence of two peak periods of interest in the gifted as the five years following *Sputnik* in 1957 and the last half of the decade of the 1970s, describing a valley of neglect between the peaks in which the public focused its attention on the disadvantaged and the handicapped. "The cyclical nature of interest in the gifted is probably unique in American education. No other special group of children has been alternately embraced and repelled with so much vigor by educators and laypersons alike" (Tannenbaum, 1983, p. 16). Many wonder if the cyclical nature to which Tannenbaum referred is not somewhat prophetic, as it appears that our field may be experiencing another downward spiral in interest as a result of current governmental initiatives and an increasing emphasis on testing and standardization of curriculum. Tannenbaum's description of a valley of neglect may describe current conditions. During the late 1980s, programming flourished during a peak of interest and a textbook on systems and models for gifted programs included 15 models for elementary and secondary programs (Renzulli, 1986). The Jacob Javits Gifted and Talented Students Education Act passed by Congress in 1988 resulted in the creation of the National Research Center on the Gifted and Talented, and dozens of model programs were added to the collective knowledge in the field in areas related to underrepresented populations and successful practices. In the 1990s, reduction or elimination of gifted programs occurred, as budget pressures exacerbated by the lingering recession in the late 1990s resulted in the reduction of services mandated by fewer than half of the states in our country.

Even during times in which more activity focused on the needs of gifted and talented students, concerns were still raised about the limited services provided to these students. In the second federal report on the status of education for our nation's most talented students entitled *National Excellence: A Case for Developing America's Talent* (Ross, 1993), "a quiet crisis" was described in the absence of attention paid to this population: "Despite sporadic attention over the years to the needs of bright students, most of them continue to spend time in school working well below their capabilities. The belief espoused in school reform that children from all economic and cultural backgrounds must reach their full potential has not been extended to America's most talented students. They are under-challenged and therefore underachieve" (p. 5). The report further indicates that our nation's gifted and talented students have a less rigorous curriculum, read fewer demanding books, and are less prepared for work or postsecondary education than the most talented students in many other industrialized countries. Talented children who come from economically disadvantaged homes or are members of minority groups are especially neglected, the report also indicates, and many of them will not realize their potential without some type of intervention.

In this anniversary series of volumes celebrating the evolution of our field, noted scholars introduce a collection of the most frequently cited articles from the premiere journal in our field, *Gifted Child Quarterly*. Each volume includes a collection of thoughtful, and in some cases, provocative articles that honor our past, acknowledge the challenges we face in the present, and provide hopeful guidance for the future as we seek the optimal educational experiences for all talented students. These influential articles, published after a rigorous peer review, were selected because they are frequently cited and considered seminal in our field. Considered in their entirety, the articles show that we have learned a great deal from the volume of work represented by this series. Our knowledge has expanded over several decades of work, and progress has been made toward reaching consensus about what is known. As several of the noted scholars who introduce separate areas explain in their introductions, this series helps us to understand that some questions have been answered, while others remain. While we still search for these answers, we are now better prepared to ask questions that continue and evolve. The seminal articles in this series help us to resolve some issues, while they highlight other questions that simply refuse to go away. Finally, the articles help us to identify new challenges that continue to emerge in our field. Carol Tomlinson suggests, for example, that the area of curriculum differentiation in the field of gifted education is, in her words, an issue born in the field of gifted education, and one that continues to experience rebirth.

Some of the earliest questions in our field have been answered and time has enabled those answers to be considered part of our common core of knowledge. For example, it is widely acknowledged that both school and home experiences can help to develop giftedness in persons with high potential and that a continuum of services in and out of school can provide the greatest likelihood that this development will occur. Debates over other "hot" issues such as grouping and acceleration that took place in the gifted education community 30 years ago are now largely unnecessary, as Linda Brody points out in her introduction to a series of articles in this area. General agreement seems to have been reached, for example, that grouping, enrichment and acceleration are all necessary to provide appropriate educational opportunities for gifted and talented learners. These healthy debates of the past helped to strengthen our field but visionary and reflective work remains to be done. In this series, section editors summarize what has been learned and raise provocative questions about the future. The questions alone are some of the most thoughtful in our field, providing enough research opportunities for scholars for the next decade. The brief introductions below provide some highlights about the series.

DEFINITIONS OF GIFTEDNESS (VOLUME 1)

In Volume 1, Robert Sternberg introduces us to seminal articles about definitions of giftedness and the types of talents and gifts exhibited by children and youth. The most widely used definitions of gifts and talents utilized by educators generally follow those proposed in federal reports. For example, the Marland Report (Marland, 1972) commissioned by the Congress included the first federal definition of giftedness, which was widely adopted or adapted by the states.

The selection of a definition of giftedness has been and continues to be the major policy decision made at state and local levels. It is interesting to note that policy decisions are often either unrelated or marginally related to actual procedures or to research findings about a definition of giftedness or identification of the gifted, a fact well documented by the many ineffective, incorrect, and downright ridiculous methods of identification used to find students who meet the criteria in the federal definition. This gap between policy and practice may be caused by many variables. Unfortunately, although the federal definition was written to be inclusive, it is, instead, rather vague, and problems caused by this definition have been recognized by experts in the field (Renzulli, 1978). In the most recent federal report on the status of gifted and talented programs entitled *National Excellence* (Ross, 1993), a newer federal definition is proposed based on new insights provided by neuroscience and cognitive psychology. Arguing that the term *gifted* connotes a mature power rather than a developing ability and, therefore, is antithetic to recent research findings about children, the new definition "reflects today's knowledge and thinking" (p. 26) by emphasizing talent development, stating that gifted and talented children are children and youth with outstanding talent performance or show the potential for performing at remarkably high levels of accomplishment when compared with others of their age, experience, or environment. These children and youth exhibit high performance capability in intellectual, creative, and/or artistic areas, possess an unusual leadership capacity, or excel in specific academic fields. They require services or activities not ordinarily provided by the schools. Outstanding talents are present in children and youth from all cultural groups, across all economic strata, and in all areas of human endeavor. (p. 26)

Fair identification systems use a variety of multiple assessment measures that respect diversity, accommodate students who develop at different rates, and identify potential as well as demonstrated talent. In the introduction to the volume, Sternberg admits, that just as people have bad habits, so do academic fields, explaining, "a bad habit of much of the gifted field is to do research on giftedness, or worse, identify children as gifted or not gifted, without having a clear conception of what it means to be gifted." Sternberg summarizes major themes from the seminal articles about definitions by asking key questions about the nature of giftedness and talent, the ways in which we should study giftedness, whether we should expand conventional notions of giftedness, and if so, how that can be accomplished; whether differences exist between giftedness and talent; the validity of available assessments; and perhaps most importantly, how do we and can we develop giftedness and talent. Sternberg succinctly summarizes points of broad agreement from the many scholars who have contributed to this section, concluding that giftedness involves more than just high IQ, that it has noncognitive and cognitive components, that the environment is crucial in terms of whether potentials for gifted performance will be realized, and that giftedness is not a single thing. He further cautions that the ways we conceptualize giftedness greatly influences who will have opportunities to develop their gifts and reminds readers of our responsibilities as educators. He also asks one of the most critical questions in our field: whether gifted and talented individuals will use their knowledge to benefit or harm our world.

IDENTIFICATION OF HIGH-ABILITY STUDENTS (VOLUME 2)

In Volume 2, Joseph Renzulli introduces what is perhaps the most critical question still facing practitioners and researchers in our field, that is how, when, and why should we identify gifted and talented students. Renzulli believes that conceptions of giftedness exist along a continuum ranging from a very conservative or restricted view of giftedness to a more flexible or multi-dimensional approach. What many seem not to understand is that the first step in identification should always be to ask: identification for what? For what type of program or experience is the youngster being identified? If, for example, an arts program is being developed for talented artists, the resulting identification system must be structured to identify youngsters with either demonstrated or potential talent in art.

Renzulli's introductory chapter summarizes seminal articles about identification, and summarizes emerging consensus. For example, most suggest, that while intelligence tests and other cognitive ability tests provide one very important form of information about one dimension of a young person's potential, mainly in the areas of verbal and analytic skills, they do not tell us all that we need to know about who should be identified. These authors do not argue that cognitive ability tests should be dropped from the identification process. Rather, most believe that (a) other indicators of potential should be used for identification, (b) these indicators should be given equal consideration when it comes to making final decisions about which students will be candidates for special services, and (c) in the final analysis, it is the thoughtful judgment of knowledgeable professionals rather than instruments and cutoff scores that should guide selection decisions.

Another issue addressed by the authors of the seminal articles about identification is what has been referred to as the distinction between (a) convergent and divergent thinking (Guilford, 1967; Torrance, 1984), (b) entrenchment and non-entrenchment (Sternberg, 1982), and (c) schoolhouse giftedness versus creative/productive giftedness (Renzulli, 1982; Renzulli & Delcourt, 1986). It is easier to identify schoolhouse giftedness than it is to identify students with the potential for creative productive giftedness. Renzulli believes that progress has been made in the identification of gifted students, especially during the past quarter century, and that new approaches address the equity issue, policies, and practices that respect new theories about human potential and conceptions of giftedness. He also believes, however, that continuous commitment to research-based identification practices is still needed, for "it is important to keep in mind that some of the characteristics that have led to the recognition of history's most gifted contributors are not always as measurable as others. We need to continue our search for those elusive things that are left over after everything explainable has been explained, to realize that giftedness is culturally and contextually imbedded in all human activity, and most of all, to value the value of even those things that we cannot yet explain."

ACCELERATION AND GROUPING, CURRICULUM, AND CURRICULUM DIFFERENTIATION (VOLUMES 3, 4, 5)

Three volumes in this series address curricular and grouping issues in gifted programs, and it is in this area, perhaps, that some of the most promising practices have been implemented for gifted and talented students. Grouping and curriculum interact with each other, as various forms of grouping patterns have enabled students to work on advanced curricular opportunities with other talented students. And, as is commonly known now about instructional and ability grouping, it is not the way students are grouped that matters most, but rather, it is what happens within the groups that makes the most difference.

In too many school settings, little differentiation of curriculum and instruction for gifted students is provided during the school day, and minimal opportunities are offered. Occasionally, after-school enrichment programs or Saturday programs offered by museums, science centers, or local universities take the place of comprehensive school programs, and too many academically talented students attend school in classrooms across the country in which they are bored, unmotivated, and unchallenged. Acceleration, once a frequently used educational practice in our country, is often dismissed by teachers and administrators as an inappropriate practice for a variety of reasons, including scheduling problems, concerns about the social effects of grade skipping, and others. Various forms of acceleration, including enabling precocious students to enter kindergarten or first grade early, grade skipping, and early entrance to college are not commonly used by most school districts.

Unfortunately, major alternative grouping strategies involve the reorganization of school structures, and these have been too slow in coming, perhaps due to the difficulty of making major educational changes, because of scheduling, finances, and other issues that have caused schools to substantially delay major change patterns. Because of this delay, gifted students too often fail to receive classroom instruction based on their unique needs that place them far ahead of their chronological peers in basic skills and verbal abilities and enable them to learn much more rapidly and tackle much more complex materials than their peers. Our most able students need appropriately paced, rich and challenging instruction, and curriculum that varies significantly from what is being taught in regular classrooms across America. Too often, academically talented students are "left behind" in school.

Linda Brody introduces the question of how to group students optimally for instructional purposes and pays particular concern to the degree to which the typical age-in-grade instructional program can meet the needs of gifted students—those students with advanced cognitive abilities and achievement that may already have mastered the curriculum designed for their age peers. The articles about grouping emphasize the importance of responding to the learning needs of individual students with curricular flexibility, the need for educators to be flexible when assigning students to instructional groups, and the need to modify those groups when necessary. Brody's introduction points out that the debate about grouping gifted and talented learners together was one area that brought the field together, as every researcher in the field supports some type of grouping option, and few would disagree with the need to use grouping and accelerated learning as tools that allow us to differentiate content for students with different learning needs. When utilized as a way to offer a more advanced educational program to students with advanced cognitive abilities and achievement levels, these practices can help achieve the goal of an appropriate education for all students.

Joyce VanTassel-Baska introduces the seminal articles in curriculum, by explaining that they represent several big ideas that emphasize the values and relevant factors of a curriculum for the gifted, the technology of curriculum development, aspects of differentiation of a curriculum for the gifted within core subject areas and without, and the research-based efficacy of such curriculum and related instructional pedagogy in use. She also reminds readers of Harry Passow's concerns about curriculum balance, suggesting that an imbalance exists, as little evidence suggests that the affective development of gifted students is occurring through special curricula for the gifted. Moreover, interdisciplinary efforts at curriculum frequently exclude the arts and foreign language. Only through acknowledging and applying curriculum balance in these areas are we likely to be producing the type of humane individual Passow envisioned. To achieve balance, VanTassel-Baska recommends a full set of curriculum options across domains, as well as the need to nurture the social-emotional needs of diverse gifted and talented learners.

Carol Tomlinson introduces the critical area of differentiation in the field of gifted education that has only emerged in the last 13 years. She believes the diverse nature of the articles and their relatively recent publication suggests that this area is indeed, in her words, "an issue born in the field of gifted education, and one that continues to experience rebirth." She suggests that one helpful way of thinking about the articles in this volume is that their approach varies, as some approach the topic of differentiation of curriculum with a greater emphasis on the distinctive mission of gifted education. Others look at differentiation with a greater emphasis on the goals, issues, and missions shared between general education and gifted education. Drawing from an analogy with anthropology, Tomlinson suggests that "splitters" in that field focus on differences among cultures while "lumpers" have a greater interest in what cultures share in common. Splitters ask the question of what happens for high-ability students in mixed-ability settings, while lumpers question what common issues and solutions exist for multiple populations in mixed-ability settings.

Tomlinson suggests that the most compelling feature of the collection of articles in this section—and certainly its key unifying feature—is the linkage between the two areas of educational practice in attempting to address an issue likely to be seminal to the success of both over the coming quarter century and beyond, and this collection may serve as a catalyst for next steps in those directions for the field of gifted education as it continues collaboration with general education and other educational specialties while simultaneously addressing those missions uniquely its own.

UNDERREPRESENTED AND TWICE-EXCEPTIONAL POPULATIONS AND SOCIAL AND EMOTIONAL ISSUES (VOLUMES 6, 7, 8)

The majority of young people participating in gifted and talented programs across the country continue to represent the majority culture in our society. Few doubts exist regarding the reasons that economically disadvantaged, twice-exceptional, and culturally diverse students are underrepresented in gifted programs. One reason may be the ineffective and inappropriate identification and selection procedures used for the identification of these young people that limits referrals and nominations and eventual placement. Research summarized in this series indicates that groups that have been traditionally underrepresented in gifted programs could be better served if some of the following elements are considered: new constructs of giftedness, attention to cultural and contextual variability, the use of more varied and authentic assessments, performance-based identification, and identification opportunities through rich and varied learning opportunities.

Alexinia Baldwin discusses the lower participation of culturally diverse and underserved populations in programs for the gifted as a major concern that has forged dialogues and discussion in *Gifted Child Quarterly* over the past five decades. She classifies these concerns in three major themes: *identification/selection, programming,* and *staff assignment and development.* Calling the first theme **Identification/Selection**, she indicates that it has always been the Achilles' heel of educators' efforts to ensure that giftedness can be expressed in many ways through broad identification techniques. Citing favorable early work by Renzulli and Hartman (1971) and Baldwin (1977) that expanded options for identification, Baldwin cautions that much remains to be done. The second theme, **Programming**, recognizes the abilities of students who are culturally diverse but often forces them to exist in programs designed "for one size fits all." Her third theme relates to **Staffing and Research,** as she voices concerns about the diversity of teachers in these programs as well as the attitudes or mindsets of researchers who develop theories and conduct the research that addresses these concerns.

Susan Baum traces the historical roots of gifted and talented individuals with special needs, summarizing Terman's early work that suggested the gifted were healthier, more popular, and better adjusted than their less able peers. More importantly, gifted individuals were regarded as those who could perform at high levels in all areas with little or no support. Baum suggests that acceptance of these stereotypical characteristics diminished the possibility that there could be special populations of gifted students with special needs. Baum believes that the seminal articles in this collection address one or more of the critical issues that face gifted students at risk and suggest strategies for overcoming the barriers that prevent them from realizing their promise. The articles focus on three populations of students: twice-exceptional students—gifted students who are at risk for poor development due to difficulties in learning and attention;

gifted students who face gender issues that inhibit their ability to achieve or develop socially and emotionally, and students who are economically disadvantaged and at risk for dropping out of school. Baum summarizes research indicating that each of these groups of youngsters is affected by one or more barriers to development, and the most poignant of these barriers are identification strategies, lack of awareness of consequences of co-morbidity, deficit thinking in program design, and lack of appropriate social and emotional support. She ends her introduction with a series of thoughtful questions focusing on future directions in this critical area.

Sidney Moon introduces the seminal articles on the social and emotional development of and counseling for gifted children by acknowledging the contributions of the National Association for Gifted Children's task forces that have examined social/emotional issues. The first task force, formed in 2000 and called the Social and Emotional Issues Task Force, completed its work in 2002 by publishing an edited book, *The Social and Emotional Development of Gifted Children: What Do We Know?* This volume provides an extensive review of the literature on the social and emotional development of gifted children (Neihart, Reis, Robinson, & Moon, 2002). Moon believes that the seminal studies in the area of the social and emotional development and counseling illustrate both the strengths and the weaknesses of the current literature on social and emotional issues in the field of gifted education. These articles bring increased attention to the affective needs of special populations of gifted students, such as underachievers, who are at risk for failure to achieve their potential, but also point to the need for more empirical studies on "what works" with these students, both in terms of preventative strategies and more intensive interventions. She acknowledges that although good counseling models have been developed, they need to be rigorously evaluated to determine their effectiveness under disparate conditions, and calls for additional research on the affective and counseling interventions with specific subtypes of gifted students such as Asian Americans, African Americans, and twice-exceptional students. Moon also strongly encourages researchers in the field of gifted education to collaborate with researchers from affective fields such as personal and social psychology, counseling psychology, family therapy, and psychiatry to learn to intervene most effectively with gifted individuals with problems and to learn better how to help all gifted persons achieve optimal social, emotional, and personal development.

ARTISTICALLY AND CREATIVELY TALENTED STUDENTS (VOLUMES 9, 10)

Enid Zimmerman introduces the volume on talent development in the visual and performing arts with a summary of articles about students who are talented in music, dance, visual arts, and spatial, kinesthetic, and expressive areas. Major themes that appear in the articles include perceptions by parents, students, and teachers that often focus on concerns related to nature versus nurture in arts talent development; research about the crystallizing experiences of artistically talented students; collaboration between school and community members about identification of talented art students from diverse backgrounds; and leadership issues related to empowering teachers of talented arts students. They all are concerned to some extent with teacher, parent, and student views about educating artistically talented students. Included also are discussions about identification of talented students from urban, suburban, and rural environments. Zimmerman believes that in this particular area, a critical need exists for research about the impact of educational opportunities, educational settings, and the role of art teachers on the development of artistically talented students. The impact of the standards and testing movement and its relationship to the education of talented students in the visual and performing arts is an area greatly in need of investigation. Research also is needed about students' backgrounds, personalities, gender orientations, skill development, and cognitive and affective abilities as well as cross-cultural contexts and the impact of global and popular culture on the education of artistically talented students. The compelling case study with which she introduces this volume sets the stage for the need for this research.

Donald Treffinger introduces reflections on articles about creativity by discussing the following five core themes that express the collective efforts of researchers to grasp common conceptual and theoretical challenges associated with creativity. The themes include **Definitions** (how we define giftedness, talent, or creativity), **Characteristics** (the indicators of giftedness and creativity in people), **Justification** (Why is creativity important in education?), **Assessment** of creativity, and the ways we **Nurture** creativity. Treffinger also discusses the expansion of knowledge, the changes that have occurred, the search for answers, and the questions that still remain. In the early years of interest of creativity research, Treffinger believed that considerable discussion existed about whether it was possible to foster creativity through training or instruction. He reports that over the last 50 years, educators have learned that deliberate efforts to nurture creativity are possible (e.g., Torrance, 1987), and further extends this line of inquiry by asking the key question, "What works best, for whom, and under what conditions?" Treffinger summarizes the challenges faced by educators who try to nurture the development of creativity through effective teaching and to ask which experiences will have the greatest impact, as these will help to determine our ongoing lines of research, development, and training initiatives.

EVALUATION AND PUBLIC POLICY (VOLUMES 11, 12)

Carolyn Callahan introduces the seminal articles on evaluation and suggests that this important component neglected by experts in the field of gifted education for at least the last three decades can be a plea for important work by both evaluators and practitioners. She divides the seminal literature on evaluation, and in particular the literature on the evaluation of gifted programs into four categories, those which (a) provide theory and/or practical guidelines, (b) describe or report on specific program evaluations, (c) provide stimuli for the discussion of issues surrounding the evaluation process, and (d) suggest new research on the evaluation process. Callahan concludes with a challenge indicating work to be done and the opportunity for experts to make valuable contributions to increased effectiveness and efficiency of programs for the gifted.

James Gallagher provides a call-to-arms in the seminal articles he introduces on public policy by raising some of the most challenging questions in the field. Gallagher suggests that as a field, we need to come to some consensus about stronger interventions and consider how we react to accusations of elitism. He believes that our field could be doing a great deal more with additional targeted resources supporting the general education teacher and the development of specialists in gifted education, and summarizes that our failure to fight in the public arena for scarce resources may raise again the question posed two decades ago by Renzulli (1980), looking toward 1990: "Will the gifted child movement be alive and well in 2010?"

CONCLUSION

What can we learn from an examination of our field and the seminal articles that have emerged over the last few decades? First, we must **respect the past** by acknowledging the times in which articles were written and the shoulders of those persons upon whom we stand as we continue to create and develop our field. An old proverb tells us that when we drink from the well, we must remember to acknowledge those who dug the well, and in our field the early articles represent the seeds that grew our field. Next, we must **celebrate the present** and the exciting work and new directions in our field and the knowledge that is now accepted as a common core. Last, we must **embrace the future** by understanding that there is no finished product when it comes to research on gifted and talented children and how we are best able to meet their unique needs. Opportunities abound in the work reported in this series, but many questions remain. A few things seem clear. Action in the future should be based on both qualitative and quantitative research as well as longitudinal studies, and what we have completed only scratches the surface regarding the many variables and issues that still need to be explored. Research is needed that suggests positive changes that will lead to more inclusive programs that recognize the talents and gifts of diverse students in our country. When this occurs, future teachers and researchers in gifted education will find answers that can be embraced by educators, communities, and families, and the needs of all talented and gifted students will be more effectively met in their classrooms by teachers who have been trained to develop their students' gifts and talents.

We also need to consider carefully how we work with the field of education in general. As technology emerges and improves, new opportunities will become available to us. Soon, all students should be able to have their curricular needs preassessed before they begin any new curriculum unit. Soon, the issue of keeping students on grade-level material when they are many grades ahead should disappear as technology enables us to pinpoint students' strengths. Will chronological grades be eliminated? The choices we have when technology enables us to learn better what students already know presents exciting scenarios for the future, and it is imperative that we advocate carefully for multiple opportunities for these students, based on their strengths and interests, as well as a challenging core curriculum. Parents, educators, and professionals who care about these special populations need to become politically active to draw attention to the unique needs of these students, and researchers need to conduct the experimental studies that can prove the efficacy of providing talent development options as well as opportunities for healthy social and emotional growth.

For any field to continue to be vibrant and to grow, new voices must be heard, and new players sought. A great opportunity is available in our field; for as we continue to advocate for gifted and talented students, we can also play important roles in the changing educational reform movement. We can continue to work to achieve more challenging opportunities for all students while we fight to maintain gifted, talented, and enrichment programs. We can continue our advocacy for differentiation through acceleration, individual curriculum opportunities, and a continuum of advanced curriculum and personal support opportunities. The questions answered and those raised in this volume of seminal articles can help us to move forward as a field. We hope those who read the series will join us in this exciting journey.

REFERENCES

Baldwin, A.Y. (1977). Tests do underpredict: A case study. *Phi Delta Kappan, 58,* 620-621.

Gallagher, J. J. (1979). Issues in education for the gifted. In A. H. Passow (Ed.), *The gifted and the talented: Their education and development* (pp. 28-44). Chicago: University of Chicago Press.

Guilford, J. E. (1967). *The nature of human intelligence.* New York: McGraw-Hill.

Marland, S. P., Jr. (1972). *Education of the gifted and talented: Vol. 1. Report to the Congress of the United States by the U.S. Commissioner of Education.* Washington, DC: U.S. Government Printing Office.

Neihart, M., Reis, S., Robinson, N., & Moon, S. M. (Eds.). (2002). *The social and emotional development of gifted children: What do we know?* Waco, TX: Prufrock.

Renzulli, J. S. (1978). What makes giftedness? Reexamining a definition. *Phi Delta Kappan, 60*(5), 180-184.

Renzulli, J. S. (1980). Will the gifted child movement be alive and well in 1990? *Gifted Child Quarterly, 24*(1), 3-9. **[See Vol. 12.]**

Renzulli, J. (1982). Dear Mr. and Mrs. Copernicus: We regret to inform you . . . *Gifted Child Quarterly, 26*(1), 11-14. **[See Vol. 2.]**

Renzulli, J. S. (Ed.). (1986). *Systems and models for developing programs for the gifted and talented.* Mansfield Center, CT: Creative Learning Press.

Renzulli, J. S., & Delcourt, M. A. B. (1986). The legacy and logic of research on the identification of gifted persons. *Gifted Child Quarterly, 30*(1), 20-23. **[See Vol. 2.]**

Renzulli J., & Hartman, R. (1971). Scale for rating behavioral characteristics of superior students. *Exceptional Children, 38,* 243-248.

Ross, P. (1993). *National excellence: A case for developing America's talent.* Washington, DC: U.S. Department of Education, Government Printing Office.

Sternberg, R. J. (1982). Nonentrenchment in the assessment of intellectual giftedness. *Gifted Child Quarterly, 26*(2), 63-67. **[See Vol. 2.]**

Tannenbaum, A. J. (1983). *Gifted children: Psychological and educational perspectives.* New York: Macmillan.

Torrance, E. P. (1984). The role of creativity in identification of the gifted and talented. *Gifted Child Quarterly, 28*(4), 153-156. **[See Vols. 2 and 10.]**

Torrance, E. P. (1987). Recent trends in teaching children and adults to think creatively. In S. G. Isaksen (Ed.), *Frontiers of creativity research: Beyond the basics* (pp. 204-215). Buffalo, NY: Bearly Limited.

Social and Emotional Issues, Underachievement, and Counseling

Sidney M. Moon

Purdue University

T he National Association for Gifted Children has made the social and emotional development of gifted children a high priority for the twenty-first century by creating two task forces to examine social/emotional issues. The first task force was formed in 2000 and called the Social and Emotional Issues Task Force. It completed its work in 2002 by publishing an edited book, *The Social and Emotional Development of Gifted Children: What Do We Know?*, that provides an extensive review of the literature on the social and emotional development of gifted children (Neihart, Reis, Robinson, & Moon, 2002). In 2002, the Affective Curriculum Task Force was formed to develop a companion book which will provide a conceptual framework for creating educational curricula to promote positive affective development among gifted and talented children.

More is known about the social and emotional characteristics of gifted children than is known about methods of facilitating optimal affective development in such children. The sixteen seminal articles included here provide a sampling of work published in *Gifted Child Quarterly* on the social and emotional characteristics of gifted students, in general, and underachievers, in particular. They also provide an introduction to the clinical literature on counseling the gifted, although much of that literature has been published in journals outside the field. These sixteen seminal articles will be discussed in three groupings: social and emotional issues, underachievement, and counseling.

SOCIAL AND EMOTIONAL ISSUES

This volume includes nine empirical articles published in *Gifted Child Quarterly* on social and/or emotional characteristics of gifted students. The research designs utilized vary considerably. Seven of the studies are quantitative; two are qualitative. Five of the quantitative studies compare gifted students to average students on social/emotional variables. Only one of these included a mental age comparison group as well as an average chronological age comparison group, a recommended design for gifted education (Robinson, Zigler, & Gallagher, 2000). Several of the studies examined within-group differences among gifted students. Two of the studies explored affective differences students with different levels of giftedness (Baker, 1995; Sayler & Brookshire, 1993). Three studies investigated within-group differences among gifted students by creating subgroups of the gifted population on the basis of social/emotional variables like popularity (Cornell, 1990), loneliness (Kaiser & Berndt, 1985), or adjustment (Sowa & May, 1997).

Together these studies provide an illustrative sampling of the research on social and emotional issues among high ability youth. These articles are not exhaustive because many research studies on social and emotional issues have been published in journals outside the field of gifted education. Nonetheless, the nine articles in this volume represent seminal studies on the social and emotional issues experienced by high ability youth and illustrate both the strengths and the weaknesses of the current literature on social and emotional issues in the field of gifted education. Each of the nine studies is briefly described below in the context of the larger literature. The studies are discussed in two broad categories: quantitative comparison studies and descriptive and modeling studies. Then, directions for future research are suggested.

Quantitative Comparison Studies

Much of the empirical literature on social and emotional issues of gifted students uses causal comparative designs to compare characteristics of students who have been identified as gifted with one or more comparison groups. Sometimes the comparison groups are students who are achieving at average levels; at other times the comparison groups are subpopulations of gifted students. Some studies include both types of comparisons. Studies comparing subpopulations of gifted students have created groupings based on variables such as level of giftedness and psychological characteristics. The studies in this volume are good examples of the quantitative comparison literature.

Comparisons to Average Achievers. Early studies on social and emotional issues tended to focus on comparing the social and emotional characteristics of academically gifted students and students who were achieving or functioning at average levels. The oldest study in this collection of seminal studies was one of the first studies of this type to focus on young children (Lehman & Erdwins, 1981).

Lehman and Erdwins compared third-grade students enrolled in a gifted program in a suburban public school with children in the same school in grades three and six who had average IQ scores (range = 90-110), a gifted student versus chronological age comparison group vs. mental age comparison or CA-MA design. They found that gifted students exhibited excellent personal and social adjustment, especially with respect to their CA peers. With respect to their MA peers, gifted third graders were superior to the sixth graders on several personal and social variables (such as self-esteem, sense of personal freedom, family relations, lack of antisocial tendencies) and similar on others (such as self-direction, withdrawal tendencies, social standards, and social skills). The only area where the gifted students showed less positive adjustment than their MA peers was on nervous symptoms. These findings suggest that gifted children who are participating in gifted programs in suburban school districts have strong families and self-esteem and precocious social and self-direction skills.

Four other studies in this collection compared the adjustment of gifted students with that of average students and found that the gifted students exhibited similar or superior adjustment. One of these studies compared scores of gifted students ages 11-12 from the National Educational Longitudinal Study with those of average students on locus of control, self-concept, popularity, and behavior problems and found that the gifted students exhibited generally superior adjustment (Sayler & Brookshire, 1993). Another compared academically achieving high school students with students with an average class ranking and found no statistically significant differences in incidence of depression (Baker, 1995). A third study reported no statistically significant differences from norms in the scores of gifted adolescents on measures of depression, anger, and stress. The fourth, and most recent, study of this type compared the social competence of the top 3% of third grade students from a National Head Start project to the remaining students and found that the top students were perceived by both teachers and parents as superior in personal and social adjustment (Robinson, Lanzi, Weinberg, Ramey, & Ramey, 2002).

These four studies are consistent with the overall comparison literature in finding that gifted students generally exhibit similar or superior adjustment when compared to average-ability peers (Keiley, 1997; Neihart, 2002a, 2002b). Robinson and Lanzi, et al.'s (2002) study is one of the few that has examined investigated personal and social adjustment among high ability students from poverty backgrounds.

Comparisons of subtypes of gifted students. Four of the comparison studies examined differences among subgroups of gifted students. One study compared gifted eighth grade students who had been accelerated with gifted students who were in gifted classes and found no differences in their perceptions of social relationships, emotional development, or frequency of behavior problems (Sayler & Brookshire, 1993). Another compared highly gifted thirteen-year-olds (top 1% in scores on off-grade level SAT) with academically gifted high school students (top 5% of class rankings in suburban high schools) and found no differences in the incidence of depression (Baker, 1995). These studies are typical. Most studies comparing students with different levels or types of giftedness, have found no differences on mental health variables such as depression (Metha & McWhirter, 1997; Pearson & Beer, 1991) and behavior problems (Cornell, Delcourt, Bland, Goldberg, & Oram, 1994).

However, comparison studies have found differences among students with different levels and types of giftedness in the area of peer relationships and friendships (Dauber & Benbow, 1990; Swiatek, 1995). Highly intellectually gifted students and verbally gifted students appear to have more difficulty with peer relationships and fewer friends than more moderately or mathematically gifted students. In addition, highly gifted children have been found to have more mature conceptions of friendship than their chronological age peers (Gross, in press).

In contrast, subtype comparison research consistently finds group differences when gifted students are grouped by social and emotional variables. For example, gifted students differ in their ways of coping with the "stigma of giftedness" (Cross, Coleman, & Terhaar-Yonkers, 1991) and exhibit different emotional responses to self-contained programming (Moon, Swift, & Shallenberger, 2002).

The seminal studies in this volume illustrate some of the methods of studying individual differences among gifted students on social and emotional variables. One common methodology is to assess gifted students on a social or emotional variable and then create comparison groups based on these scores. This was done in the study of unpopular gifted students included in this volume (Cornell, 1990). First, gifted students were categorized as having high, average, or low popularity using combined peer nomination and peer rating scores. Then popular and unpopular groups were compared on self-reported personality variables such as self-concept, emotional autonomy, and anxiety, as well as on teacher ratings of academic self-esteem. The researchers found that unpopular high ability students differed from the average and popular students in family social status, social self-concept, and academic self-esteem. They did not differ in emotional autonomy or anxiety. Descriptive studies, such as this one, can inform counseling, program development, and policy.

Similarly, Kaiser and Berndt (1985) assessed a group of high school students attending a Governor's school on a variety of emotional variables including anger, depression, stressful life changes, and loneliness. Although they found the group to be relatively well-adjusted overall, 15-20% reported significant distress on one or more of the measures used. These researchers then moved beyond description to prediction. Using regression analyses, they were able to determine that depression, stress, and anger predicted loneliness among these gifted students. This method of studying within group differences has three advantages. First, it demonstrates that even though most gifted students are well-adjusted, a minority may be at risk for social/emotional problems. Second, regression designs retain all of the information in continuous variables and most social/emotional assessment scales are continuous in nature. Third, prediction models may be able to identify specific gifted students who are at risk for social/emotional adjustment problems and/or might benefit from counseling.

Descriptive and Modeling Studies

The final category of studies is descriptive and modeling studies. Some of these studies used survey methods (Moon, Kelly, & Feldhusen, 1997), while others used qualitative methods (Coleman, 2001; Sowa & May, 1997). These studies were designed to describe social and emotional characteristics of gifted students and their social systems or develop models of adjustment processes among high ability students. Because the focus is exclusively on high ability students, these studies are more likely to be published in journals within the field of gifted education than in journals in related fields such as counseling or psychology. Hence, some of the best examples of such studies are those included in this volume.

The survey study investigated adult perceptions of the need for differentiated counseling services (Moon et al., 1997). Parents of gifted students, coordinators of K-12 gifted education programs, community counselors, and professors were surveyed. All groups believed that gifted youth and their families could benefit from specialized counseling and guidance services. The social and emotional issues that were perceived to warrant specialized and differentiated counseling services included peer relationships, emotional adjustment, social adjustment, stress management, and underachievement.

These strong perceptions of the need for counseling services for gifted students are somewhat at odds with the group comparison literature discussed earlier which suggests that gifted students are as well or better adjusted than most other students. There are two possible explanations for these apparently conflicting results. First, the adults in this study may have been thinking of the minority of gifted and talented students that the within group comparison studies discussed above clearly indicate do have social/emotional issues. Second, the adults might have been commenting on the need for differentiation of the counseling process when counseling is provided, rather than saying that all gifted students need counseling. This interpretation is supported by the strong support respondents voiced for training programs for teachers, principals, counselors, and psychologists.

Sowa and May (1997) used qualitative research to create a prediction model for functional and dysfunctional patterns of adjustment among gifted students. Their model was based on observations of students and interviews with families, teachers, and friends about coping styles. Although their sample was small, as is typical in qualitative research, it was one of the few samples in the social/emotional literature that was diverse. Out of 20 students 7 (35%) were ethnic minorities. The model they developed uses both environmental variables (family functioning) and individual variables (adjustment mechanisms) to predict social/emotional adjustment. Like the within-group comparison studies, this study reminds us that gifted students are diverse with respect to social/emotional variables, with some being well adjusted and others having adjustment problems. This study also provides guidance on family and psychological risk factors that can increase the chances that gifted students will experience adjustment difficulties. It provides a theoretical framework for developing and evaluating interventions to increase the resilience of gifted students by targeting family functioning and/or individual coping styles.

The final descriptive study used ethnography to conduct an in-depth investigation of the social system that existed at a state high school for gifted students (Coleman, 2001). More than any other study in this collection, this one gets inside the heads of gifted adolescents, helping us to understand what they experience in an academically rigorous, residential environment. The study suggests that residential schools for gifted adolescents can facilitate the creation of an atypical adolescent social system with many positive characteristics such as appreciation of diversity, support for academic achievement, and absence of physical violence. The study also highlights some of the stressors that gifted students can experience in this type of environment such as busy schedules, omnipresent deadlines, and pressure.

Directions for Future Research

Group comparison studies. Researchers have consistently found few differences or differences favoring the gifted group when comparing gifted students to norms. However, most of the studies comparing gifted students to average students have focused on gifted students attending fee-based summer programs or predominately Caucasian samples from suburban gifted programs, limiting generalizability of the findings to other populations of gifted students such as those who have never had the opportunity to participate in a gifted program or who are not Caucasian. Hence, future research of this type should include more ethnically diverse populations of gifted students and gifted students who are not receiving any special programming.

In addition, future research should focus on within-group differences among the gifted using a wide variety of grouping variables including gender, age, type of giftedness, level of giftedness, availability and type of GT programming, ethnicity, and characteristics of motivation, emotions, personality, and family. This research should create complex models that will predict when specific subtypes of gifted students are likely to experience social or emotional stress.

Deficit model vs. positive psychology. Most of the studies in this collection come from a deficit model of psychological functioning, i.e., they are investigating vulnerability and psychological problems. Future research should also be conducted from within the positive psychology framework and investigate factors that increase resilience (Neihart, 2002c) or personal talent (Moon, 2002, November) among gifted students. The Sowa and May (1997) study moves in this direction because it identified processes that influenced both positive and negative adaptation to stress. Future research should go even further, looking for factors that facilitate optimal or extraordinary psychosocial development among gifted students.

Cross-sectional vs. longitudinal. Most of the studies in this volume, like the rest of the social and emotional literature, are short-term, cross-sectional studies. Since psychosocial development is a process that takes place across time, longitudinal studies are needed to fully understand the social and emotional issues of gifted students (Peterson, 2002; Robinson, Reis, Neihart, & Moon, 2002). Methods like growth analysis could be used to illuminate patterns of change over time on social and emotional variables among gifted students. Longitudinal studies would also facilitate more accurate prediction of risk and resilience factors.

UNDERACHIEVEMENT

The underachievement of gifted students is a puzzling phenomenon that has been the subject of sporadic attention in the field of gifted education for many years (Dowdall & Colangelo, 1982; Reis & McCoach, 2000; Rimm, 1995; Whitmore, 1980). Research on underachievement is hindered by lack of a consensus on how underachievement should be defined, the small number of gifted students who underachieve, the hidden nature of much underachievement, and the complexity of the phenomenon (Reis & McCoach, 2000). There is little conclusive research in this area but there are some interesting possibilities, some of which are suggested by the five papers on underachievement in this volume.

The only quantitative study in the group compares achieving and underachieving gifted high school students on satisfaction with school, aspirations, and need for services (Colangelo, Kerr, Christensen, & Maxey, 1993). This study is from the "comparison of subtypes of gifted students" tradition discussed in the previous section. The other three empirical studies are all qualitative investigations of interventions to reverse underachievement (Baum, 1995; Emerick, 1992; Hebert & Olenchak, 2000). The final paper in the set is a comprehensive review of the literature. These papers answer three questions about underachievement: (a) What is it? (b) What factors are associated with underachievement among gifted individuals? (c) How can we reverse poor school performance among gifted students when it occurs?

Definitions and Models of Underachievement

In their comprehensive review of the literature on underachievement, Reis and McCoach (2000) address all three of these questions. To answer the "What is it?" question they note that many operational and conceptual definitions of underachievement have been proposed in the literature, all of which have problems of one kind or another. They recommend widespread adoption of an operational definition of underachievement as a severe discrepancy between expected achievement (measured by tests) and actual classroom achievement (measured by grades and teacher evaluations) that persists over time and is not the result of a diagnosed learning disability. All four of the studies in this volume used some variation of this definition to select their underachieving subjects. Although this definition may not be relevant to underachievement in nonschool settings and will miss hidden gifted students who are underachieving, such as gifted students who are unable to show their abilities on standardized achievement tests, it is a good working definition for research on poor school performance among gifted students.

Several authors have proposed models of underachievement to answer the question "What factors are associated with it?" (Baker, Bridger, & Evans, 1998; Rimm, 2003). Generally, these models propose that individual, family, and school factors can all cause underachievement, singly or in combination. The Reis and McCoach (2000) review suggests that the situation is actually more complex than these models suggest. Peers can also influence underachievement. In addition, although many individual characteristics have been found to be associated with underachievement, these characteristics are so varied and idiosyncratic that it is not possible to identify a single underachieving personality (Baum, 1995). The influence of the three areas (family, individual, and school) also appears to vary greatly. For example, there is no consistent evidence that all gifted underachievers come from dysfunctional families or experience inappropriate schooling. Finally, these models do not capture the role that culture, ethnicity, and socialization can play in underachievement, particularly among minority populations. Hence, new models are needed that can take these additional complexities into account.

Characteristics of Underachievers

One stream of research on underachievers has examined the individual characteristics of the students. This research tradition is represented in this collection both in the review paper (Reis & McCoach, 2000) and in the quantitative comparison paper (Colangelo et al., 1993). Table 5 in the review paper provides a comprehensive summary of research on personality characteristics, internal mediators, differential thinking styles, maladaptive strategies, and positive attributes that have been found to be associated with poor performance in school by bright children. Most of the characteristics are negative and many of them are also associated with learning disabilities and/or AD/HD, suggesting that it is important to assess gifted underachievers for hidden disabilities as a first step in intervention. Colangelo et al.'s study suggests that underachievers also have fewer out-of-class accomplishments and lower educational aspirations than their high achieving peers.

A second stream of research on underachievers has examined the characteristics of their families (Fine & Holt, 1983; Fine & Pitts, 1980; Green, Fine, & Tollefson, 1988; Moon & Hall, 1998; Rimm & Lowe, 1988; Zuccone & Amerikaner, 1986). This research is not well represented in this volume, probably because research on families is still not a major theme in gifted education so the studies published in *GCQ* from this stream would tend not to be cited as often as those from the individual characteristics stream. In addition, some of the research from the family literature has been published outside the field of gifted education in journals that focus on families and family interventions.

In both the individual and the family streams, the characteristics research is primarily descriptive. Only a few studies have attempted to determine causality (Dias, 1998). Most of the studies are cross-sectional so we know little about how underachievement changes over time except through a handful of retrospective (Emerick, 1992; Peterson, 2001b; Peterson & Colangelo, 1996) and longitudinal (Peterson, 2000, 2001a, 2002) studies. There is a great need for more longitudinal research on underachievement from an eco-systemic perspective, that is, research that follows achievers and underachievers over time, assessing not only their individual characteristics but also the characteristics of their families, peers, and schools. A good exemplar of this type of research is Peterson's (2002) fascinating study of the post–high school development for fourteen gifted adolescents who were at risk for underachievement. By following the students for four years from an eco-systemic perspective, Peterson was able to observe and report on their development as it unfolded after high school. There is also a need for more studies of specific subpopulations of underachievers, especially those from populations that have been historically underrepresented in gifted programs (Dias, 1998; Ford, 1996).

Reversing Underachievement

Increasing numbers of studies of underachievement have focused on interventions to reverse the poor school performance. As might be expected from the models of underachievement described above, this research also has three streams. It includes studies of *educational interventions* (Whitmore, 1980), *family interventions* (Fine & Pitts, 1980; Moon & Hall, 1998; Moon & Thomas, 2003; Wendorf & Frey, 1985; Zuccone & Amerikaner, 1986), and *personal interventions* (Siegle & McCoach, 2002). A few studies, especially the retrospective ones, have examined all three of these types of interventions at once (Emerick, 1992; Peterson, 2001b).

This collection includes three studies of educational and personal interventions to reverse underachievement: one retrospective, eco-systemic study of reversals of underachievement without formal intervention programs (Emerick, 1992) and two studies of the effectiveness of planned interventions (Baum, 1995; Hébert & Olenchak, 2000). Emerick investigated 10 students aged 14-20 who had demonstrated a sustained period of average or below average school performance followed by a sustained reversal that produced above average school performance. Her qualitative investigation yielded six emergent themes that describe factors related to the reversal of underachievement: out-of-school interests, supportive parents, classes with specific characteristics, career goals, caring and enthusiastic teachers, and personal growth. Baum et al.

investigated the effectiveness of Type III investigations in reversing poor academic performance among 17 students aged 8-13 who had diverse profiles of factors contributing to their underachievement. They found that 82% of the participants experienced a sustained reversal of poor school performance during the year of the intervention and the year immediately following. Improvement was noted both in grades and in behavior, especially self-regulated and classroom behavior. Hébert and Olenchak (2000) investigated the effectiveness of mentors in reversing poor school performance in three male students of widely different ages (elementary school to college). They found that mentorship relationships could reverse underachievement when the mentor was open and nonjudgmental, provided consistent and personalized support, and created strength and interest-based intervention strategies. Taken together, these three studies suggest that individualized, approaches based on student interests and strengths can help underachieving gifted students reverse patterns of poor school performance. Such interventions can be implemented by a variety of caring adults including parents, educators, and mentors.

COUNSELING GIFTED STUDENTS

The field of gifted education has focused much more time and energy on researching the need for and the efficacy of differentiated educational services for gifted and talented youth than it has on differentiated counseling services. As a result, little is known about the types of counseling services that could provide the greatest benefit to specific gifted students at specific points in their development.

Most of the literature that does exist on counseling gifted students is clinical rather than empirical. It consists of reports by clinicians on their practice rather than investigations of the efficacy of specific counseling strategies with gifted and talented students. In addition, much of this literature has been published in books (Kerr, 1991; Silverman, 1993; VanTassel-Baska, 1990; Webb & DeVries, 1993) or in journals outside the field of gifted education, especially journals for counselors or psychologists such as *The Journal of Counseling and Development* (McMann & Oliver, 1988; Myers & Pace, 1986; Peterson & Colangelo, 1996; Zuccone & Amerikaner, 1986), *The Journal of Counseling Psychology* (Kerr & Cheryl, 1991), *The Journal of Marital and Family Therapy* (Moon & Hall, 1998), and *The School Counselor* (Lester & Anderson, 1981). Hence, the three seminal papers in this volume represent only a small part of the existing literature.

Counseling Needs

As noted above, there are contradictions in the literature regarding the need for specialized counseling services for gifted students. On the one hand, clinicians who work with gifted children and their families report that they need assistance in addressing affective concerns related to giftedness such as identity development, multipotentiality, perfectionism, introversion, peer relationships, and sensitivity (Jackson & Peterson, 2003; Mahoney, 1997; Mendaglio, 2003; Peterson, 2003; Silverman, 1993). There is also some clinical evidence that giftedness can mask symptoms of mental health problems such as behavior and depressive disorders (Jackson & Peterson, 2003; Kaufmann, Kalbfleisch, & Castellanos, 2000; Kaufmann & Castellanos, 2000). On the other hand, as noted earlier, studies comparing gifted students with average students on affective variables generally find that the gifted students meet or exceed norms on these variables.

The survey study discussed in the section on social/emotional development provides a different perspective on counseling needs (Moon et al., 1997). In this study parents, school personnel, and related counseling professionals were surveyed to determine their perceptions of the needs of gifted students for specialized counseling services. The results supported the clinical literature more than the group comparison literature. All three groups felt that gifted students would benefit from specialized and differentiated counseling services. Recommended services included career assessments, talent assessments, and guidance for both parents and students. This study supported the need for differentiation of counseling services to address unique issues of gifted individuals. Unfortunately, very few empirical studies have been conducted on how to differentiate counseling when working with gifted and talented students.

Counseling Models

The remaining two papers on counseling in this volume proposed models based on clinical practice (Buescher, 1987; Dettman & Colangelo, 1980). These papers are typical of the large, clinical literature on counseling gifted students that spans a continuum from prevention to intervention (Moon, 2002, 2003). The models included here represent the preventative end of the continuum.

One of the models suggested that differentiated, affective curricula can help gifted adolescents address four critical issues: adolescent development, identity and stress, relationships, and career development (Buescher, 1987). This curricular approach is similar to that proposed in dimensions one and two of the Autonomous Learner Model (Betts & Kercher, 1999; Betts, 1985). The goal is to help gifted adolescents understand themselves and develop personal talent (Moon, 2002, November, 2002, October). The NAGC Affective Curriculum Task Force is currently working along similar lines to develop a comprehensive framework for affective curricula that will promote the social, emotional, and personal development of gifted individuals.

The other paper, one of the oldest in the collection, provided a model for school counselors to use in working with parents of gifted students (Colangelo & Dettman, 1981). The model was based on a review of the early literature on the needs of parents of the gifted (Colangelo & Dettmann, 1983) and described three approaches school counselors could take in assisting parents of gifted students: the parent-centered approach, the school-centered approach, and the partnership approach. The partnership approach was recommended because it encompassed the strengths of the other two approaches and promoted joint responsibility for the welfare of gifted children. Although this model makes intuitive sense, it has never been empirically tested or validated and provides only very general guidance to school counselors on how to create parent-school partnerships.

There are no papers in this volume representing the intervention end of the counseling model continuum, probably because there have not been very many studies of therapeutic interventions with gifted individuals. The handful of studies that have been conducted have often been published elsewhere, i.e., in therapy journals (Adams-Byers, Whitsell, & Moon, 2004; Moon, Nelson, & Piercy, 1993; Thomas, 1999; Wendorf & Frey, 1985) or other journals in the field of gifted education (Bourdeau & Thomas, 2003).

CONCLUSION

Clearly, there is a need for more attention to the affective development of all gifted students, as well as for increased attention to the affective needs of special populations of gifted students, such as underachievers, who are at risk for failure to achieve their potential. There is also a need for more empirical studies on "what works" with these students, both in terms of preventative strategies such as affective curricula, and with regard to more intensive interventions such as individual, group, or family therapy. Good counseling models have been developed, but they need to be rigorously evaluated to determine the conditions under which they are most effective. In addition, research is needed on affective and counseling interventions with specific subtypes of gifted students such as Asian Americans, African Americans, and twice-exceptional students (Ford, Harris, & Schuerger, 1993, March/April; Moon, Zentall, Grskovic, Hall, & Stormont, 2001; Plucker, 1996; Zuccone & Amerikaner, 1986). For this to happen, researchers in the field of gifted education will need to collaborate with researchers from affective fields such as personal and social psychology, counseling psychology, family therapy, and psychiatry. Working together, we can learn how to intervene most effectively with gifted individuals who have mental health problems and how to help all gifted persons achieve optimal social, emotional, and personal development.

REFERENCES

Adams-Byers, J., Whitsell, S. S., & Moon, S. M. (2004). Gifted students' perceptions of the academic and social/emotional effects of homogeneous and heterogeneous grouping. *Gifted Child Quarterly, 48*(1), 7-20.

Baker, J. A. (1995). Depression and suicidal ideation among academically gifted adolescents. *Gifted Child Quarterly, 39*(4), 218-223. **[See Vol. 8, p. 21.]**

Baker, J. A., Bridger, R., & Evans, K. (1998). Models of underachievement among gifted preadolescents: The role of personal, family, and school factors. *Gifted Child Quarterly, 42*(1), 5-15.

Baum, S. M., Renzulli, J. S., & Hébert, T. P. (1995). Reversing underachievement: Creative productivity as a systematic intervention. *Gifted Child Quarterly, 39*(4), 224-235. **[See Vol. 8, p. 133.]**

Betts, G., & Kercher, J. (1999). *Autonomous learning model: Optimizing ability.* Greely, CO: ALPS.

Betts, G. T. (1985). *Autonomous learner model for the gifted and talented.* Greeley, CO: ALPS.

Bourdeau, B., & Thomas, V. (2003). Counseling gifted clients and their families: Comparing clients' and counselors' perspectives. *Journal for Secondary Gifted Education, 14*(2), 114-126.

Buescher, T. M. (1987). Counseling gifted adolescents: A curriculum model for students, parents, and professionals. *Gifted Child Quarterly, 31*(2), 90-94. **[See Vol. 8, p. 221.]**

Colangelo, N., & Dettman, D. F. (1981). A conceptual model of four types of parent-school interactions. *Journal for the Education of the Gifted, 5*(2), 120-126.

Colangelo, N., & Dettmann, D. F. (1983). A review of research on parents and families of gifted children. *Exceptional Children, 50*(1), 20-27.

Colangelo, N., Kerr, B., Christensen, P., & Maxey, J. (1993). A comparison of gifted underachievers and gifted achievers. *Gifted Child Quarterly, 37*(4), 155-160. **[See Vol. 8, p. 119.]**

Coleman, L. J. (2001). A "rag quilt": Social relationships among students in a special high school. *Gifted Child Quarterly, 45*(3), 164-173. **[See Vol. 8, p. 63.]**

Cornell, D. G. (1990). High ability students who are unpopular with their peers. *Gifted Child Quarterly, 34*(4), 155-160. **[See Vol. 8, p. 31.]**

Cornell, D. G., Delcourt, M. B., Bland, L. D., Goldberg, M. D., & Oram, G. (1994). Low incidence of behavior problems among elementary school students in gifted programs. *Journal for the Education of the Gifted, 18*(1), 4-19.

Cross, T. L., Coleman, L. J., & Terhaar-Yonkers, M. (1991). The social cognitiion of gifted adolescents in schools: Managing the stigma of giftedness. *Journal for the Education of the Gifted, 15*, 44-55.

Dauber, S. L., & Benbow, C. P. (1990). Aspects of personality and peer relations of extremely talented adolescents. *Gifted Child Quarterly, 34*(1), 10-15.

Dettman, D. F., & Colangelo, N. (1980). A functional model for counseling parents of gifted students. *Gifted Child Quarterly, 24*(3), 158-161. **[See Vol. 8, p. 213.]**

Dias, E. I. (1998). Perceived factors influencing the academic underachievement of talented students of Puerto Rican descent. *Gifted Child Quarterly, 42*(2), 105-122.

Dowdall, C. B., & Colangelo, N. (1982). Underachieving gifted students: Review and implications. *Gifted Child Quarterly, 26*(4), 179-184.

Emerick, L. J. (1992). Academic underachievement among the gifted: Students' perceptions of factors that reverse the pattern. *Gifted Child Quarterly, 36*(3), 140-146.

Fine, M. J., & Holt, P. (1983). Intervening with school problems: A family systems perspective. *Psychology in the Schools, 20*, 59-66.

Fine, M. J., & Pitts, R. (1980). Intervention with underachieving gifted children: Rationale and strategies. *Gifted Child Quarterly, 24*(2), 51-55.

Ford, D. Y. (1996). *Reversing underachievement among gifted black students: Promising practices and programs.* New York: Teachers College Press.

Ford, D. Y., Harris, J., & Schuerger, J. M. (1993, March/April). Racial identity development among gifted black students: Counseling issues and concerns. *Journal of Counseling and Development, 71*(March/April), 409-417.

Green, K., Fine, M. J., & Tollefson, N. (1988). Family systems characteristics and underachieving gifted. *Gifted Child Quarterly, 32*(2), 267-272.

Gross, M. (in press). From "play partner" to "sure shelter": How do conceptions of friendship differ between average-ability, moderately gifted, and highly gifted children?, *Proceedings of the 5th Biennial Henry B. and Jocelyn National Wallace Research Symposium on Talent Development*. Scottsdale, AZ: Gifted Psychology Press.

Hebert, T. P., & Olenchak, F. R. (2000). Mentors for gifted underachieving males: Developing potential and realizing promise. *Gifted Child Quarterly, 44*(3), 196-207. **[See Vol. 8, p. 157.]**

Jackson, P. S., & Peterson, J. S. (2003). Depressive disorder in highly gifted students. *Journal For Secondary Gifted Education, 14*(3), 175-186.

Kaiser, C. R., & Berndt, D. J. (1985). Predictors of loneliness in the gifted adolescent. *Gifted Child Quarterly, 29*(2), 74-77. **[See Vol. 8, p. 43.]**

Kaufmann, F., Kalbfleisch, M. L., & Castellanos, F. X. (2000). *Attention deficit disorders and gifted students: What do we really know?* Storrs, CT: NRC/GT.

Kaufmann, F. A., & Castellanos, F. X. (2000). Attention-Deficit/Hyperactivity Disorder in gifted students. In K. A. Heller, F. J. Monks, & R. J. Sternberg, & R. F. Subotnik (Eds.), *International Handbook of Giftedness and Talent* (2nd ed., pp. 621-632). Amsterdam: Elsevier.

Keiley, M. K. (1997). Affect regulation in adolescents: Does the management of feelings differ by gender and/or by method of measurement. *Unpublished Manuscript.*

Kerr, B. (1991). *A handbook for counseling the gifted and talented.* Alexandria, VA: American Counseling Association.

Kerr, B., & Cheryl, E. (1991). Career counseling with academically talented students: Effects of a value-based intervention. *Journal of Counseling Psychology, 38*(3), 309-314.

Lehman, E. B., & Erdwins, C. J. (1981). The social and emotional adjustment of young, intellectually-gifted children. *Gifted Child Quarterly, 25*(3), 134-137. **[See Vol. 8, p. 1.]**

Lester, C. F., & Anderson, R. S. (1981). Counseling with families of gifted children: The school counselor's role. *School Counselor, 29*(2), 147-151.

Mahoney, A. S. (1997). In search of gifted identity: From abstract concept to workable counseling constructs. *Roeper Review, 20*(3), 222-227.

McMann, N., & Oliver, R. (1988). Problems in families with gifted children: Implications for counselors. *Journal of Counseling and Development, 66*, 275-278.

Mendaglio, S. (2003). Heightened multifaceted sensitivity of gifted students: Implications for counseling. *Journal for Secondary Gifted Education, 14*(2), 72-82.

Metha, A., & McWhirter, E. H. (1997). Suicide ideation, depression, and stressful life events among gifted adolescents. *Journal for the Education of the Gifted, 20*(3), 284-304.

Moon, S. M. (2002). Counseling needs and strategies. In M. Neihart, S. M. Reis, N. M. Robinson, & S. M. Moon (Eds.), *The social and emotional development of gifted children: What do we know?* (pp. 213-222). Waco, TX: Prufrock Press.

Moon, S. M. (2002, November). *Personal talent.* Paper presented at the National Association for Gifted Children, Denver, CO.

Moon, S. M. (2002, October). *Developing personal talent.* Paper presented at the European Council for High Ability, Rhodes, Greece.

Moon, S. M. (2003). Counseling families. In N. Colangelo & G. A. Davis (Eds.), *Handbook of gifted education* (pp. 388-402). Boston: Allyn and Bacon.

Moon, S. M., & Hall, A. S. (1998). Family therapy with intellectually and creatively gifted children. *Journal of Marital and Family Therapy, 24*(1), 59-80.

Moon, S. M., Kelly, K. R., & Feldhusen, J. F. (1997). Specialized counseling services for gifted youth and their families: A needs assessment. *Gifted Child Quarterly, 41*(1), 16-25. **[See Vol. 8, p. 229.]**

Moon, S. M., Nelson, T. S., & Piercy, F. P. (1993). Family therapy with a highly gifted adolescent. *Journal of Family Psychotherapy, 4*(3), 1-16.

Moon, S. M., Swift, S., & Shallenberger, A. (2002). Perceptions of a self-contained class of fourth- and fifth-grade students with high to extreme levels of intellectual giftedness. *Gifted Child Quarterly, 46*(1), 64-79.

Moon, S. M., & Thomas, V. (2003). Family therapy with gifted and talented adolescents. *Journal of Secondary Gifted Education, 14*(2), 107-113.

Moon, S. M., Zentall, S. S., Grskovic, J. A., Hall, A., & Stormont, M. (2001). Emotional and social characteristics of boys with AD/HD and/or giftedness: A comparative case study. *Journal for the Education of the Gifted, 24*(3), 207-247.

Myers, R. S., & Pace, T. M. (1986). Counseling gifted and talented students: Historical perspectives and contemporary issues. *Journal of Counseling and Development, 64,* 548-551.

Neihart, M. (2002a). Delinquency and gifted children. In M. Neihart, S. M. Reis, N. M. Robinson, & S. M. Moon (Eds.), *The social and emotional development of gifted children: What do we know?* (pp. 103-112). Waco, TX: Prufrock.

Neihart, M. (2002b). Gifted children and depression. In M. Neihart, S. M. Reis, N. M. Robinson, & S. M. Moon (Eds.), *The social and emotional development of gifted children: What do we know?* (pp. 93-102). Waco, TX: Prufrock Press.

Neihart, M. (2002c). Risk and resilience in gifted children: A conceptual framework. In M. Neihart & S. M. Reis & N. M. Robinson & S. M. Moon (Eds.), *The social and emotional development of gifted children: What do we know?* (pp. 113-122). Waco, TX: Prufrock.

Neihart, M., Reis, S., Robinson, N., & Moon, S. M. (Eds.). (2002). *The social and emotional development of gifted children. What do we know?* Waco, TX: Prufrock.

Pearson, M., & Beer, J. (1991). Self-consciousness, self-esteem, and depression of gifted school children. *Psychological Reports, 66,* 960-962.

Peterson, J. S. (2000). A follow-up study of one group of achievers and underachievers four years after high school graduation. *Roeper Review, 22*(4), 217-224.

Peterson, J. S. (2001a). Gifted and at risk: Four longitudinal case studies of post-high school development. *Roeper Review, 24*(1), 31-39.

Peterson, J. S. (2001b). Successful adults who were adolescent underachievers. *Gifted Child Quarterly, 45*(4), 236-250.

Peterson, J. S. (2002). A longitudinal study of post-high-school development in gifted individuals at risk for poor educational outcomes. *Journal for Secondary Gifted Education, 14*(1), 6-18.

Peterson, J. S. (2003). An argument for proactive attention to affective concerns of gifted adolescents. *Journal for Secondary Gifted Education, 14*(2), 62-71.

Peterson, J. S., & Colangelo, N. (1996). Gifted achievers and underachievers: A comparison of patterns found in school files. *Journal of Counseling and Development, 74,* 399-407.

Plucker, J. A. (1996). Gifted Asian-American students: Identification, curricular, and counseling concerns. *Journal for the Education of the Gifted, 19*(3), 314-343.

Reis, S. M., & McCoach, D. B. (2000). The underachievement of gifted students: What do we know and where do we go? *Gifted Child Quarterly, 44*(3), 152-170. **[See Vol. 8, p. 181.]**

Rimm, S. (1995). *Why bright kids get poor grades and what you can do about it.* New York: Crown.

Rimm, S. B. (2003). Underachievement: A national epidemic. In N. Colangelo & G. A. Davis (Eds.), *Handbook of gifted education* (pp. 424-443). Boston: Allyn and Bacon.

Rimm, S. B., & Lowe, B. (1988). Family environments of underachieving gifted students. *Gifted Child Quarterly, 32*, 353-359.

Robinson, N. M., Lanzi, R. G., Weinberg, R. A., Ramey, S. L., & Ramey, C. T. (2002). Family factors associated with high academic competence in former Head Start children at third grade. *Gifted Child Quarterly, 46*(4), 278-290. **[See Vol. 8, p. 83.]**

Robinson, N. M., Zigler, E., & Gallagher, J. J. (2000). Two tails of the normal curve: Similarities and differences in the study of mental retardation and giftedness. *American Psychologist, 55*(12), 1413-1425.

Sayler, M. F., & Brookshire, W. K. (1993). Social, emotional, and behavioral adjustment of accelerated students, students in gifted classes, and regular students in eighth grade. *Gifted Child Quarterly, 37*(4), 150-154. **[See Vol. 8, p. 9.]**

Siegle, D., & McCoach, D. B. (2002). Promoting positive achievement attitude with gifted and talented students. In M. Neihart, S. M. Reis, N. M. Robinson, & S. M. Moon (Eds.), *The social and emotional development of gifted children: What do we know?* (pp. 237-249). Waco, TX: Prufrock.

Silverman, L. K. (1993). *Counseling the Gifted and Talented*. Denver, CO: Love.

Sowa, C. J., & May, K. M. (1997). Expanding Lazarus and Folkman's paradigm to the social and emotional adjustment of gifted children. *Gifted Child Quarterly, 41*(2), 36-43. **[See Vol. 8, p. 51.]**

Swiatek, M. A. (1995). An empirical investigation of the social coping strategies used by gifted adolescents. *Gifted Child Quarterly, 39*(3), 154-161.

Thomas, V. (1999). David and the family bane: Therapy with a gifted child and his family. *Journal of Family Psychology, 10*(1), 15-24.

VanTassel-Baska, J. (Ed.). (1990). *A practical guide to counseling the gifted in a school setting* (2nd. ed.). Reston, VA: Council for Exceptional Children.

Webb, J. T., & DeVries, A. R. (1993). *Training manual for facilitators of SENG model guided discussion groups*.

Wendorf, D. J., & Frey, J. (1985). Family therapy with the intellectually gifted. *The American Journal of Family Therapy, 13*(1), 31-38.

Whitmore, J. R. (1980). *Giftedness, conflict, and underachievement*. Boston: Allyn & Bacon.

Zuccone, C. F., & Amerikaner, M. (1986). Counseling gifted underachievers: A family systems approach. *Journal of Counseling and Development, 64*, 590-592.

1

The Social and Emotional Adjustment of Young, Intellectually Gifted Children

Elyse Brauch Lehman

Carol J. Erdwins

Since Terman's longitudinal investigation of gifted children, there have been numerous additional studies comparing the gifted with their average IQ peers on intellectual, academic, and achievement criteria (e.g., Flanagan & Cooley, 1966; Gallagher & Crowder, 1957; Klausmeier & Check, 1962; Klausmeier & Loughlin, 1961; Terman, Baldwin, & Bronson, 1925). Much less attention has been paid to how the intellectually gifted child may compare to his/her chronological or mental age mates on social and emotional adjustment characteristics. This is in spite of the fact that several early theorists (Jung, 1954; Lombroso, 1891) suggested that the gifted may be predisposed to emotional

Editor's Note: From Lehman, E. B., & Erdwins, C. J. (1981). The social and emotional adjustment of young, intellectually gifted children. *Gifted Child Quarterly*, 25(3), 134-137. © 1981 National Association for Gifted Children. Reprinted with permission.

instability. More recent studies have unanimously rejected this assumption and consistently find no evidence of greater emotional disturbance in gifted populations (Kennedy, 1962; Ramaseshan, 1957, Warren & Heist, 1960; Wrenn, Ferguson, & Kennedy, 1962). These studies as well as others (Haier & Denham, 1976; Lucito, 1964; Milgram & Milgram, 1976) have, in fact, found gifted students scoring higher than their average IQ peers on such traits as self-sufficiency, dominance, independence, originality, nonconformity, positive self-concept, and internal locus of control. Most of this research, however, has been done with high school or college-aged students and has used same-aged peers or normative data as the comparison group. Only one study thus far has attempted to compare younger gifted children with an older population as well as their chronological age mates. Lessinger and Martinson (1961) found a group of gifted eighth graders to be much more similar in their responses on the California Psychological Inventory to both a group of gifted high school students and the general adult population than they were to their same-aged peers.

The present study attempted to focus on the emotional and social development of the younger gifted child. Since gifted children have frequently been found to function intellectually and academically several years ahead of their chronological peers, it might be hypothesized that in the emotional and social spheres of their lives they will also be more similar to their mental age mates. This hypothesis was tested by comparing a group of intellectually gifted third graders with groups of average IQ third- and sixth-grade students on two personality measures which yield a variety of scores relevant to emotional and social adjustment.

METHOD

Subjects

Three groups of middle-class, mainly Caucasian children participated in the study. The first group consisted of sixteen very bright third graders (9 boys and 7 girls) who were enrolled in a program for the gifted and talented in a suburban public school. These children were in classrooms with other equally bright children of similar age, although "regular" third-grade classes also existed in the same school. Their Stanford-Binet (Form L-M) IQ scores ranged from 141 to 165 (mean = 152.6).

Children selected by their principals on the basis of their having IQ scores between 90 and 110 comprised the two average IQ groups: one with third graders, the other with sixth graders (8 boys and 8 girls at each level). They attended elementary and middle schools in a suburban county adjoining the one in which the gifted children resided. Mean chronological ages in years for the groups were 8–6, 8–11, and 12–8, respectively.

Procedure

The California Test of Personality—Form AA: Primary and Elementary (Thorpe, Clark, & Tiegs, 1953) and the Children's Social Attitude and Value Scales (Solomon, Kendall, & Oberlander, 1976) were administered to the children as part of a battery of tests. The intellectually gifted children were tested individually in their homes after school hours, while the average IQ children worked on the tests in small groups at school. Although the gifted children were tested in a more familiar environment, the home testing was also more subject to distractions not present in the school setting. For all groups the testing was closely supervised. Individual items were periodically read out loud to or by the children, the children were encouraged to ask questions when the items were unclear, and two experimenters were always present during the group testing to provide more individualized attention.

The personality test requires a Yes/No decision to be made on a series of statements which are divided into twelve subtests (half measuring personal adjustment and half assessing social adjustment). These subtests are listed in Table 2. The individual statements are brief and are geared to the child's reading level. Examples taken from the Primary version are: "Do you usually finish the games you start?," "Do the children think you can do things well?," and "Is it hard for you to talk to new people?" Reliability coefficients for the individual subtests computed with the Kuder-Richardson formula range from .59 to .83 (Thorpe et al., 1953). While paper and pencil personality measures are sometimes thought to be subject to positive distortion, Thorpe et al. (1953) suggest that there is little likelihood of this occurring in elementary school children. In addition, an attempt was made in constructing the test to phrase items in a non-threatening way.

On the attitude inventory children responded to each statement on a 4-point scale from "strongly agree" to "strongly disagree." Eleven scales surveying opinions on self-direction, cooperation, concern for others, etc., comprise this inventory. These scales are listed in Table I. Examples of statements from the scale are: "When you want to make something, it is best to start with some help or advice from a teacher," "It spoils the fun to let people who don't know the rules play games," and "School is nice only if everybody shares everything." Internal consistency reliability coefficients for the individual scales range from .38 to .79 (Solomon et al., 1976).

RESULTS

Figure 1 presents the standard scores on the subtests of the California Test of Personality for the three groups of children. Higher scores reflect better adjustment. Scores on the Children's Social Attitude and Value Scales for these groups are listed in Table 1, where higher scores can be interpreted as indicating greater agreement with a particular social value. Examination of these results indicates

Table 1   Means and Univariates *Fz* Tests for the Children's Social Attitude and Value Scales

Scale	Means			F	P
	Grade 3 average	Grade 3 gifted	Grade 6 average		
Self-direction	12.81	11.63	12.27	1.11	—
Assertion responsibility	12.38	12.31	11.60	0.55	—
Willingness to compromise	13.25	9.81	12.27	3.42	.042
Equality of representation	9.56	11.06	11.07	2.43	—
Equality of participation	11.25	12.63	11.00	4.32	.019
Group activities	30.13	32.94	34.60	3.26	.048
Cooperation	23.13	24.31	22.00	3.34	.045
Decision-making autonomy	24.19	21.81	21.93	0.67	—
Tolerance for differences	10.67	12.44	10.67	1.75	—
Concern for others	22.19	22.94	21.87	0.48	—
Self-esteem	45.81	50.06	44.40	3.80	.030

Note.—df = 2, 44. Empty cells indicate nonsignificance.

that the intellectually gifted children were quite well-adjusted. On many of the scales they had higher adjustment scores than their chronological age mates. They even scored higher than their mental age mates on some of the social adjustment subtests. Additionally, in comparison with normative data provided by Thorpe et al. (1953) for the California Test of Personality, the gifted group as a whole scored above the fiftieth percentile on ten of the twelve subtests. No normative data were available for the children's Social Attitude and Value scales.

Two multivariate one-way analyses of variance were used to assess the differences among the three groups of children. One tested for an effect on the California Test of Personality, using scores on the twelve subtests as variates; the second used scores on the eleven scales of the Children's Attitude and Value Scales as variates. Subsequently, univariate *F*-tests were used to discern which variates most contributed to the effect. Tables 1 and 2 summarize these univariate *F*-tests for each variable. Finally, to aid in describing the gifted group and in answering the original question concerning the similarity of the gifted children to other groups, Newman-Keuls post hoc analyses were performed for each of the variables which were significant on the univariate *F*-tests.

Personality

The overall MANOVA on the California Test of Personality was statistically significant using three different criteria: Pillais $F = 2.70$ (df = 24, 70), $p < .00067$, Hotellings $F = 3.13$ (df = 24, 66), $p < .00013$, and Wilks-Roys $F = 2.91$ (dr = 24, 68), $p < .00029$. Six of the subtests produced significant univariate *Fs*: Sense of

Figure I   Mean standard scores on the California test of personality for three groups of children: grade 3 gifted (G3G), grade 3 average IQ (G3A), and grade 6 average IQ (G6A). The subscales are: self-reliance (SRe), personal worth (PW), personal freedom (PF), feeling of belonging (B), withdrawal tendencies (WT), nervous symptoms (NS), social standards (SSt), social skills (SSk), anti-social tendencies (ASt), family relations (FR), school relations (SRs), and community relations (CR).

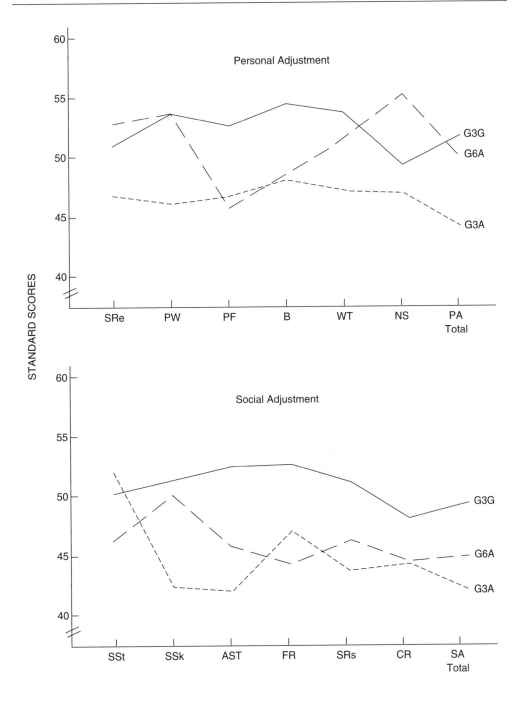

Table 2 Univariate *F* Tests for the California Test of Personality

Subtest	F	p
Personal adjustment		
Self-reliance	2.62	–
Sense of personal worth	4.41	.018
Sense of personal freedom	3.34	.045
Feeling of belonging	2.74	–
Withdrawal tendencies	2.66	–
Nervous symptoms	4.60	.015
Social adjustment		
Social standards	2.71	–
Social skills	3.88	.028
Anti-social tendencies	4.06	.024
Family relations	3.08	–
School relations	4.74	.014
Community relations	1.62	–

Note.—df = 2, 45. Empty cells indicate nonsignificance.

personal worth, Sense of personal freedom, Nervous symptoms, Social skills, Anti-social tendencies, and School relations. Subsequent post hoc tests ($p < .05$) indicated that the gifted children and the sixth graders scored higher than the average IQ third graders on Sense of personal worth and on Social skills, the gifted children higher than both other groups on Sense of personal freedom, the gifted children higher than the average IQ third graders on Anti-social tendencies and on School relations, and the sixth graders higher than both other groups on Nervous symptoms.

Social Attitudes and Values

The overall MANOVA on the Children's Attitude and Value Scales was also statistically significant using all three criteria: Pillais $F = 1.95$ (df = 22, 70), $p < .019$, Hotellings $F = 2.18$ (df = 22, 66), $p < .0079$, and Wilks-Roys $F = 2.07$ (df = 22, 68), $p < .012$. Table 1 presents the five significant univariate Fs: Willingness to compromise, Equality of participation, Group activities, Cooperation, and Self-esteem. Subsequent post hoc tests ($p < .05$) showed that the gifted children obtained higher scores than both average IQ groups on Equality of participation, higher than the sixth graders on Cooperation and on Self-esteem, and lower than the average IQ third graders on Willingness to compromise. In addition, the sixth graders scored higher than the average IQ third graders on Group activities.

DISCUSSION

In general, the differences on these two personality inventories suggest that intellectually gifted children do, in fact, differ significantly from their chronological age mates more than from their mental age mates on measures of personal and social adjustment. However, the pattern of differences is not a consistent one. On some scales the bright children performed more like their CA mates (e.g., Nervous symptoms, Cooperation), on other more like their MA mates (e.g., Sense of personal worth, Social skills), and on still others like neither (e.g., Sense of personal freedom, Willingness to compromise, Equality of participation, Self-esteem).

The picture of gifted children which emerges from these comparisons is a positive one. They appear to feel comfortable with themselves and with interpersonal relationships. The gifted children in the present study, for example, reported more positive feelings about themselves whether the test items were couched in terms of what they thought about themselves or what others thought about them. This is consistent with Milgram and Milgram's (1976) study which also found more positive self-concepts in their gifted population of fourth and eighth graders. The bright group also reported having greater personal freedom than did the average IQ third graders. Perhaps because these gifted children demonstrate greater maturity in their interactions they are accorded more freedom by their families. They do, in fact, feel quite secure in their families and in school. The gifted children scored significantly higher than the sixth graders on positive family relationships and higher than the average IQ third graders on school relationships.

Evidence of maladjustment in the gifted group was negligible. The incidence of physical complaints such as dizzy spells, cold, and upset stomachs and of nervous symptoms such as bad dreams and biting fingernails was the same for all third graders, although both of these groups reported more such complaints than the sixth graders. On the other CTP measure of maladjustment (anti-social tendencies), the gifted children showed significantly better adjustment than their chronological age mates. That is, they were less aggressive and destructive, and performed fewer acting out behaviors.

The gifted also appear to have social skills which are helpful in interpersonal relationships. They scored higher than their age mates on a measure of social skills assessing the child's ability to interact tactfully with others, perhaps putting the other person's needs before his/her own. They also appear to value cooperative, as opposed to competitive, and democratic forms of peer group interaction more strongly than children of average intelligence, although sixth graders feel more positively about working in groups. At the same time they describe themselves as being less willing to compromise, suggesting that, while they are able to interact with some thoughtfulness towards others, they are by no means always acquiescent.

In summary, it seems that these young gifted children, while differing significantly from the groups of average IQ children on several scales, do not vary in any consistent manner from either their chronological or mental age peers. What is clear is that when they do differ from the others, the young gifted children, as had been reported in earlier studies for older gifted children, score consistently more positively on measures of social and emotional adjustment. They report more positive feelings about themselves, more maturity in interactions with others, and better relations with others.

REFERENCES

Flanagan, J. C., & Cooley, W. W. *Project talent one-year follow-up studies*. Pittsburgh, PA: University of Pittsburgh, 1966.

Gallagher, J. J., & Crowder, T. The adjustment of gifted children in the regular classroom. *Exceptional Children*, 1957, 23, 306–312; 317–319.

Haier, R. J., & Denham, S. A. A summary profile of the nonintellectual correlates of mathematical precocity in boys and girls. In D. P. Keating (Ed.), *Intellectual talent: Research and development*. Baltimore: The Johns Hopkins University Press, 1976, 225–241.

Jung, C. G. The gifted child. In H. Read, M. Fordham, & G. Adler (Eds.), *The collected work of C. G. Jung* (Vol. 17). NYC: Pantheon Books, 1954.

Kennedy, W. A. MMPI profiles of gifted adolescents. *Journal of Clinical Psychology*, 1962, 18, 148–149.

Klausmeier, H. J., & Check, J. Retention and transfer in children of low, average, and high intelligence. *Journal of Educational Research*, 1962, 55, 319–322.

Klausmeier, H. J., & Loughlin, L. T. Behavior during problem solving among children of low, average and high intelligence. *Journal of Educational Psychology*, 1961, 52, 148–152.

Lessinger, L. M., & Martinson, R. The use of the California Psychological Inventory with gifted pupils. *Personnel and Guidance Journal*, 1961, 39, 572–575.

Lombroso, C. *The man of genius*. London: Scott, 1891.

Lucito, L. J. Independence-conformity behavior as a function of intellect: Bright and dull children. *Exceptional Children*, 1964, 31, 5–13.

Milgram, R. M., & Milgram, N. A. Personality characteristics of gifted Israeli children. *The Journal of Genetic Psychology*, 1976, 129, 185–194.

Ramaseshan, P. H. The social and emotional adjustment of the gifted. Doctoral dissertation, University of Nebraska, 1957.

Solomon, D., Kendall, A. J., & Oberlander, M. I. Children's social attitude and value scales. In O. G. Johnson (Ed.), *Tests and measurements in child development* (Vol. 2). San Francisco: Jossey-Bass, 1976, 1074–1075.

Terman, L. M., Baldwin, B. T., & Bronson, E. Mental and physical traits of a thousand gifted children. *Genetic studies of genius* (Vol. 1). Stanford, CA: Stanford University Press, 1925.

Thorpe, L. P., Clark, W. W., & Tiegs, E. W. *California Test of Personality*. Monterey, CA: McGraw-Hill, 1953.

Warren, J. R., & Heist, P. A. Personality attributes of gifted college students. *Science*, 1960, 132, 330–337.

Wrenn, G. C., Ferguson, L. W., & Kennedy, J. L. Intelligence level and personality. *Journal of Social Psychology*, 1962, 7, 301–308.

2

Social, Emotional, and Behavioral Adjustment of Accelerated Students, Students in Gifted Classes, and Regular Students in Eighth Grade

Michael F. Sayler and William K. Brookshire

University of North Texas

This study investigated differences in the social emotional, and behavioral adjustment of gifted and regular eighth-grade students. Three groups were identified: (a) gifted students who entered school early or skipped at least one grade K-7, (b) students enrolled in eighth-grade gifted classes, and (c) regular eighth-grade students. Data were self-reported in the

Editor's Note: From Sayler, M. F., & Brookshire, W. K. (1993). Social, emotional, and behavioral adjustment of accelerated students, students in gifted classes, and regular students in eighth grade. *Gifted Child Quarterly*, 37(4), 150-154. © 1993 National Association for Gifted Children. Reprinted with permission.

National Education Longitudinal Study (NELS) from the National Center for Educational Statistics (NCES) (Ingels et al., 1989). Results indicated that accelerated students and students in gifted classes had better perceptions of their social relationships and emotional development and tended to have fewer serious school behavior problems than regular students. Contrary to commonly held beliefs, most students who entered school early or skipped elementary grades did not report unusual social isolation or experience profound emotional difficulties. They had serious behavioral problems less frequently than regular students.

The use of acceleration as an educational option for gifted students has a long history in this country. Used extensively prior to 1900 (Panel on Youth, 1974), acceleration has experienced several periods of waxing and waning interest this century (Brody & Stanley, 1991). Recently, a national survey of gifted programs found 9% to 16% of public schools allowed moderate or radical acceleration (Cox, Daniel, & Boston, 1985).

The academic benefits of acceleration are generally positive (Brody & Benbow, 1987; Daurio, 1979; Southern & Jones, 1991). A meta-analysis of 26 studies on acceleration found that the accelerated students were successful academically and achieved test scores exceeding those of their age peers and equal to those of talented older students in the advanced grades (Kulik & Kulik, 1984). Allowing gifted students to enter school early or skip grades provides developmentally appropriate education to these students (Elkind, 1988). Many experts recognize acceleration as a viable option for certain gifted students (Benbow, 1991; Cox et al., 1985; Feldhusen, 1989; National Commission on Excellence in Education, 1983; VanTassel-Baska, 1986).

Although many forms of acceleration exist (Brody & Stanley, 1991), only two are examined in this study: early school entrance and grade skipping. Early school entrance allows children to enter formal schooling at a younger chronological age than usual. Grade skipping allows students already in school to bypass one or more grade levels. Although the practices are different, practitioners view early admission and grade skipping as the same process with the same perceived problems and weaknesses (Southern, Jones, & Fiscus, 1989).

Although individuals recognize the positive academic benefits of acceleration, they often question the social or emotional effect acceleration will have on students (Cornell, Callahan, Bassin, & Ramsay, 1991; Gagné, 1983). The arguments put forward by opponents of acceleration are often based not on empirical evidence but on vague generalities and half-truths (Southern et al., 1989). Preconceived opinions rather than facts or personal experiences form the basis of most of these objections (Daurio, 1979). Interestingly, attitudes toward acceleration improve dramatically and fears subside when school officials (Southern et al., 1989) or parents (Hoffman, 1989; Howley & Howley, 1985) have personal or family experiences with acceleration.

Current research on potential social and emotional adjustment difficulties has suffered from several design problems. Much of the research on acceleration lacked appropriate cross-sectional or longitudinal orientations (Janos & Robinson, 1985). Often reference or control groups were not present, especially groups of equally gifted nonparticipants (Richardson & Benbow 1990). There is a need for studies with sample sizes that are large enough and representative enough of the population to yield clearer results (Stanley, 1991).

This study explored the social and emotional adjustment of three groups of students from a large, nationally representative sample of eighth-grade students. The three groups studied were: (a) students who had entered school early or had skipped one or more grades K-7, (b) students in gifted classes in Grade 8, and (c) regular eighth-grade students.

Putting the Research to Use

The use of acceleration for certain gifted and talented students continues to be controversial. Many parents and educators fear that an accelerated child will not do well socially or will suffer emotional adjustment problems if allowed to accelerate. This study does not provide all of the answers needed to address these fears, but it does give one more indication that acceleration works well for many children. The large stratified national sample gives us a snapshot of many accelerated students in many places and situations. Although this kind of study, with its broad focus, cannot tell us about the adjustment of each individual accelerant, in general, accelerants report feeling good about their social and emotional adjustment and are well-behaved. On most variables, their self-ratings were higher than those of regular students and as high or almost as high as those of students in gifted classes who were not accelerated.

Data used came from the first stage of the National Education Longitudinal Study: 1988 (NELS:88) from the National Center for Educational Statistics (Ingels et al., 1989). The Center will follow this cohort of eighth graders as they leave elementary school (Grade 8) through high school (Grades 10 and 12) and into college and careers (2 years after high school graduation). The schools ($N = 1,052$) and students ($N = 24,599$) were selected using a two-stage nationally representative stratified procedure: first a selection of schools was drawn and then students were sampled from the schools. The sample included both public and private schools. Students in this study completed a survey and took a battery of achievement tests. One parent of each student completed a survey. School administrators completed surveys about the schools in which the students were enrolled. Two randomly selected teachers from each school completed surveys. These teachers came from two of four subject areas: language arts, math, science, or social studies.

The current study was a post hoc analysis of the NELS:88 data. Using an existing data base limited the researchers' flexibility in selecting instruments, questions, and data-gathering techniques and in creating research questions. These limitations were offset by the large size and national representativeness of the subjects. Given the post hoc limitations, social and emotional adjustment were operationalized from the existing NELS:88 data in four areas: self-concept, locus of control, gross behavior problems, and self-reporting peer relationships and reference groups.

Locus of control and self concept were composite scales from the NELS:88 data (see Figure 1). The self concept scale provided a measure of global self-concept. Scores for the two scales were average z scores of the associated question-naire items. Coefficient alpha was calculated for each scale (locus of control = .68, self-concept = .79). Validity data for the two scales were not presented in the NELS:88 technical manuals. Items were selected by the National Center for Educational Statistics (Ingels et al., 1989) because of their construct validity and their comparability to the two other major studies of the Center (The National Longitudinal Study, NLS-72; High School and Beyond, HS&B, cited in Ingels et al., 1989).

Although the NELS:88 study did not specifically address behavioral adjustment problems of gifted students, two gross measures of behavioral adjustment were available: being sent to the principal's office for behavioral problems or having a warning sent to the parents concerning behavioral problems. These self-reporting measures were limited indicators of behavioral adjustment problems. Usually, only the most egregious problems result in being called to the principal's office or in a letter being sent to the parents. Perceived social adjustment was assessed through self-report of how the respondents thought their classmates viewed them (popular, athletic, good student, important, or trouble maker).

The total score from a battery of achievement tests, language arts, mathematics, science, and social studies, designed for the NELS:88 (Rock & Pollack, 1991) assessed the achievement of the students in each group. The subscales that comprised the composite scale had coefficient alpha reliabilities ranging from .75 to .90.

METHOD

Subjects

Three groups were drawn from the NELS:88 data base of 24,599 eighth-grade students. First, the accelerated students in the sample were identified. An initial group of accelerated students was located based on self-reporting of acceleration (a survey item). This produced a sample that included large

Figure 1   Locus-of-Control and Self-Concept Items

Locus-of-Control Items

- I don't have enough control over the direction my life is taking
- In my life, good luck is more important than hard work for success
- Every time I try to get ahead, something or somebody stops me
- My plans hardly ever work out, so planning only makes me unhappy
- *When I make plans, I am almost certain I can make them work*
- Chance and luck are very important for what happens in my life

Self-Concept Items

- *I feel good about myself*
- *I feel I am a person of worth, the equal of other people*
- *I am able to do things as well as most other people*
- *On the whole, I am satisfied with myself*
- I certainly feel useless at times
- I feel I do not have much to be proud of

Reverse scored items

---

numbers of nongifted students, individuals who had been retained in the early grades and later "accelerated" back to their original cohort group. An alternative strategy was then developed to identify accelerated gifted students. All subjects who were younger than 11 years old in September of 1988 were included as accelerants. These students were at least 2 years younger than regular eighth graders. Additionally, students who were 12 and who had birthdays after January 1, 1974, were included. January 1 was selected as a safe date, indicating kindergarten entrance at age 5 with a January 1 birthday. Finally, students who turned 12 between September 1, 1988, and January 1, 1989, and who reported they had been accelerated were included in the accelerated group. This three-part process produced an accurate but conservative sample of accelerants ($n = 365$); some accelerants were probably not identified by this process. Another group that could not be identified were those gifted students who had been accelerated and because of adjustment or academic problems were later held back. Such accelerants would appear as gifted or regular students using these selection criteria.

Two comparison groups, approximately equal in size to the accelerated group, were randomly selected (gifted, $n = 334$ and regular students, $n = 323$). This provided equally weighted groups for analysis. The gifted group of students was a computer-generated random sample of the 4,633 students in the NELS:88 study who reported they participated in gifted classes during Grade 8. Students who had been included in the accelerated group were excluded from the set of those in gifted programs before the random sample was taken. The regular group of students included a computer-generated random sample of all 24,599 eighth graders in the study excluding those who were selected as accelerants or those in gifted classes.

Procedures

Sources of data on students included items from a survey, scales derived from items in the survey, and separate achievement tests. Parents completed surveys only. Pertinent items, composite self-concept and locus of control scales, and achievement tests were analyzed.

RESULTS

There was a significant difference in gender distribution among the three groups, although the effect size was small (χ^2 = 9.142, p = .01; effect size = .09). The percentage of males in the gifted group was higher (56% male) than in the entire sample of students in the study (48% male). The accelerated group had more females (55% female) than the group as a whole (52% females).

The socioeconomic status (SES) of the regular group was evenly distributed across all 4 quartiles (25.5%, 24.6%, 27.1%, 22.8%). Most students in the accelerated (71.6%) and gifted groups (65.1%) came from the upper 2 quartiles. The parents of students in the accelerated group graduated from college more frequently (52%) than parents of students in gifted classes (45%), or the parents of students in regular classes (24%) (χ^2 = 70.346, effect size = .26).

On average, students in the accelerated group had the highest level of internal locus of control, followed by students in the gifted and regular groups (see Table 1). The global self-concepts of both the gifted and accelerated groups were higher than those of the regular group sample.

The accelerated group had higher composite achievement scores than did either the gifted group or the regular group (see Table 1). Both the accelerated and gifted groups were about one half of one standard deviation above the mean of the entire NELS:88 sample.

Multivariate analysis of variance was used to analyze the differences in the variables: locus of control, self-concept, and composite achievement test score. Wilks' lambda was 0.929 (F = 12.66, df = 6,2014, p = .0001), showing a significant difference among the three groups on the three variables. Univariate analysis of variance was used after the significant multivariate analysis. Tukey (HSD) pairwise comparison identified both the accelerated group and gifted group means as higher than the regular group mean (see Table 1) on all three variables. Slight but significant differences were found for locus of control (F = 9.80, df = 2,1009, p = .0001; effect size = .14), self-concept (F = 4.09, df = 2,1009, p = .017; effect size = .09), and composite achievement (F = 35.65, df = 2,1009, p = .0001; effect size = .27).

The gifted students said their peers saw them as good students, popular, important, and athletic more often than regular or accelerated students did (see Table 2). Accelerated students reported that they were more likely than regular students to be seen as good students by their peers, but not as often as students in the gifted group did. The accelerated group reported being seen as troublemakers significantly less than the regular group.

Table 1   Average Locus-of-Control, Self-Concept, And Achievement Levels

Variable Label	n	Mean (z-scores)	SD	Range
Locus of Control				
Accelerated	365	0.162	0.614	−2.450 to 1.280
Gifted	343	0.127	0.674	−2.090 to 1.280
Regular	323	−0.055	0.656	−2.300 to 1.280
Self-Concept				
Accelerated	365	0.113	0.707	−2.690 to 1.210
Gifted	344	0.133	0.680	−2.510 to 1.210
Regular	323	−0.015	0.690	−2.690 to 1.210
Composite Score on Achievement Test				
Accelerated	362	0.603	1.046	−2.180 to 2.098
Gifted	337	0.514	1.158	−2.127 to 2.098
Regular	317	−0.034	0.959	−2.110 to 1.971

Subjects reported the number of times they were sent to the office for misbehaving or their parents received a warning about their behavior. The accelerated group was sent to the office fewer times than were students in the regular group. There was no significant difference among the groups in the frequency of parents receiving a warning about behavior (see Table 3).

DISCUSSION

This study explored the social and emotional adjustment of three groups of students from a large, nationally representative, cross-sectional sample of eighth-grade students. Comparisons were made among groups on demographic, academic, social, adjustment, and gross behavioral variables. Groups studied included students who entered school early or skipped at least one grade K-7, students in gifted classes in Grade 8, and regular eighth-grade students.

The large cross-sectional nature of the study provided clearer evidence of the appropriateness of acceleration than was available from previous studies with smaller, program-specific subject pools. All geographic areas of the country, income levels, ethnic groups, rural and urban schools, and public and private schools were sampled. This added a level of validity and generalizability to the findings not easily produced with smaller samples.

The fear that acceleration usually or inevitably leads to academic, social, or emotional maladjustment was not supported. The accelerated students, on average, were not disadvantaged by early entrance or grade skipping prior to

Table 2   Peer Perceptions (Percentages)

Variable Group	Very	Somewhat	Not at All	Pairwise Comparison
Seen as popular				
Accelerated	17.09	59.38	23.53	A = G ($p < .001$)
Gifted	23.88	63.88	12.24	A = R ($p = .487$)
Regular	15.02	63.90	21.09	G = R ($p = .001$)
Chi-square		20.95 ($p < .001$)		
Seen as athletic				
Accelerated	18.38	50.97	30.64	A = G ($p < .001$)
Gifted	35.82	44.78	19.40	A = R ($p = .242$)
Regular	23.70	47.73	28.57	G = R ($p = .001$)
Chi-square		31.82 ($p < .001$)		
Seen as good student				
Accelerated	47.65	46.54	5.82	A = G ($p = .004$)
Gifted	60.06	34.91	5.03	A = R ($p < .001$)
Regular	32.59	58.86	8.54	G = R ($p < .001$)
Chi-square		49.79 ($p < .001$)		
Seen as important				
Accelerated	21.62	62.22	15.83	A = G ($p = .015$)
Gifted	30.21	59.21	10.57	A = R ($p = .140$)
Regular	16.77	63.23	20.00	G = R ($p < .001$)
Chi-square		22.62 ($p < .001$)		
Seen as troublemaker				
Accelerated	3.90	15.60	80.50	A = G ($p = .321$)
Gifted	4.85	19.39	75.76	A = R ($p = .006$)
Regular	6.11	24.12	69.77	G = R ($p = .235$)
Chi-square		10.42 ($p = .034$)		

eighth grade. They displayed levels of emotional adjustment and feelings of acceptance by others that were higher than those of regular students and about the same as those of older students identified as gifted.

At least one alternative interpretation of the preception of peer acceptance data is possible. The self-reporting of peer relationships may be an indicator of the students' self-concept. The acceptance variables (important, popular, good student, athletic) might represent distinct elements of multifaceted self-concepts (Griffin, Classin, & Young, 1981). Using the hypothesis that the self-reporting of peer relationships is really a measure of multifaceted self-concept, evidence of academic self-concept is found in the students' answer to whether others saw them as good students. Students in gifted classes expressed more confidence that others saw them as good students, evidence of a strong academic self-concept. Likewise, accelerated students' answers evidenced better academic self-concepts than those of regular students but not as high as those of the older students in gifted classes. Students in gifted classes had significantly

Table 3   Self-Reported Records of Behavioral Problems

	Never	Once or Twice	More Than Twice	
Sent to office for misbehaving				
Accelerated	77.35	18.78	3.87	A = G (p = .070)
Gifted	74.78	17.30	7.92	A = R (p = .006)
Regular	67.59	24.07	8.33	G = R (p = .085)
Chi-square		13.00 (p = .011)		
Parents received warning about behavior				
Accelerated	83.47	12.67	3.86	A = G (p = .070)
Gifted	76.54	18.18	5.28	A = R (p = .308)
Regular	78.95	15.79	5.26	G = R (p = .711)
Chi-square		5.56 (p = .235)		

higher self-ratings for being seen as athletic, evidence for a better than average athletic self-concept. Accelerated and regular students did not seem to differ on this variable. Students in gifted classes reported higher ratings for popularity and importance, possibly indicating a social self-concept that was higher than that of accelerated or regular students. Again, accelerated and regular students rated these items about the same. The sensitivity of all of these measures and the power of this hypothesis are limited; each conjecture is based on one or two self-reported items.

This study provided a snapshot of the pervasiveness of early school entrance or grade skipping prior to eighth grade in American schools in 1988. Only 1.3% of eighth-grade students in this study could be identified as being accelerated. A study by Cox et al. (1985) found that acceleration was rarely used as an educational option: between 9% and 16% of schools responding to a national survey allowed either moderate or radical acceleration. The current study suggests that even if 9% to 16% of schools allow acceleration, few students in those schools are ever accelerated.

This study illustrates a continuing problem in identifying gifted students: the low incidence of children from families with lower socioeconomic status among accelerants and in gifted programs. The students in the accelerated and gifted groups came mainly from families with income, resources, and experiences that placed them in the top half of families nationally. Unlike students in the regular group, accelerated students and students in gifted classes were more likely to have at least one parent who had a college education.

This study has several limiting factors. Due to the post hoc nature of the analysis, some accelerants and gifted students may have been missed. Students in the gifted group were identified only through self-reporting. No qualitative analysis of the types of gifted programs these students attended was possible.

The study does not address the social, emotional, or behavioral characteristics of accelerants who experienced adjustment problems and were retained, becoming on-grade again. Although the total number of accelerants who later were held back would seem to be a small portion of the few students who ever accelerate, the characteristics of these one-time accelerants need to be explored. A case study approach might best identify and illuminate the factors that differentiate unsuccessful accelerants from successful ones.

The data in the current study provide a basis for future analysis and discussion of the social and emotional impact of acceleration on gifted students. Our understanding of the social and emotional adjustment of accelerated students will improve as the students in this study are followed through their secondary and postsecondary education. Future analyses will monitor the accelerated students identified in this study, add students accelerated after Grade 8, look for students who were accelerated before eighth grade but held back after eighth grade, and compare and contrast the accelerants with high and low self-concepts and adjustment.

REFERENCES

Benbow, C. P. (1991). Meeting the needs of gifted students through acceleration. In M. C. Wang, M. C. Reynolds, & H. J. Walberg (Eds.), *Handbook of special education* (Vol. 4, pp 23–36). Elmsford, NY: Pergamon.

Brody, L. E., & Benbow, C. P. (1987). Accelerative strategies: How effective are they for the gifted? *Gifted Child Quarterly, 31*, 105–109.

Brody, L. E., & Stanley, J. C. (1991). Young college students: Assessing factors that contribute to success. In W. Southern & E. Jones (Eds.), *Academic acceleration of gifted children* (pp. 102–132). New York: Teachers College Press.

Cornell, D. G., Callahan, C. M., Basin, L. E., & Ramsay, S. G. (1991) Affective development in accelerated students. In W. Southern & E. Jones (Eds.). *Academic acceleration of gifted children* (pp. 74–101). New York: Teachers College Press.

Cox, J., Daniel, N., & Boston, B. O. (1985). *Educating able learners.* Austin, TX: University of Texas Press.

Daurio, S. P. (1979). Educational enrichment versus acceleration: A review of the literature. In W. C. George, S. J. Cohn, & J. C. Stanley (Eds.), *Educating the gifted* (pp. 13–63). Baltimore, MD: The Johns Hopkins University Press.

Elkind, D. (1988). Mental acceleration. *Journal for the Education of the Gifted, 11*(4), 19–31.

Feldhusen, J. F. (1989). Synthesis of research on gifted youth. *Educational Leadership, 46*, 6–11.

Gagné, F. (1983). Perceptions of programs for gifted children: Agreement on principles, but disagreement over modalities. *Journal of Special Educational, 7*(2), 51–56.

Griffin, N., Classin, L., & Young, R. D. (1981). Measurement of global self-concept versus multiple role-specific self-concepts in adolescents. *Adolescence, 26*(1), 49–56.

Hoffman, S. G. (1989). What the books don't tell you about grade skipping. *Gifted Child Today, 12*(1) 37–39.

Howley, C. B., & Howley, A. A. (1985). A personal record: Is acceleration worth the effort? *Roeper Review, 8*(1), 43–45.

Ingels, S. J., Abraham, S. Y., Rasinski, K., Kan, R., Spencer, B. D., & Frankel, M. R. (1989). *User's manual: National education longitudinal study of 1988* (NCES Publication No. 90–404). Washington, DC: U.S. Department of Education, Office of Educational Research and Improvement.

Janos, P. M., & Robinson, N. R. (1985). The performance of students in a program of radical acceleration at the university level. *Gifted Child Quarterly, 29*, 175–179.

Kulik, J. A., & Kulik, C.-L. C. (1984). Effects of accelerated instruction on students. *Review of Educational Research, 54*, 409–426.

National Commission on Excellence in Education (1983). *A nation at risk: The imperative for educational reform.* Washington, DC: U.S. Government Printing Office.

Panel on Youth of the President's Science Advisory Committee (1974). History of age grouping in America. In J. S. Coleman et al. (Eds.), *Youth: Transition to adulthood* (pp. 9–29). Chicago, IL: University of Chicago Press.

Richardson, T. M., & Benbow, C. P. (1990). Long-term effects of acceleration on the social emotional adjustment of mathematically precocious youths. *Journal of Educational Psychology, 82*(3), 464–470.

Rock, D. A., & Pollack, J. M. (1991). *Psychometric report for the NELS:88 base year test battery: Contractor report* (NCES Publication No. 91–468). Washington, DC: U.S. Department of Education. Office of Educational Research and Improvement.

Southern, W. T., & Jones, E. D. (Eds.). (1991). *The academic acceleration of gifted children.* New York: Teachers College Press.

Southern, T. W., Jones, E. D., & Fiscus, E. D. (1989). Practitioner objections to the academic acceleration of gifted children. *Gifted Child Quarterly, 33*, 29–35.

Stanley, J. C. (1991). Critique of "Socioemotional adjustment of adolescent girls in a residential acceleration program." *Gifted Child Quarterly, 35*, 67–70.

VanTassel-Baska, J. C. (1986). Acceleration. In C. J. Maker (Ed.), *Critical issues in gifted education, defensible programs for the gifted* (pp. 179–190). Rockville, MD: Aspen.

3

Depression and Suicidal Ideation Among Academically Gifted Adolescents

Jean A. Baker

University of Georgia

Depression and suicidal ideation among academically gifted adolescents, exceptionally gifted adolescents, and adolescents average in academic performance were examined. No significant differences were detected among the three groups in level, severity, or nature of distress experienced. Results are discussed in light of the supportive interventions appropriate for high school students and the need for further research with subgroups of gifted students more likely to experience psychological distress.

Editor's Note: From Baker, J. A. (1995). Depression and suicidal ideation among academically gifted adolescents. *Gifted Child Quarterly*, 39(4), 218-223. © 1995 National Association for Gifted Children. Reprinted with permission.

DEPRESSION AND SUICIDAL IDEATION AMONG ACADEMICALLY GIFTED ADOLESCENTS

Educators are becoming increasingly aware of the mental health needs of students. Of special concern are depression and suicidal behavior among adolescents. This awareness is due to the prevalence and seriousness of these problems. Epidemiological evidence shows that approximately 10–12% of high school students experience clinically significant levels of depression. Similarly, thoughts about suicide, or suicidal ideation, affect approximately the same percentage of adolescents, with 11% of adolescents in public high schools exhibiting some kind of suicidal behavior (Kovacs, 1989; Reynolds, 1990). To date there is a paucity of research in this area specific to gifted and talented students. Although educators often feel these students to be "at-risk," little empirical evidence exists to substantiate this claim.

Depression in Gifted Adolescents

Depression is best conceptualized as a cluster of symptoms or syndrome (Kendall, Cantwell & Kazdin, 1989) characterized predominantly by sadness and a loss of interest in everyday activities (American Psychiatric Association, 1994). A substantial body of literature documents the course and nature of depression in adolescents (Reynolds, 1992). However, very little of this is specific to gifted and talented students.

A decade ago, preliminary research efforts reported that gifted students obtained average or below average scores on a depression measure (Berndt, Kaiser & Van Aalst, 1982; Kaiser & Berndt, 1985). However, these studies involved a select group of gifted students and did not compare depression in this group to that of typical adolescents or to gifted students from public school settings. We do not have current, well-controlled empirical efforts describing the prevalence, severity, or nature of depression in gifted adolescents.

Suicidal Ideation in Gifted Adolescents

Suicidal behaviors are conceptualized along a continuum, with morbid thoughts and vague wishes for death at one end and completed suicides at the other (Reynolds, 1988). There are no well-controlled studies of suicidal ideation of attempts of suicide in gifted adolescents. Lajoie and Shore (1981) reviewed the suicide literature as it pertains to giftedness and concluded that there appears to be no empirical support for differences in IQ between suicidal and nonsuicidal persons. The authors cite a below-average suicide rate in reviewing Lewis Terman's longitudinal data on gifted children. However, Delisle (1984) states that over-representation of suicides and suicidal behaviors among high-achieving college students and high school students participating in "cluster" suicides is possible. It is unclear if suicidal risk results from giftedness or from other environmental or personal factors. Despite the lack of empirical evidence, concern is voiced that gifted students may be at high risk for suicide (e.g., Hayes Sloat, 1989; Smith, 1990).

Purpose of the Study

This study explored the prevalence and nature of depression and suicidal ideation in samples of academically talented students and their general cohort of peers. It was hypothesized that very few differences would emerge between gifted students, exceptionally gifted students, and a general cohort comparison group.

Putting the Research to Use

This study suggests that academically gifted adolescents, even exceptionally gifted students, are not more at risk for depression or suicidal ideation than their general cohort of peers. However, neither are they less depressed. The implications of this finding are that educators of the gifted can expect to find approximately 10% of their high school–aged students experiencing clinically significant levels of depressive symptoms. Teachers need to be alerted to signs of depression in adolescents and appropriate school-based prevention or intervention efforts seem warranted for high school students.

METHOD

Subjects

A total of 146 subjects from Midwestern communities participated in this study.

"Exceptionally" gifted students. A group of 32 "exceptional" students were recruited from students scoring above 900 on the Scholastic Aptitude Test (SAT) taken at approximately age thirteen as part of the Northwest Talent Search Program. Students scoring above 900 are generally considered exceptionally talented and comprise the top 1% of academically gifted students of this age (E. Schatz, personal communication, October, 1992; VanTassel-Baska, 1984). Students were primarily from the 9th grade (25 students; of the remaining, 6 were in junior high and 1 was in 11th grade). The sample was 56% male and 44% female. The sample was 90% Caucasian, 3% Asian, 3% Hispanic, and 3% other. Based on student reports of their parents' occupations, 84% reported at least one parent in one of the two highest SES levels [using Hollingshead's (1975) indices].

Gifted students. Forty-six (46) students whose academic achievement placed them in the upper 5% of their class rankings from two suburban public high schools were recruited as the "academically gifted" group for this study. The students were in grades 9 through 11.

An additional twelve (12) students selecting to take the SAT and scoring 600 or less from the Talent Search group were also included in this group. They had scored above the 95th percentile on standardized achievement tests but did not distinguish themselves on out-of-level testing. The twelve students did not differ from the public school gifted sample in this study on any demographic variable other than age. On the whole they were slightly younger, ranging from 7th to 10th grade, with the majority in the ninth grade. Because the norms of all of the measures used in this study accommodate 7th through 12th graders, with the exception of the suicidal ideation questionnaire, data from these students were collapsed into the "gifted" public school sample for all but the suicidal ideation analyses.

Thus, a total of 58 students constituted the "gifted" group for this study. The sample was 29% male and 71% female. The disproportionate number of females in this group reflected the composition of the top 5% of students in these schools. The sample was 95% Caucasian, 3% Asian, and 2% Hispanic. Based on student reports of their parent's occupations, 80% reported at least one parent in one of the two highest SES levels.

Academically average group. Fifty-six (56) students in grades 9 through 11 from the public high schools were selected from around the midpoint of their class rankings. This group constituted an average comparison group. The sample was 55% male and 45% female. The sample was 96% Caucasian, 2% African-American, and 2% Hispanic. Based on student reports of their parents' occupations, 70% reported at least one parent in one of the two highest SES levels.

The exceptional, gifted, and average groups were comparable on all demographic variables assessed with some exceptions. The exceptional group was younger than both the average and gifted groups. More females than males were represented in the gifted group.

Procedure

Public school samples. Active parental consent was obtained from all participating students via a permission letter sent home to parents. Parents were informed that names of students scoring above the clinical cut-off for the measures would be given to the school's guidance staff who would notify them and follow-up with affected students. There was a 64% return rate for the gifted students and a 45% return rate for the average students. These parental consent return rates were typical for research conducted in these schools.

All data were collected in school during the regular school day. The questionnaires were administered to students in a classroom or study hall, and students were given an opportunity to withdraw their participation at any time.

All students completed the questionnaire packets. The depression and suicidal ideation questionnaires were administered as part of a larger protocol examining the nature of stress in gifted students. Following data collection, students were provided with an information sheet discussing teen stress and listing school and community counseling resources. The schools were notified of students scoring above the clinical cut-off on the depression or suicidal ideation measures.

Northwest Talent Search sample. Students and parents living within a 200-mile radius were invited to a university campus for data collection in conjunction with an enrichment activity. Again, only students with active parental consent were included. There was a much lower participation rate for these students (15%), attributable primarily to the distance and the active parental involvement required to drive these students to campus. Parents were notified of students scoring above the clinical cut-off on any of the distress measures.

Instrumentation

The *Reynolds Adolescent Depression Scale* (RADS; Reynolds, 1987) was utilized to measure depression. The RADS is a 30-item self-report inventory of depressive symptomatology for 7th through 12th graders. The manual reports well-established reliability and validity data for the scale. Its internal consistency reliability (Cronbach alpha) in this study was .92. Although the RADS is best utilized as a strong unitary measure of depression, factor analyses suggest that it measures four types of depressive symptomatology with items reflective of cognitive, somatic, mood, and despondency characteristic of depression.

Suicidal ideation was measured using the *Suicidal Ideation Questionnaire* (SIQ; Reynolds, 1988). The SIQ measures suicidal thoughts ranging from mild ideas about death to extreme intentions to harm oneself. It has both a 30-item senior-high form (SIQ) and a 10-item junior high form (SIQJr). The manual reports excellent reliability and validity data for both of this measure. Internal consistency reliabilities in this study were .97 and .90 for the senior and junior high forms, respectively.

RESULTS

Means and standard deviations for each of the measures by group and gender are reported in Table 1. Data analysis was planned separately for males and females because of the significant gender differences noted on the measures used in this study.

Differences in Level of Depression and Suicidal Ideation

It was hypothesized that few differences would exist between gifted, exceptionally gifted, and average students in their self-reported level of depression

Table 1   Means (M) and Standard Deviations (SD) for Measures by Group and by Gender

Measure	Average		Group Gifted		Exceptional	
	M n = 30	F 25	M 17	F 41	M 18	F 14
RADS	M = 55.63	65.40	57.00	61.51	54.89	65.50
	SD = 10.14	13.67	9.79	14.33	10.01	12.64
SIQ	M = 16.12	24.28	13.58	22.67		
	SD = 12.78	28.23	11.05	26.72		
SIQJr	M =		12.20	13.13	12.59	18.15
	SD =		8.23	12.87	5.77	16.15

and suicidal ideation. This was indeed the case. Planned comparisons using the Dunn procedure for comparing means of nested contrasts were calculated separately for each dependent measure (see Table 2). Each nest was afforded an alpha level of .05; all tests were two-tailed. Data were analyzed separately for boys and girls by nesting group in sex. For the RADS data, comparisons were made between gifted and average students (G/A), average and exceptional students (A/E), and gifted to exceptional students (G/E). For the SIQ, the senior high school form allowed comparisons between gifted and average (G/A) students drawn from the public school sample. Comparisons between exceptional and gifted (G/E) students in level of suicidal ideation were made using the Talent Search students' reports on the SIQJr. An examination of Table 2 reveals no significant difference in level of depression or suicidal ideation between groups.

Gender differences within groups were also calculated using Dunn planned comparisons by nesting gender in group (see Table 3). All tests were one-tailed because of the significant gender differences expected on these measures. Expected differences were found on the RADS, with girls reporting more depression than boys for all but the average group. No significant differences were noted between genders on the suicidal ideation questionnaires.

Prevalence of Depression Across Groups

Perhaps of more interest clinically than mean differences between groups were differences in the proportion of students reporting clinically significant levels of depression or suicidal ideation between groups. For the RADS, no significant difference was noted between groups for proportions of students scoring above the clinical cutoff score of 77 (Chi-square = .38, 2 df, $p = .82$). Similarly, no differences were noted for students scoring above the SIQ cutoff score of 41 (Chi-square = .25, 1 df, $p = .62$) or for students scoring above the SIQJr. cutoff score of 31 (Chi-square = .02, 1 df, $p = .90$).

Table 2 *t* Values for Nested Contrasts by Group in Gender for Measures

| Measure (df) | Group | | | | | |
| | Girls | | | Boys | | |
	G/A	A/E	G/E	G/A	A/E	G/E
RADS (6,144)	1.25	− 0.02	− 1.05	− 0.37	0.02	0.51
SIQ (1,97)	.42			.10		
SIQJr (1,42)			.60			.70

*p < .05

Table 3 *t* Values for Nested Contrasts by Gender in Group for Measures

| Measure (df) | M v. F | | |
	GT	Av	Ex
RADS (3,144)	2.93*	1.27	2.42*
SIQ (1,97)	1.76	1.72	
SIQJr (1,42)	.60		.84

*p < .05

Nature of Depression

Whether or not depression was experienced differently by gifted students relative to their average ability peers was also of interest in this study. Differences between groups on the four types of depressive symptomatology measured by the RADS were calculated using nested planned comparisons. Means and standard deviations are reported in Table 4. Table 5 presents the Dunn test statistic, values by group for the cognitive, despondency, somatic, and mood factors of the RADS (all tests were two-tailed). No significant differences were found among groups on the four factors of the RADS.

DISCUSSION

The question of whether or not academically talented students are at risk for mental health problems has been of concern for educators of the gifted. The major finding from this study is that academically able and exceptionally able students are not distinguishable from average students by differences in levels of depression or suicidal ideation. This supports the general findings from previous research (e.g., Berndt et al., 1982) that found gifted adolescents did not show elevated levels of depression. This research differs from previous work

Table 4   Means (M) and Standard Deviations (SD) for RADS Factors by Group and by Gender

Factor	Average M n = 30	Average F 25	Group Gifted M 17	Group Gifted F 41	Exceptional M 18	Exceptional F 14
Cog.	M = 13.07	16.24	13.53	13.88	12.72	14.29
	SD = 3.48	5.68	3.68	4.92	4.03	4.60
Desp.	M = 19.43	23.12	20.00	23.56	19.44	24.36
	SD = 4.30	4.42	4.33	6.10	4.72	5.11
Mood.	M = 8.63	9.16	8.47	8.39	8.17	9.14
	SD = 1.73	2.25	1.55	1.73	2.23	1.96
Som.	M = 12.00	14.12	12.59	13.29	12.17	14.86
	SD = 2.83	3.53	3.36	4.01	2.07	3.63

Table 5 t Values for Nested Contrasts by Group in Gender for RADS Factors

Group	Cog.	Desp.	Mood	Som.
Girls				
G vs. A	2.05	− 0.35	1.60	0.99
A vs. E	1.29	− 0.74	0.03	− 0.65
G vs. E	− 0.29	− 0.51	− 1.28	− 1.51
Boys				
G vs. A	− 0.34	− 0.30	0.28	− 0.57
A vs. E	0.25	− 0.01	0.82	− 0.16
G vs. E	0.53	0.33	0.47	0.37

* $p < .05$

with adolescents that noted less depression in gifted students when their performance was compared to the measure's norms (Berndt et al., 1982; Kaiser & Berndt, 1985). Academically able students in this study were not less depressed than their average peers. This finding is significant for educators working with gifted students as they may expect to see their students struggle with the same level of affective distress as expected for adolescents in general. In this study, 8% of the gifted adolescents, 9% of the average adolescents, and 12% of the exceptional adolescents were experiencing significant levels of depression.

Also of interest in this study was the nature of depression in gifted adolescents. There is some concern that gifted students may overintellectualize and experience distress via cognitive distortions. Berndt and his colleagues (1982, 1985) noted cognitive features of depression as prominent in their sample of academically talented, depressed students. However, the finding from this study was the similarity between groups in the way depressive symptoms are experienced. The main implication from this finding is that therapeutic interventions for depressed adolescents should be applicable to affected gifted and talented students. However, further comparisons with clinical samples of gifted and average ability students are needed to support this contention.

These data do not support the contention that able students are more at risk for suicidal ideation than their general cohort peers. This research suggests more similarities than differences between average and able students. However, survey research is not sensitive to patterns of individual differences. Future research into distress in gifted adolescents using methodology that is more idiopathic may be helpful in describing patterns of distress in gifted adolescents.

Before generalizing from these results, several cautions must be made due to the nature of the sample. Potential selection bias, resulting from the active parental consent required for participation, poses a threat to the validity of research on children's psychological distress. It is possible there was an undersampling of distressed children in this study because of the parental consent requirement. That selection bias is especially true for the exceptional students whose parents actively participated by driving them to campus for data collection.

Although selection bias is of concern in all depression research, it was not felt to unduly influence the results from this study. The participating students' scores on the depression and suicidal ideation measures, and the proportion of students experiencing distress, were comparable to those from previous studies. It is noteworthy that comparability holds for the exceptional students whose participation rate is the most problematic in this study.

Another potential limitation is the heterogeneity and size of the groups. The exceptional group was younger than the others. Because the norms of the measures accommodated the full age and grade spread in the study, age differences were not considered a grave concern. However, the gifted group oversampled girls by a 2-to-1 margin. The low number of gifted boys in the study limits the utility of this study in helping us understand depression in this group or possible gender differences among gifted adolescents. Further work with larger representations of gifted boys may be needed to elucidate possible gender differences.

Finally, it is important to note that this study evaluated distress among highly achieving students from schools with long-standing, well-supported programs for gifted students. We would not expect comparable data from underachieving students or from students in schools offering little academic support.

Several implications for educators are readily apparent from these data. First, although depression was not an excessive problem for able students, they experienced much the same prevalence rate as did their average peers. This suggests that educators of the gifted should be alerted that approximately 10% of their students may be suffering from clinically significant levels of depression. This finding supports the need for teachers to receive training in recognizing and intervening with depressed students in their classrooms (Baker & Reynolds, 1994). Secondly, gifted students, like their average peers, could benefit from preventive affective education or from support to understand their affective development and to cope with stressors and psychological distress. Given the incidence of depressive symptomatology in adolescents, school-based curricula seem warranted to address the mental health needs of high school students.

REFERENCES

American Psychiatric Association. (1994). *Diagnostic and statistical manual of mental disorders* (4th edition). Washington, DC: Author:

Baker, J. A., & Reynolds, W. M. (1994). *Enhancing teachers' recognition of depressed children in their classrooms: A teacher training model.* Manuscript in preparation.

Berndt, D., Kaiser, C., & Van Aalst, F. (1982). Depression and self-actualization in gifted adolescents. *Journal of Clinical Psychology, 38,* 142–150.

Delisle, J. R. (1984). Death with honors: Suicide among gifted adolescents. *Journal of Counseling and Development, 64,* 558–560.

Hayes, M. L., & Sloat, R. S. (1989). Gifted students at risk for suicide. *Roeper Review, 12,* 102–207.

Hollingshead, A. B. (1975). *Four factor index of social position.* New Haven, CT: Author.

Kaiser, C., & Berndt, D. (1985). Predictors of loneliness in the gifted adolescent. *Gifted Child Quarterly, 29,* 74–77.

Kendall, P. C., Cantwell, D. P. & Kazdin, A. E. (1989). Depression in children and adolescents: Assessment issues and recommendations. *Cognitive Therapy and Research, 13,* 109–146.

Kovacs, M. (1989). Affective disorders in children and adolescents. *American Psychologist, 44,* 209–215.

Lajoie, S. P., & Shore, B. M. (1981). Three myths? The over-representation of the gifted among dropouts, delinquents and suicides. *Gifted Child Quarterly, 25,* 138–143.

Reynolds, W. M. (1987). *The Reynolds Adolescent Depression Scale.* Odessa, FL.: Psychological Assessment Resources.

Reynolds W. M. (1988). *The Suicidal Ideation Questionnaire.* Odessa, FL: Psychological Assessment Resources.

Reynolds, W. M. (1990). Depression in children and adolescents: Nature, diagnosis, assessment and treatment. *School Psychology Review, 19,* 158–173.

Reynolds, W. M. (1992). Depression in children and adolescents. In W. M. Reynolds (Ed.), *Internalizing disorders in children and adolescents* (pp. 149–254). New York: Wiley & Sons.

Smith, K. (1990). Suicidal behavior in school-aged youth. *School Psychology Review, 19,* 186–195.

VanTassel-Baska, J. (1984). The talent search as an identification model. *Gifted Child Quarterly, 28,* 172–176.

4

High Ability Students Who Are Unpopular With Their Peers

Dewey G. Cornell

University of Virginia

Although previous studies have found that high ability students generally enjoy favorable peer status, few studies have investigated those high ability students who are unpopular even with peers of comparable ability. The present study compared unpopular high ability students with average and popular groups on measures of achievement, family social status, and personality adjustment. Results indicate relatively few differences between average and popular students, but unpopular students are distinguished by lower social self-concept and academic self-esteem, as well as by less prestigious paternal occupations. There was no evidence that unpopular students were academically less capable, less mature, or more anxious than their more popular peers.

Editor's Note: From Cornell, D. G. (1990). High ability students who are unpopular with their peers. *Gifted Child Quarterly*, 34(4), 155-160. © 1990 National Association for Gifted Children. Reprinted with permission.

Peer relations is a critically important factor in child development. Theorists from Piaget to Erikson have emphasized that the child's interactions with peers provide a context for cognitive development, the growth of social skills, the evolution of self-concept, and the establishment of moral and social values (Erikson, 1963; Piaget, 1965). Harry Stack Sullivan (1953) contended that peer relations fulfilled a fundamental human need and provided an essential basis for the transition from childish egocentrism to a more mature, reciprocal perspective on interpersonal relations.

Numerous investigators have confirmed that childhood difficulties in peer relations are associated with serious maladjustment in adulthood (Parker & Asher, 1987). Accordingly, there has been a recent resurgence of research interest in peer relations (Mueller & Cooper, 1986; Parker & Asher, 1987), as well as efforts to identify and treat children with problems in peer relations (Schneider, Rubin & Ledingham, 1985). Children who are unpopular with their peers in one setting often continue to have difficulties making friends in the future (Rubin & Mills, 1988).

Peer Relations of High Ability Youth

Almost all research on the peer relations of high ability youth has focused on refuting the stereotype that they are social misfits who are rejected by their classmates (Austin & Draper, 1981; Montemayor, 1984; but see also Schneider, 1987). The design of such studies usually involves obtaining peer ratings from the regular classroom peers of gifted program students. These studies have found that children identified as gifted have average or above-average peer status, although the findings are less consistent for adolescents (Austin & Draper, 1981; Gallagher, 1958; Schneider, 1987; Schneider, Clegg, Byrne, Ledingham, & Crombie, 1989).

The high popularity ratings of gifted program students as a group mask information about those high ability students who *do* have peer problems. Previous research is limited on this issue in two ways. First, it is usually not clear whether a child's unpopularity is due to the child's personality and behavior or to prejudicial attitudes in the classroom or school. In schools where there is a positive attitude toward achievement, high ability students may be well received, but in other schools they may be less popular, regardless of their personal characteristics.

Second, previous research does not shed much light on differences within the group of high ability students, specifically, what distinguishes those who are popular from those who are not. This is an important question because it can lead to ways to help less popular students improve their peer relations.

Putting the Research to Use

Although most high ability students get along well with their peers, little is known about the minority of high ability students who have trouble making friends or getting along with others. It is sometimes hard to tell whether a child is rejected by peers because of some stigma associated with his/her exceptional abilities or school placement in a gifted program, or because of social skill problems. The present study adds to our knowledge by investigating high ability students who were unpopular with peers of equally high ability, all of whom attended a two week residential summer enrichment program.

The study found that unpopular students as a group do not have pervasive signs of psychological adjustment problems. For example, they are not more anxious or more emotionally dependent than their peers, and while they score lower on a measure of their social self-concept, they do not score lower on academic, athletic, or physical appearance self-concepts. Teacher ratings of unpopular students indicated inappropriate or unassertive classroom behavior. These findings suggest that assessment and counseling of unpopular students should focus on their social self-concept and perhaps their social skills, rather than on their general personality or academic ability.

The Present Study

Differences in popularity within a group of high ability students were the focus of this study. If a student is unpopular with other classmates in a gifted program, the problem cannot be due to prejudicial attitudes toward the program or the special status of being identified as "gifted." Differences between unpopular and popular students of comparable ability can be examined. Therefore, the present study examined the peer status or popularity of students attending gifted classes, in this case, a residential university-based summer enrichment program. Students identified as unpopular with their peers were compared to two other groups, average and popular gifted program classmates.

A variety of personal characteristics might be associated with peer status differences among high ability students. Several authors have suggested that students with extremely high ability lack true peers even among other gifted program students (Hollingworth, 1942; Janos & Robinson, 1985; Schneider, 1987). Students from families with lower socioeconomic status may experience less favorable status among their peers. Poor self-concept may impair the student's ability to get along with peers (although this relationship may well be bi-directional). Other authors have identified aspects of the student's personality and emotional adjustment which might impact on peer relations, including the student's emotional maturity and social competence (Kurdek & Krile, 1982; Montemayor, 1984; Steinberg & Silverberg, 1986).

The present study examined the relationship between peer status and the following factors: 1) student academic achievement and ability; 2) family social status; 3) self-report measures of student self-concept and teacher ratings of self-esteem; and 4) measures of emotional maturity and freedom from anxiety.

METHOD

Sample: The sample consisted of students in grades 5 through 11 who attended the University of Virginia Summer Enrichment Program. Parents were mailed a request that they complete a family questionnaire. Students were asked to complete a series of questionnaires during the two-week summer program. Of the 795 families contacted, 486 (61%) consented to participate in the study. Subjects were drawn from 319 students who attended the second or third session of the summer program (because peer nomination data were not collected during the first session).

Description of the enrichment program: The summer enrichment program is a two-week residential experience in which students participate in a variety of academic and social activities. Groups of 7 to 9 students live together in dormitory suites with a young adult counselor who provides supervision when students are not in classes. During each weekday, the students attend a 3-hour morning class on a single enrichment subject, such as psychology, computer programming, or humanities. The courses emphasize in dependent learning skills and in-depth study of issues and topics not ordinarily available in regular school curricula. There are 15 to 20 students per class; these were the classrooms used in this study. (Afternoon classes involve a variety of special topics seminars on subjects ranging from astronomy to zoology. Evenings are spent in social activities.)

Students were admitted to the program on the basis of a teacher's recommendation, school grades, standardized test scores (if available), and student responses to a series of questions concerning personal interests and activities, including reasons for applying to the program. The program attempts to admit a diverse group of high ability youth without placing primary emphasis on any single criterion.

MEASURES

Peer status: Peer status was assessed approximately 11–12 days into the two- week period. There are two widely accepted, reliable, and valid ways to measure peer status: peer nominations and peer ratings (Asher & Hymel, 1981). Peer nominations were obtained by giving students a list of all the students in their morning class and asking them to circle the names of their three best friends. Peer status by this method is measured by the number of times a student has been chosen as a friend.

While students could nominate anyone in their class, only nominations by same-sex peers were counted because of the well-established sex bias in socio-metric assessments of peer preference. One risk of this procedure is that nominations might be skewed in some manner if there were only a few boys or a few girls in a classroom. For example, a boy in a classroom with just five other boys would be rated by fewer peers than another boy in a classroom with more boys. (Whether this would lead to more nominations because there are fewer same-sex rivals for nominations, or fewer nominations because there are fewer same-sex peers to make nominations, is not clear.) Therefore, the range and distribution of scores were examined, but little evidence of skewed results was observed. In this sample, students received 0 to 8 nominations, although only 10 students received more than 5 nominations. The average number of nominations was 2.4. Peer nominations were grouped into three broad categories, further reducing the effects of any extreme scores.

One further limitation of the peer nomination method is that if a child is not nominated by anyone, it is not clear whether the child is disliked, ignored, or simply overlooked by the other students. To address this limitation, the peer ratings method was employed. Peer ratings were obtained by asking students to rate each student on a 5-point scale from 5 (liked a lot) to 1 (not liked at all). Each student's peer rating score is the average of ratings received from the other students in the class. Again, only same-sex ratings were counted. The weakness of this method is that students could give identical ratings to everyone.

The two methods do not lead to identical results. The correlation between peer ratings and peer nominations was only .54 ($p < .01$), which accounts for only about 29 of the variance. Peer nominations and peer ratings were combined in order to identify distinct groups of unpopular, average, and popular students. Students were classified into the top third, middle third, and bottom third of peer ratings. Students who fell into the bottom third of peer ratings (below a cut-off of 3.60) and received no peer nominations were classified as "unpopular" ($n = 43$). These students clearly have peer relations difficulties; their classmates gave them low ratings and no one named them as a friend. Students with peer ratings in the middle third (between 3.60 and 4.09) and peer nominations from 2 or 3 students were classified as "average" ($n = 54$). Students with top third peer ratings (above 4.09) and 4 or more nominations were designated "popular" ($n = 43$). The remaining 189 students were not included in the analysis in order to maximize group differences. The average age of these students was 12.4 years, with no significant age differences among groups. Approximately 40% of the students were male, with no significant association between group and sex.

Academic achievement and ability: Academic achievement and ability were assessed by school records of reading and mathematics scores (national percentiles) and Estimated Ability Scores (EAS) from the Science Research Associates (SRA) achievement tests.

Family social status: Information on family social status was obtained from a parent questionnaire (including information not reported in this study) completed by mail prior to the summer program. Social status was assessed using the standard scales for occupation and education of both parents presented by Hollingshead (1975).

Self-concept, emotional autonomy, and anxiety: Three self-report personality questionnaires were administered within the first 2–3 days of each two-week session. Self-concept was assessed using Harter's (1982) Perceived Self-Competence Scale for Children (PSCS), a 36-item self-report questionnaire. Four PSCS scales selected for use in this study assessed the following areas: 1) academic self-concept; 2) social self-concept; 3) physical appearance self-concept; and 4) athletic self-concept. Evidence of adequate reliability and validity for the PSCS is reported elsewhere (Harter, 1982, 1985).

   Students completed an experimental measure of emotional autonomy, the Emotional Autonomy Scale devised by Steinberg and Silverberg (1986). This 20-item questionnaire assesses the degree to which a student has become emotionally autonomous from his or her parents and is capable of making independent decisions. There are four scales (sample items in parentheses): Parent Deidealization ("I try to have the same opinions as my parents" [negative]); Perceives Parents as People ("I have often wondered how my parents act when I'm not around"); Individuation ("There are some things about me that my parents don't know"); and Nondependency on Parents ("It's better for kids to go to their best friend than to their parents for advice on some things"). Steinberg and Silverberg (1986) report adequate reliability and evidence of validity for the Emotional Autonomy Scale.

   Students also completed the Children's Manifest Anxiety Scale (RCMAS; Reynolds & Richmond, 1985), based on the idea that more troubled, nervous students would have problems with peer status. The RCMAS is a 37-item yes/no questionnaire that provides an overall measure of chronic anxiety levels (Reynolds & Richmond, 1985). Scholwinski and Reynolds (1985) factor-analyzed the RCMAS with national normative samples of both regular classroom children ($n = 5,507$) and gifted program children ($n = 584$). They identified three factors in each sample: Physiological Anxiety, Worry/Oversensitivity, and Concentration Anxiety. The present study scores RCMAS subscales according to the factor loadings generated by gifted program students.

Teacher ratings of academic self-esteem: Teachers completed the Behavioral Academic Self-Esteem (BASE) questionnaire (Coopersmith & Gilberts, 1979) after each two-week session. The BASE is a 16-item rating scale which provides measures of student classroom behavior in five areas: Student Initiative (student is self-directed and independent in the classroom); Social Attention (student does not demand excessive attention in class); Success/Failure (student tolerates failure and does not overreact to criticism); and Self-Confidence (student expresses opinions readily and has good appreciation for his/her work). Information on the psychometric characteristics of the BASE is reported elsewhere (Coopersmith & Gilberts, 1979).

RESULTS

Group comparisons were conducted by multivariate analyses of variance (MANOVA) for instruments with multiple scales and the same sample size. (Sample sizes differed across analyses because of missing data for some subjects.) When MANOVAs were significant or not appropriate, univariate analyses with post hoc comparisons (Student-Newman Keuls) were conducted. Descriptive information and F values for all analyses are reported in Tables 1 and 2.

Academic achievement: Despite the selective nature of the sample, there was adequate range of achievement scores to justify statistical analysis. Reading scores ranged from the 75th to the 99th percentile, mathematics scores ranged from the 46th to the 99th percentile, and ability scores (EAS) ranged from 103 to 145. Group differences in SRA reading and math achievement were not significant. In addition, there were no significant group differences on the SRA Estimated Ability Score.

Social status: The MANOVA for family social status was significant, $F = 2.20$, $p < .05$. Follow-up univariate analyses indicated that students whose fathers had more prestigious occupations had higher peer status. Paternal occupations of average students were higher than paternal occupations of unpopular students, and those of popular students were higher than those of average students.

Personality measures: The MANOVA for the four self-concept scales was significant, $F = 5.23$, $p < .01$. The follow-up analyses identified only one significant scale, Social Acceptance. Unpopular students evidenced a significantly lower social self-concept than both of the other groups.

The MANOVA for the BASE was significant, $F = 2.45$, $p < .01$. The follow-up analyses identified significant group differences on four of five scales. In each instance, post hoc analyses indicated that the unpopular students were lower than the other two groups, but that average and popular groups did not differ from one another. The MANOVA for Emotional Autonomy was nonsignificant, $F = 0.96$, as was the MANOVA for Anxiety, $F = 1.87$.

Table I   Group Comparisons on Student Achievement and Family Social Status

	Unpopular			Average			Popular			
	Mean	(SD)	n	Mean	(SD)	n	Mean	(SD)	n	F Value
SRA Achievement										
Reading	93.6	(6.3)	30	93.7	(6.2)	46	95.2	(5.7)	34	0.44
Math	93.3	(6.4)	30	93.3	(10.6)	46	94.5	(5.8)	34	0.77
SRA Ability (EAS)	127.2	(8.2)	20	129.4	(7.7)	33	127.2	(9.3)	23	0.51
Social Status										
Mother										
Education	5.81	(.87)	21	6.00	(1.2)	30	5.97	(.86)	32	0.25
Occupation	7.19	(.87)	21	7.10	(1.5)	30	6.69	(1.3)	32	1.25
Father										
Education	5.85	(1.2)	21	6.20	(.96)	30	6.50	(.88)	32	2.73
Occupation	6.90	(1.7)	21	7.53	(1.6)	30	8.03	(1.2)	32	3.58*

Note: * $p < .05$

Table 2   Group Comparisons on Personality Measures

	Unpopular			Average			Popular			
	Mean	(SD)	n	Mean	(SD)	n	Mean	(SD)	n	F Value
Self-concept										
Academic	18.6	(2.8)	33	19.8	(2.8)	54	19.2	(3.0)	43	1.86
Social	14.5	(3.8)	33	18.3	(3.4)	54	19.0	(2.8)	43	19.97**
Athletic	15.3	(3.9)	33	15.8	(4.0)	54	16.8	(4.2)	43	1.38
Physical Appearance	16.1	(4.0)	33	16.6	(3.8)	54	16.1	(4.4)	43	0.23
Academic Self-Esteem										
Initiative	22.5	(5.2)	31	24.7	(4.1)	51	25.0	(4.5)	41	3.47*
Social Attention	11.5	(2.9)	31	12.8	(2.3)	51	13.0	(2.0)	41	4.02*
Success/Failure	7.4	(1.9)	31	8.3	(1.4)	51	8.3	(1.6)	41	3.86*
Social Attraction	10.0	(2.5)	31	11.4	(2.2)	51	12.2	(2.4)	41	8.06**
Self-Confidence	7.9	(1.6)	31	8.3	(1.2)	51	8.2	(1.5)	41	0.62
Emotional Autonomy										
Deidealization	13.9	(2.8)	31	14.1	(2.4)	53	12.9	(2.6)	43	
Parents	15.5	(2.3)	31	14.9	(3.4)	53	14.4	(2.6)	43	
Individuation	14.1	(3.2)	31	13.9	(2.7)	53	13.4	(2.6)	43	
Nondependency	13.9	(2.8)	31	14.1	(2.4)	53	12.9	(2.6)	43	
Anxiety										
Physiological	2.2	(1.7)	32	2.1	(1.6)	54	1.9	(1.5)	43	
Oversensitivity	4.2	(3.4)	32	4.0	(2.7)	54	3.7	(2.8)	43	
Concentration	4.0	(2.7)	32	2.9	(2.1)	54	2.5	(2.4)	43	

Note: *$p < .05$ **$p < .01$ Univariate F tests are not reported for Emotional Autonomy and Anxiety scales because the multivariate F values were not significant.

DISCUSSION

Unpopular students differed from average and popular students in family social status, social self-concept, and academic self-esteem. They did not differ on measures of achievement or on measures of emotional autonomy or anxiety. Each of these findings contributes to an understanding of peer status difficulties in high ability students and suggests directions for future research.

Fathers of unpopular students had lower occupational status than other fathers. On the 9-point occupation scale, the average rating for fathers of unpopular students was 6.90; for fathers of average students it was 7.53; and for fathers of popular students it was 8.03. Examples of occupations for different levels of the scale are: Level 6, technicians and secretaries; Level 7, managers and computer programmers; Level 8, administrators and secondary school teachers; Level 9, lawyers and physicians.

It was troubling to observe a relationship between father's occupation and peer status. The reason for this relationship is not clear and calls for further research. It seems doubtful that students had widespread knowledge of the occupations of one another's fathers or that this knowledge directly influenced their peer relationships. However, students may have responded to other peer characteristics associated with paternal occupational status. It is possible that the students differed in clothing, speech patterns (content, style, or articulation), feelings of confidence or assertiveness, or other behavior that is indirectly associated with both family social status and peer status. The association between race and peer status is analyzed in a separate report; results suggest that black students do not experience less favorable peer status than white students, with or without controlling for family social status (Cooley, Cornell, & Lee, in press).

Unpopular students scored just as well as the other students on measures of academic achievement and ability. Of course there is some natural restriction of range on these measures because all of the students qualified for the summer program (there were no specific cut-off scores in the admission process, but most students were high achieving). Nevertheless, it is notable that unpopular students were not comparatively low achievers, even though an association between underachievement and peer problems has been observed by others (Whitmore, 1980).

Unpopular students were not comparatively high scorers on achievement tests, but this does not resolve the question of whether *exceptionally* high intelligence is associated with poor peer relations for a subgroup of students. Achievement tests such as the ones used in this study do not have sufficiently high ceilings to distinguish students in the extreme upper ranges hypothesized in the literature to be associated with peer problems (Hollingworth, 1942; Janos & Robinson, 1985). Anecdotally, there were several unpopular students whose application materials reported individual IQs more than three standard deviations above the mean (148 on the Stanford-Binet, 145 on the Wechsler Intelligence Scale for Children, Revised), but more direct study of this issue is needed.

Personality findings: It is not surprising that unpopular students had relatively poorer social self-concepts. This scale asks students to assess how easily they make friends and whether they feel they have enough friends. Although the self-concept questionnaires were completed approximately ten days before peer status was assessed, it seems reasonable to assume that the unpopular students were aware of their problems making friends. There is probably a bi-directional relationship between social self-concept and peer status; students with peer problems develop a poor self-concept, and students with poor self-concepts are at a disadvantage in making friends (Cornell et al., in press). Unpopular students also may lack the social skills necessary to make friends (Asher & Hymel, 1986).

What is perhaps more interesting about the self-concept results is the finding that unpopular students do not have across-the-board poor self-concepts. Unpopular students generally had conceptions of their academic abilities, their physical appearance, and their athletic abilities which were comparable to those of other students. This might imply that intervention efforts with students with poor peer status should be focused on the social arena. Possible exceptions to this generalization are discussed elsewhere (Cornell et al., in press).

The negative findings for the measures of emotional autonomy and anxiety also help to narrow the focus of concern in working with students with poor peer status. Unpopular students endorsed attitudes indicative of emotional independence from their parents which were similar to those of other students. They did not report exceptional anxiety or nervousness that might make them less successful at interacting with peers. Although undoubtedly there are students whose peer status is hindered by emotional dependency or excessive anxiety, this does not appear to be a consistent problem for unpopular students in general.

The most consistent group differences emerged in the teacher ratings of academic self-esteem. On four out of five scales unpopular students were rated lower than their peers. Based on these scales, unpopular students can be characterized as lacking in initiative, especially when it comes to working independently, making decisions, and undertaking new tasks or challenges. They may have excessive needs for social attention, so that they are not appropriately quiet in class and may not cooperate well with others. They may not tolerate failure easily and may overreact to criticism. Finally, teachers observe that unpopular students do not assume leadership roles with their peers and generally do not refer to themselves in positive terms.

DIRECTIONS FOR FUTURE STUDY

The present study is one of the few attempts to distinguish high ability students who are unpopular with their gifted program classmates from other students; therefore, all of the findings presented here are in need of replication and extension. At least three main directions for further research can be identified. First, it would be useful to compare unpopular high ability students with unpopular students of average ability. If these two groups are similar, it would be further evidence that it is not productive to focus on the intelligence of these unpopular students, but rather on other factors unrelated to their abilities.

Second, it would be useful to investigate whether students who are unpopular in the summer enrichment program are also unpopular in their home schools and whether popular students in the summer program are popular at home, too. Such studies may be useful in examining whether high ability students value the same characteristics in their peers as other students do and in distinguishing unfavorable attitudes toward high ability students *as individuals* from prejudicial attitudes toward high ability students or gifted program students in general.

Finally, it is critical to study the characteristics of high ability students with poor peer status in more detail. What are the factors that contribute to the poor social self-concept of these students? Can their self-images be improved? What specific behaviors observed by the teachers in the BASE ratings can be targeted for change? Is it the case that these students lack critical social skills? The ultimate goal of this research would be to develop ways to help unpopular students to improve their social competence and thereby attain more positive and constructive relationships with their peers.

REFERENCES

Austin, A. B., & Draper, D. C. (1981). Peer relationships of the academically gifted: A review. *Gifted Child Quarterly, 25,* 129–133.

Asher, S. R., & Hymel, S. (1981). Children's social competence in peer relations: Sociometric and behavioral assessment. In J.D. Wine & M.S. Smye (Eds.), *Social competence.* New York: Guilford Press.

Asher, S. R., & Hymel, S. (1986). Coaching in social skills for children who lack friends in school. *Social Work in Education, 8,* 205–218.

Cooley, M. R., Cornell, D. G., & Lee, C. (in press). Peer acceptance and self-concept of black students in a summer gifted program. *Journal for the Education of the Gifted.*

Coopersmith, S., & Gilberts, R. (1979). *Behavioral Academic Self-Esteem: A rating scale.* Palo Alto, CA: Consulting Psychologists Press.

Cornell, D., Pelton, G., Bassin, L., Landrum, M., Ramsay, S., Cooley, M., Lynch, K., & Hamrick, E. (in press). Self-concept and peer status of gifted program youth. *Journal of Educational Psychology.*

Erikson, E. H. (1963). *Childhood and society* (2nd ed., rev.). New York: Norton.

Gallagher, J. J. (1958). Peer acceptance of highly gifted children in elementary school. *Elementary School Journal, 58,* 465–470.

Harter, S. (1982). The perceived competence scale for children. *Child Development, 53,* 87–97.

Harter, S. (1985). *Manual for the self-perception profile for children.* Denver: University of Denver.

Hollingshead, A. B. (1975). Four factor index of social status. Unpublished paper. Yale University.

Hollingworth, L. S. (1942). *Children above 180 IQ, Stanford-Binet*. New York: World Book.

Janos, P. M., & Robinson, N. M. (1985). Psychosocial development in intellectually gifted children. In F.D. Horowitz & M. O'Brien (Eds.), *The gifted and talented: Developmental perspectives* (pp. 149–195). Hyattsville, MD: American Psychological Association.

Kennedy, J. H. (1988). Issues in the identification of socially incompetent children. *School Psychology Review, 17*, 276–288.

Kurdek, L. A., & Krile, D. (1982). A developmental analysis of the relation between peer acceptance and both interpersonal understanding and perceived social self-competence. *Child Development, 53*, 1485–1491.

Montemayor, R. (1984). Changes in parent and peer relationships between childhood and adolescence: A research agenda for gifted adolescents. *Journal for the Education of the Gifted, 8*, 9–23.

Mueller, E. C., & Cooper, C. R. (Eds.). (1986). *Process and outcome in peer relationships*. Orlando: Academic Press.

Parker, J. G., & Asher, S .R. (1987). Peer relations and later personal adjustment: Are low-accepted children at risk? *Psychological Bulletin, 102*, 357–389.

Piaget, J. (1965). *The moral judgment of the child*. New York: The Free Press (Original work published 1932).

Reynolds, C. R., & Richmond, B. O. (1985). *The revised children's manifest anxiety scale*. Los Angeles: Western Psychological Services.

Rubin, K. H., & Mills, R. S. (1988). The many faces of social isolation in childhood. *Journal of Consulting and Clinical Psychology, 56*, 161–124.

Schneider, B. H. (1987). *The gifted child in peer group perspective*. New York: Springer-Verlag.

Schneider, B. H., Clegg, M. R., Byrne, B. M., Ledingham, J. E., & Crombie, G. (1989). Social relations of gifted children as a function of age and school program. *Journal of Educational Psychology, 81*, 48–56.

Scholwinski, E., & Reynolds, C. R. (1985). Dimensions of anxiety among high IQ children. *Gifted Child Quarterly, 29*, 125–130.

Steinberg, L., & Silverberg, S. B. (1986). The vicissitudes of autonomy in early adolescence. *Child Development, 57*, 841–851.

Sullivan, H. S. (1953). *The interpersonal theory of psychiatry*. New York: Norton.

Whitmore, J. R. (1980). *Giftedness, conflict, and underachievement*. Boston: Allyn & Bacon.

5

Predictors of Loneliness in the Gifted Adolescent

Charles F. Kaiser

College of Charleston

David J. Berndt

Michael Reese Hospital and Medical Center and University of Chicago

Gifted adolescents reported degree of loneliness to be a function of anger, depression, and stressful life changes. Furthermore, the most salient aspects of depression for predicting loneliness were helplessness, social introversion, and low self-esteem. The relationship between loneliness and depression suggests further evidence of a possible success depression in certain gifted adolescents. The results help to clarify the complex relationship between loneliness and other dysphoric states in these youths.

Editor's Note: From Kaiser, C. F., & Berndt, D. J. (1985). Predictors of loneliness in the gifted adolescent. *Gifted Child Quarterly*, 29(2), 74-77. © 1985 National Association for Gifted Children. Reprinted with permission.

PREDICTORS OF LONELINESS
IN THE GIFTED ADOLESCENT

Loneliness is a common and distressing problem for many people (Bradburn, 1969). It has been implicated as a central factor in depression (Ortega, 1969), suicide (Wenz, 1977), and a variety of individual and social problems including alcoholism (Nerviado & Gross, 1976), delinquent behavior (Ostrov & Offer, 1978), physical illness, overutilization of health care services (Lynch, 1977), and general maladjustment (Goswick & Jones, 1981; Ostrov & Offer, 1978). The current research examined loneliness and other dysphoric states in gifted adolescents.

Popular conceptualizations treat loneliness as an unpleasant psychological state resulting from dissatisfaction with the number and quality of one's social and emotional relationships (Peplau & Perlman, 1979; Young, 1981). It is said to be accompanied by anger, self-disappointment, unhappiness, and pessimism (Young, 1979). Young (1981) described lonely individuals as being without caring person(s) to depend on, to love and to understand, to trust and to share meaningful values and interests. They experience alienation—feeling different from others; exclusion—not belonging to a desired group; feeling unloved—unattractive and unaccepted; and constriction—harboring thoughts and feelings they cannot express to others.

Only relatively recently has research focused on correlates, predictors, and consequences of loneliness. This research has been spearheaded by development of self-assessment devices such as the revised UCLA Loneliness Scale (Russell, Peplau, & Cutrona, 1980), and the Young Loneliness Inventory (Young, 1979).

An examination of studies based primarily on college students reveals that loneliness is correlated with depression (Berndt, 1981; Bragg, 1979; Russell, Peplau, & Cutrona, 1980; Young, 1979), and with characteristics frequently associated with self-reported depression, including dissatisfaction with self and low self-esteem (Goswick & Jones, 1981), social and general anxiety (Jones, Freemon, & Goswick, 1981), introversion, low assertiveness, feelings of alienation, external locus of control (Hojat, 1982), reduced social and nonsocial activity, perceived unfairness of the world (Jones et al., 1981), hyperalertness or spectator behavior (Weiss, 1973), shyness (Cheek & Busch, 1981; Maroldo, 1981), and boredom and restlessness (Russell et al., 1980).

Adolescence is a time of marked psychological and physiological changes that may accentuate loneliness. As aptly put by Ostrov and Offer (1978), the process of separation and individuation has loneliness as its cutting edge. Certainly the gifted adolescent might be expected to be at this edge. However, loneliness has not been systematically investigated in this population. In a recent study by Berndt, Kaiser, and van Aalst (1982), it was noted that a subgroup of gifted adolescents appeared to have the adolescent equivalent of a success depression. The gifted sample as a whole was more introverted than adolescent peers, as measured by the Multiscore Depression Inventory (MDI)

(Berndt, Petzel, & Berndt, 1980). Guilt, low self-esteem, helplessness, and cognitive difficulty were prominent symptoms for what appeared to be a success depression subgroup of gifted adolescents. Seligman (1975) clarified recent theories of success depression within the framework of learned helplessness: Persons who believe they are being unjustly rewarded are susceptible to depression because they have a belief that their achievements are reinforced for reasons unrelated to their own initiative or talent.

The current study looked at the question of loneliness in gifted adolescents who had been subjects in earlier research (Berndt, Kaiser, & van Aalst, 1982). First, we were interested in determining which facets of depression, as measured by the MDI, were most related to loneliness in this group. We also investigated the relationship between increased stress, depression, anger, and loneliness in gifted adolescents.

METHOD

Subjects

Subjects were 175 junior and senior high school students ranging in age from 14–17 years who attended the Governor's School of South Carolina, a select summer academic program held at the College of Charleston. Eighty-five males and 90 females participated in the study. Participants, chosen in proportion to enrollment from public and private schools statewide, ranked at or above the top 5% of their class, or scored equivalently on standardized ability or achievement tests. They were identified by their schools as the most intellectually and creatively gifted. Other characteristics of these gifted adolescents and the complex screening process have been described elsewhere (e.g., Berndt, Kaiser, & van Aalst, 1982; Kaiser & Bryant, 1982). Because the sample was a group with extreme scores on some tests, a restricted range on many of the variables probably reduced the magnitude of relationships obtained in the study.

Procedure

Subjects completed the following instruments during a group administration: the Young (1979) Loneliness Inventory, the Novaco (1977) Anger Inventory, the Dimensions of Anger Reactions (Novaco, 1977), the short form of the Multiscore Depression Inventory (SMDI) (Berndt, Berndt, & Kaiser, 1984; Berndt, Petzel, & Kaiser, 1983), and the Coddington (1972) adolescent adaptation of the Holmes and Rahe (1967) Schedule of Recent Events (SRE) measure of stress. All instruments were administered on the first day of the formal group session.

The SMDI is a brief version of the Multiscore Depression Inventory (Berndt, 1981; Berndt & Berndt, 1980; Berndt, Berndt, & Byars, 1983; Berndt, Petzel, & Berndt, 1980), a self-report measure of severity of depression which provides scores for different symptoms of depression as well as a global score. The MDI was designed for youth with a reading ability of 7th grade or above (Berndt, Schwartz, & Kaiser, 1983).The 47-item short form shows adequate validity and reliability (Berndt, 1982; Berndt, Berndt, & Kaiser, 1984; Berndt, Petzel, & Kaiser, 1983; Joy, 1981) for both the full scale and nine subscales: Guilt, Social Introversion, Irritability, Sad Mood, Low Self-Esteem, Energy Level, Instrumental Helplessness, Pessimism, and Cognitive Difficulty.

The Young (1979) Loneliness Inventory has been shown to be highly related to the other major loneliness scale (Russell, Peplau, & Cutrona, 1980). Although the measurement of stressors has progressed considerably since Holmes and Rahe (1967) introduced the SRE methodology, the Coddington (1972) remains the only well-validated checklist of stressors appropriate for adolescence.

RESULTS

Table 1 gives the means and standard deviations for the full 175 subjects. Differences between males and females were nonsignificant and were combined for subsequent analyses. The means and standard deviations are comparable to scores reported for normal adolescents (e.g., Berndt, Berndt, & Kaiser, 1984; Coddington, 1972; Novaco, 1977). Although slightly more depression, stress, loneliness, and anger are reported by the gifted adolescents, none of these are significantly greater than the scores of their adolescent peers. The group as a whole, however, demonstrated a consistent selection phenomenon resulting in a restriction of range, with most gifted students scoring low on measures relevant to psychopathology. Nevertheless, between 15% and 20% of the gifted students self-reported significant distress on one or more of the measures in Table 1. Twelve percent were at least one standard deviation above the mean on loneliness, depression, and one of the measures of anger.

The results of this study do not, then, indicate any clear difficulties with dysphoric states for gifted adolescents as a group. However, if loneliness is conceptualized as on a continuum, then subsequent analyses reported in this study, while predicting loneliness, are generalizable only to the gifted population studied. Furthermore, if a success depression group does indeed exist, as suggested by Berndt, Kaiser, & van Alst (1982) the results of the current study can only be understood if success depression in gifted adolescents is conceptualized as on a continuum.

Two stepwise (forward) regression analyses were used to determine predictors of loneliness (Lewis-Beck, 1980). First, in order to clarify which aspects of depression were most characteristic of loneliness in the gifted, the nine subscales of the SMDI, along with severity of stress, were entered in a stepwise forward regression analysis. Four of the ten variables were entered into a regression equation that was significant at $F(4,170) = 37.91$, $p < .001$. The order in which they were entered is the order listed in Table 2. The standardized regression weights, the amount of variance accounted for by each variable, the increment in variance contributed, and the significance levels (based on analysis

Table 1   Means and Standard Deviations on Measures of Depression, Anger, and Stress

Measures	Mean	SD
Multiscore Depression Inventory (Short Form)	11.61	9.98
Novaco Anger Inventory	250.34	59.72
Young Loneliness Scale	9.41	6.43
Dimensions of Anger Reactions	16.95	10.31
Number of Stressful Life Events	6.89	6.24
Coddington Stress Score	252.60	136.85

Note. n = 175.
Restriction of range was a mild to moderate problem for many of the variables.

Table 2   Life Events and Depressive Symptoms Which Significantly Contribute to the Prediction of Loneliness in Gifted Adolescents

Instruments	Beta	STD Error	R^2	R^2 Change
Coddington***	.501	.058	.286	.286
Helplessness***	.274	.455	.394	.108
Social introversion***	.196	.247	.447	.053
Self-Esteem*	.134	.263	.459	.012

Note. n = 175
***$p < .001$; * $p < .05$.

of squared semi-partial coefficients) are reported in Table 2. While stress, helplessness, social introversion, and low self-esteem each contributed significantly to the equation, the other six variables did not contribute significantly.

To further clarify the predictors of loneliness, a second regression analysis was computed with loneliness significantly predicted by a regression equation consisting of the SMDI total score, number of life event changes on the Coddington, and the Novaco Anger Inventory, $F (3,171) = 64.66$, $p < .001$. A fourth measure, the Dimensions of Anger Reactions, did not contribute significantly to the equation. The standardized regression weights, the amount of variance accounted for by each variable, the increment in variance contributed, and the levels of significance are reported in Table 3.

DISCUSSION

The correlation of loneliness with depression supports previous research indicating a substantial relationship between self-reported depression and loneliness. Further, the prominence of helplessness as measured by the MDI (Berndt,

Table 3   Significant Variables Contributing to the Prediction of Loneliness
in Gifted Adolescents

Change Instruments	Beta	STD Error	R^2	R^2 Change
Multiscore Depression Inventory***	.482	.044	.464	.464
Coddington*	.290	.068	.500	.036
Novaco Anger Inventory*	.166	.006	.521	.021

Note. $n = 175$
***$p < .001$; *$p < .05$.

Petzel, & Berndt, 1980) suggests that loneliness is characterized by frustrated dependency and recognition needs in the gifted adolescent; alienation, and cognitions of insufficient love, understanding, and social support (see Berndt, 1981). Moreover, social introversion suggests a style reflecting ambivalence and constriction in relationships which can be compatible with a strong need for achievement. Low self-esteem also suggests perceived or actual alienation from the not-so-gifted peers, as well as inadequacy in the face of social and high intellectual demands (some of which may be unrealistic) that are set by the self and important others. The results describe the lonely but gifted adolescent, perhaps stressed and reactively depressed about the burdens of his or her "success."

The relationship between stressful events and loneliness supports theories emphasizing the importance of disruption of relationships and loss of supports precipitating loneliness. Furthermore, adaptation to stress may limit opportunities for development and enhancement of social skills required for affiliation and intimate, mutually supportive relationships (Beck & Young, 1978; Lynch, 1977; Weiss, 1973).

The hypothesized relationship between tendency to anger and loneliness was also noteworthy. Although anger may be easily seen as a reaction to feeling rejected, alienated, excluded, and socially deprived, one may also see it as a manifestation of the type A behavior pattern which appears to be elevated in the gifted adolescent (Kaiser & Bryant, 1982). This behavior pattern, strongly reinforced in our society, permits compensation for perceived inadequacies in other modes of functioning and which perhaps may exacerbate loneliness.

It is evident that stressful life events and loneliness need not preclude superior academic and creative performance in the adolescent, although they may have detrimental consequences for achievement in other situations (Ponzetti & Cate, 1981). Our initial results should be viewed with appropriate caution. Relationships demonstrated here should not be seen as indicating causal ordering; in fact, they are likely to be complex and reciprocal.

For the educator, the results highlight the importance of a special sensitivity to emotional problems of the gifted adolescent. The majority of gifted adolescents are exceptionally well adjusted and find their success goes hand in hand with a healthy self-confidence and self-esteem. Our results, however, emphasize that not all gifted students are as well adjusted emotionally as they are in academic tasks. Nearly one in eight of the gifted students in our research reported not only significant loneliness but also depression and anger. A pattern of depressive symptoms (helplessness, introversion, guilt, and low self-esteem), together with high stress, should be considered indicators of a possible success depression. These students may not experience the enhanced self-esteem from their accomplishments that their peers enjoy. Either unrealistically high expectations which can never be met, or a belief that their success is due to external or unpredictable factors, may predispose these students to poor self-esteem, loneliness, and depression. Such individuals should be considered for counseling or psychotherapy. However, these problems may also reflect a transient reaction to severe stress.

REFERENCES

Beck, A. T., & Young, J. E. (1978). College blues. *Psychology Today, 12,* 80–92.

Berndt, D. J. (1981). How valid are the subscales of the multiscore depression inventory? *Journal of Clinical Psychology, 37,* 564–570.

Berndt, D. J. (1982, July). *Premature closure in the diagnosis of adolescent depression.* Paper presented at the 10th Congress of the International Association for Child and Adolescent Psychiatry and Allied Professions, Dublin, Ireland.

Berndt, D. J., & Berndt, S. M. (1980). Relationship of mild depression to psychological deficit in college students. *Journal of Clinical Psychology, 36,* 868–873.

Berndt, S. M., Berndt, D. J., & Byars, W. D. (1983). A multi-institutional study of depression in family practice. *Journal of Family Practice, 16,* 83–87.

Berndt, D. J., Berndt, S. M., & Kaiser, C. F. (1984). Multidimensional assessment of depression. *Journal of Personality Assessment, 48,* 489–494.

Berndt, D. J., Kaiser, C. F., & van Aalst, F. (1982). Depression and self-actualization in gifted adolescents. *Journal of Clinical Psychology, 38,* 142–150.

Berndt, D. J., Petzel, T., & Berndt, S. M. (1980). Development and initial evaluation of a multiscore depression inventory. *Journal of Personality Assessment, 44,* 396–404.

Berndt, D. J., Petzel, T., & Kaiser, C. F. (1983). Evaluation of a short form of the multiscore depression inventory. *Journal of Consulting and Clinical Psychology, 51,* 790–791.

Berndt, D. J., Schwartz, S., & Kaiser, C. F. (1983). Readability of self-report depression inventories. *Journal of Consulting and Clinical Psychology, 51,* 627–628.

Bradburn, N. (1969). *The structure of psychological well-being.* Chicago: Aldine.

Bragg, M. (1979, May). *A comparison of non-depressed and depressed loneliness.* Paper presented at the UCLA Research Conference on Loneliness, Los Angeles.

Cheek, J. M., & Busch, C. M. (1981). The influence of shyness on loneliness in a new situation. *Personality and Social Psychology Bulletin, 7,* 572–577.

Coddington, R. D. (1972). The significance of life events as etiologic factors in the diseases of children. *Journal of Psychosomatic Research, 16,* 205–213.

Goswick, R. A., & Jones, W. H. (1981). Loneliness, self-concept and adjustment. *Journal of Psychology, 107,* 237–240.

Hojat, M. (1982). Loneliness as a function of selected personality variables. *Journal of Clinical Psychology, 38,* 137–141.

Holmes, T. H., & Rahe, R. (1967). The social readjustment rating scale. *Journal of Psychosomatic Research, 11,* 213.

Jones, W. H., Freemon, J. E., & Goswick, R. A. (1981). The persistence of loneliness. *Journal of Personality, 49,* 27–48.

Joy, D. (1981, August). *Viewing a rape: The psychological costs to crisis intervention volunteers.* Paper presented at the 89th Annual Meeting of the American Psychological Association, Los Angeles.

Kaiser, C. F., & Bryant, L. (1982, May). *The relationship between health locus of control and type A personality in gifted adolescents.* Paper presented at the Georgia Psychological Association, Augusta, GA.

Lewis-Beck, M. S. (1980). *Applied regression: An introduction.* Beverly Hills, CA: Sage.

Lynch, J. (1977). *The broken heart: The medical consequences of loneliness.* New York: Basic Books.

Maroldo, G. K. (1981). Shyness and loneliness among college men and women. *Psychological Reports, 48,* 885–886.

Nerviado, V. J., & Gross, W. F. (1976). Loneliness and locus of control for alcoholic males. *Journal of Clinical Psychology, 32,* 479–484.

Novaco, R. W. (1977). Stress inoculation: A cognitive therapy for anger and its application to a case of depression. *Journal of Consulting and Clinical Psychology, 45,* 600–608.

Ortega, M. J. (1969). Depression, loneliness and unhappiness. In E. S. Shneidman & M. J. Ortega (Eds.), *Aspects of depression.* Boston: Little & Brown.

Ostrov, E., & Offer, D. (1978). *Adolescent youth and society.* Chicago: University of Chicago Press.

Peplau, L. A., & Perlman, D. (1979). Toward a social psychological theory of loneliness. In M. Cook & G. Wilson (Eds.), *Love and attraction.* Oxford, England: Pergamon Press.

Ponzetti, J. J., & Cate, R. M. (1981). Sex differences in the relationship between loneliness and academic performance. *Psychological Reports, 48,* 758.

Russell, D., Peplau, L. A., & Cutrona, C. (1980). The revised UCLA loneliness scale. *Journal of Personality and Social Psychology, 39,* 472–480.

Seligman, M. E. P. (1975). *Helplessness.* San Francisco: Freeman.

Weiss, R. S. (1973). *Loneliness: The experience of emotional and social isolation.* Cambridge, MA: MIT Press.

Wenz, F. V. (1977). *Seasonal suicide attempts and forms of loneliness. Psychological Reports, 40,* 807–810.

Young, J. E. (1979). Loneliness in college students: A cognitive approach. *Dissertation Abstracts, 40,* 1932.

Young, J. E. (1981). Cognitive therapy and loneliness. In G. Emery, S. D. Hollon, & R. C. Bedrosian (Eds.), *New directions in cognitive therapy.* New York: Guilford.

6

Expanding Lazarus and Folkman's Paradigm to the Social and Emotional Adjustment of Gifted Children and Adolescents (SEAM)

Claudia J. Sowa

Kathleen M. May

University of Virginia

A qualitative study of how 20 gifted children and adolescents cope with demands and pressures they experience is the basis of the model of social and emotional adjustment presented in this article. The model combines patterns in the ways the children and adolescents responded to the stressors in their lives with theoretical and empirical information from the fields of child development and personal adjustment to stress. Intrapersonal, family, school, and peer influences, as well as functional and dysfunctional patterns of social and emotional adjustment, are explained within the framework of the model.

Editor's Note: From Sowa, C. J., & May, K. M. (1997). Expanding Lazarus and Folkman's Paradigm to the social and emotional adjustment of gifted children and adolescents (SEAM). *Gifted Child Quarterly*, 41(2), 36-43. © 1997 National Association for Gifted Children. Reprinted with permission.

Understanding the social and emotional experiences of gifted youth requires identifying their cognitive development (and factors contributing to it) as it relates to the more general concepts and models from the fields of child development and psychological adjustment. Here, Rathus and Nevid's (1992) view of adjustment and Lazarus and Folkman's (1984) model of adjustment to stress set the stage for investigating these experiences.

Rathus and Nevid (1992) define adjustment mechanisms as processes people use to respond to environmental demands. Successful adjustment mechanisms allow people to meet demands, change the environment to meet their needs or tastes, regulate their behavior to bring about desired effects, believe in their abilities to achieve desired outcomes, interpret experiences such that they perceive solutions to problems and do not overly arouse negative emotions, and imitate others so that they learn many ways to influence their environment. Children and adolescents who demonstrate these characteristics represent successful social and emotional adjustment processes.

While Rathus and Nevid (1992) delineate the characteristics of adjusted persons, Lazarus and Folkman (1984) offer a model, the cognitive appraisal paradigm, wherein adjustment involves "constantly changing cognitive and behavioral efforts to manage specific external and/or internal demands that are appraised as taxing or exceeding the resources of the person" (p. 141). They define both process adjustment and achievement adjustment mechanisms. Process adjustment is the method of employing cognitive efforts to cope with the demands of the environment whereas achievement adjustment is the employment of behavioral efforts to adapt to the environment (Lazarus & Folkman, 1984).

Achievement adjustment often is reflected in the research on the gifted children's adaptation relative to their nongifted peers. Examples of this literature include comparison of gifted children and nonidentified children on self-perceptions of social competence (Chan, 1988), and comparison of gifted children's families to families of nonidentified children on characteristics of the family environment (Mathews, West, & Hosie, 1986).

Putting the Research to Use

Based on the stories of the gifted children presented in this article and the resulting paradigm, researchers, teachers, and parents need to be aware of the duality of social and emotional adjustment in these children. For gifted adolescents, the development of social and emotional adjustment may not be a parallel process, that is, gifted children may rely on behaviors reflecting social adjustment at the expense of their own emotional needs of express cognitive appraisals that suggest they are emotional adjusted even though their behaviors do not reflect social adjustment. The need to establish school and home environments that create opportunities and rewards for both the incorporation of others' opinions in decision making and the development and expression of personal opinion is important in fostering healthy social and emotional adjustment in gifted children.

Process adjustment was further delineated as problem-focused or emotion-focused cognitive appraisals by Lazarus in 1993. In problem-focused coping, the individual uses cognitive appraisal to determine behaviors that are aimed at solving a problem or reducing the stress associated with the environment. In emotional-focused coping, the cognitive appraisal process is associated with changing personal interpretations of the environment to reduce stress.

Therefore, the use of cognitive appraisal within process adjustment produces behaviors or changes in interpretation of the environment. If this appraisal process helps the individual exhibit behaviors which are adaptive within the environment, it reflects a parallel mechanism of achievement adjustment and process adjustment.

Lazarus and Folkman's (1984) cognitive appraisal paradigm has been criticized by Ryan-Wenger (1992) and Compas (1987) as primarily reflecting adults' cognitive development and function. For gifted children, however, the onset of deductive reasoning has been shown to occur as early as four years of age (Hollingworth, 1931; Morelock, 1992; Torrance, 1965). Based on the early development of deductive reasoning and the precocity of gifted children, the application of the cognitive appraisal paradigm as part of the social and emotional adjustment model presented was deemed appropriate.

This application of the cognitive appraisal paradigm to young people recognizes that children and adolescents' stressors are not the same as those of adults (Dise-Lewis, 1988). Young people's stressors often are related to experiences with parents, other family members, teachers, and social conditions beyond their control (Compas, Malcarne, & Fondacaro, 1988). Thus, an additional consideration must be the fit between the child and the environment (Compas, 1987). Therefore, the model presented in this article conceptualizes the fit between gifted adolescents and their environments through the addition of environmental characteristics of family, school, and peers to the cognitive appraisal paradigm of Lazarus and Folkman.

METHOD

Subjects

Twenty 9–14 year olds, three males and seventeen females, were recruited through advertisements in professional newsletters on gifted children and through contacts with coordinators of gifted programs. Each potential participant had been identified as gifted by his or her school district. Further selection was based on responses to open-ended questions regarding demographic characteristics and social and emotional adjustment issues. Approximately half of the sample had experienced an adjustment problem as reported by self or by parents, including lack of positive peer relationships; difficulty getting along with teachers, parents, or siblings; or frustrations with school. No student had been identified as having a psychological disorder. Final selection reflected diversity of gifted program type, geographic location, ethnicity, and socio-economic status.

All lived in the same southeastern state and attended gifted programs in their public schools representing 20 different schools. They were from lower middle, upper middle, and upper class families and represented rural, suburban, and urban schools and communities. Thirteen were Caucasian, two were Asian American, three were African American, one was Hispanic, and one was biracial.

Procedures

Students, their families, teachers, and friends were interviewed about how the gifted child adjusted and coped with stress. Students were also observed at school, home, and activities (e.g. Boy Scouts, basketball games). The interviews and observations which transpired over a year focused on social and emotional needs. Transcripts and observational records were reviewed with the subjects and other informants to clarify information and to receive feedback regarding implications drawn.

Cases were analyzed for patterns in response to school, family, peers, and for general developmental issues. As a result of the empirical evidence from the cases studied, a model of the social and emotional adjustment of gifted children and adolescents was formulated to incorporate the data and relevant theoretical information.

SOCIAL AND EMOTIONAL ADJUSTMENT MODEL (SEAM)

The following section describes three paths through SEAM: a functional adjustment path representing gifted children and adolescents who reflect characteristics of both social and emotional adjustment and two dysfunctional adjustment patterns representing those who rely on either social or emotional adjustment patterns at the expense of the other. The functional path within SEAM is presented first.

Functional Path (Figure 1)

The Gifted Child

The beginning of SEAM is the gifted child, defined as one whose development of formal operations or abstract thinking occurs at an earlier age than the child's nonidentified peers (Morelock, 1992). Stories were shared by parents of situations involving these children learning to read by age three or playing the piano by age five. The parents agreed that their children not only knew what they wanted but also knew how to seek solutions at an early age.

The Family

The interaction between the child and the parent as well as the entire family (Box 2.0) provides the stage for the social and emotional adjustment of the gifted child. In functional families (Box 2.2) a sense of belonging is balanced with a sense of having one's own unique identity (Minuchin, 1974). Functional families are described by Goldenberg and Goldenberg (1994) as providing rules to maintain order and stability while at the same time allowing flexibility in the event of changing circumstances.

Adjustment Mechanisms

The well functioning family is the basis for the child's development of simultaneous achievement adjustment and process adjustment. This balance between achievement adjustment and process adjustment is considered necessary for both social and emotional adjustments of gifted children within the model. For clarity, achievement adjustment and process adjustment are shown as two separate boxes (Boxes 3.1 and 3.2) in the figures, although they are interactive and dynamic within the adjustment mechanism (Box 3.0).

Alan typifies the use of simultaneous adjustment mechanisms. "If somebody is doing something I don't like . . . I usually just read and do something that is not strenuous . . . something I like to do and take my mind off the person." . . . I congratulate myself and say I am learning to do this, I am using my head instead of reacting." The gifted adolescent in this case uses cognitive appraisal to determine behaviors that are aimed at solving a problem and reducing the stress associated with the environment. Since this appraisal process helps Alan adapt within the environment without sacrificing a sense of self, it reflects a parallel adjustment mechanism of achievement adjustment and process adjustment.

The Interactional Mechanism

Children begin to develop self-concept through relationships with others, their development of self-knowledge, and their comparisons of themselves to others (Collins, 1984). The interactional mechanism (Box 4.0) reflects this developmental process. Self-concept is both situational, based on the identification and comparison with similar peers (Box 4.1) and global, based on the concept of personal identity (Box 4.2) (Bandura, 1986; Erikson, 1963). Previous research has shown that the comparison of self to peers is critical to the social and emotional adjustment of gifted adolescents (Cornell, et al., 1990).

A teacher working with two gifted Hispanic students told this story. A little while into the school year a gifted Hispanic student, Antonio, moved into the area. "When Antonio first came to me, I thought Juan and Antonio would be friends. I thought maybe Juan would be a good influence on Antonio. But Juan kept his distance because he knows Antonio is trouble. . . . Now in my class, they are pleasant to each other, they talk, but I would not say that Antonio is a good friend of his."

The outcome of the entire functional model is gifted young people who are socially and emotionally adjusted (Box 5.0). These youngsters exhibit the characteristics of functional adjustment as defined by Rathus and Nevid (1992) and positive self-concepts. The following story is an overview of one child whose story reflects the functional model.

Nina, a sixth grade student, is both a highly capable and creative gifted child. Nina viewed her parents as having "fair rules" and yet admitted that, at times, she disagrees with the rules. She is given responsibilities and interacts with her siblings in a normal manner. She described her relationship with her siblings as "great friends" most of the time who "get along okay" other times, and "then sometimes we just don't get along at all."

Nina brings energy and enthusiasm to each of her activities, both academic and extracurricular. She exhibits playfulness and seems to engage in a wide array of experiences for the sake of personal pleasure. Her school principal stated that she is "a sensational student. . . . She finds interest in all areas of learning and is endlessly curious about so many things. She loves learning and is energetic in her pursuit." At the same time, a teacher sees Nina as a "self-motivated and self-challenging student, who sets high standard for herself." Nina appears to be strongly goal-oriented. Nina radiates confidence regarding her ideas, abilities, and values. She views herself as unique and different. This perspective is due in part to the fact that she believes she is a creative person and that creativity makes a person different from other people. "I want to be creative cause if I was like everyone else, the world wouldn't be as cool . . . by being creative, people are different. Being creative makes everybody special, makes everybody different."

At the same time Nina enjoys being creative and unique, she enjoys her associations with her classmates and has many friends. As one teacher puts it: "She seems to be comfortable in her own skin."

Reliance on Achievement Adjustment (Figure 2)

Over-reliance on achievement adjustment may occur when the gifted child or adolescent is part of a family (Box 2.1) where a sense of belonging is emphasized to the detriment of a sense of self. Characteristics of these types of families include rigid adherence to family rules, parental domination, rewards based on conformity to the family, and family taking precedence over the individual (Lamborn, Mounts, & Steinberg, 1991). For example, in one child's family, the father is the authoritarian figure in the family. His word is final. The father feels the need to control his children and his wife and praise is based on conformity to the father's viewpoint.

Figure I   Functional Model

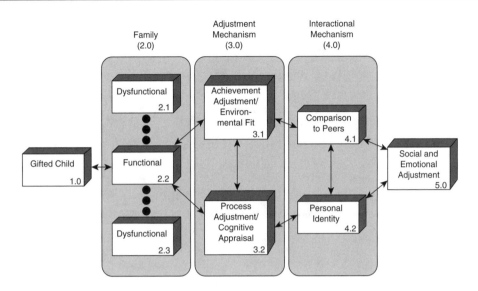

The child's involvement in this type of family results in imbalance within the simultaneous adjustment mechanism (Box 3.0). This gifted child relies on achievement adjustment (Box 3.1) as a means of coping socially and emotionally. The child produces socially accepted behaviors which include purposeful attempts to comply or adjust to the detriment of self. Teachers often describe these children as perfect. "Juan does exactly what you ask, exactly when you ask him to do it, and if there is any feedback, it is always positive."

Children's reliance on these behaviors, when they are incongruent with their cognitive appraisal of the environment, produce a conflict between personal beliefs and the actions expected by others. After starring in a school play, one gifted child received high praise from her family and friends at a celebration party and appeared to be enjoying the party. However during the party, she quietly retreated in tears to her room and stated "I was not as good as I could have been."

The reliance on achievement adjustment often is reinforced by the selection of similar peers who also fit into the environment (Box 4.1) and play by the rules of the game. The gifted child following the path illustrated in Figure 2 consistently suppresses beliefs to conform to peer expectations and may be socially adjusted at the expense of emotional adjustment, which requires a reflection of one's own beliefs in one's action. For example, Debbie's father reported that "she is very concerned socially about conforming and she doesn't want to appear apart from her peers."

June is a 13 year old 8th grader attending a public middle school in a relatively small community and represents gifted children who over-rely on achievement adjustment. At school, she serves on the yearbook staff and is a reporter for the school newspaper. For a time, she acted as manager for the school's volleyball team, then she joined the school's track and field team as a long distance runner. She is a member of the school's Odyssey of the Mind team and participates in an after school gifted and talented seminar program. Recently, June was elected by her class to be next year's class president.

Outside of school, June takes piano and ballet lessons and between these activities and her homework, she finds the time to maintain a wide variety of hobbies. She enjoys reading, is an active participant in a local theater group and enjoys both vegetable and flower gardening.

When asked to describe her family in one word, June's mother responded with "Smiths." This is a family which spends a great deal of time together. June's father describes their family as "tight knit." And each of the Smiths appears to be very satisfied with their family life and supportive of one another. June points out that her parents want what is best for her.

However, June worries that her mother works too hard and indicates that occasionally her mother becomes upset about not being able to do everything she feels that she should: "She gets upset a lot of times about the house and getting it clean." June's response to her mother's reaction is: "[I] try as hard as I can to help around the house." June points out that "When she's [mom] upset . . . it affects us all." She also reports that occasionally she and her mother have disagreements but that their anger with one another dissipates quickly: "I don't want our relationship to get hurt because she's very important to me."

Susan, June's only close friend, is very similar to June. Their friendship is based on mutual academic support. Regarding her friendship with Susan, June claims that "we have to be good friends because we take all the same classes, and I need her help and she needs my help." June's mother expressed concern that the friendship between June and Susan appears to be based solely on their academic interests.

Last year, June received her first B. "It was a big thing [at the time] . . ." In fact, it was a big enough "thing" that June, who does not cry often, cried, and her mother wrote a note to the teacher. However, June never gave this note to the teacher because "[I] didn't want to hurt [my] relationship with her [the teacher]."

According to her teachers, June is a standard, of sorts. In her classes, she acts as both a leader and a follower and is open to her classmates' and teachers' different ideas and approaches to class work. Her algebra teacher believes that June succeeds in school not only because she enjoys learning, but also because "[she] has a fierce desire to please her parents." June's case illustrates that the perfect gifted child may be at risk for emotional adjustment difficulties by continually sacrificing for others.

Reliance on Process Adjustment (Figure 3)

When a gifted child is born into a family (Box 2.3) that creates an exaggerated sense of individual importance we may see development of over-reliance on process adjustment. These types of families are characterized by erratic

Figure 2   Reliance on Achievement Adjustment

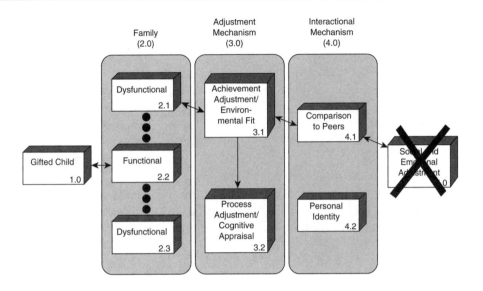

Figure 3   Reliance on Process Adjustment

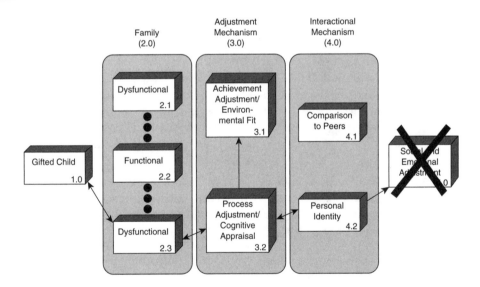

rules, individual domination (often the child is dominant), expectations of system modification to individual needs, and individuals taking precedence over family (Hollingsworth, 1990; Rimm, 1990). For example, one mother described the impact her son, Kevin, had on her relationship with her husband as "Life before Kevin, now it's Kevin, and hopefully there will be life after Kevin." A father said his gifted child was "the recipient of all his dreams and hopes."

The child's involvement in this type of family sets up a reliance on process adjustment (3.2). This child often is described as not fitting into the environment and not expressing any distress over lack of adaptation. For example, Jill, a fifth grader, often argues and debates issues in her classes. She says that she "knows other students don't like it, but it's good for them. Maybe they'll go on to be in the debate in high school or become lawyers."

Difficulties for these adolescents occur when they experience congruence between their beliefs and their behaviors, but generate actions that do not help them fit into the environment. Often these behaviors are seen by others as inappropriate. Therefore, the gifted adolescent's internal appraisal does not encourage behaviors necessary for achievement adjustment, and emotional adjustment exists at the expenses of social adjustment.

Kevin, a seventh grade student at the time this study began, is a highly intellectual child with an IQ of 180 on the Slosson Intelligence Test. Kevin's interviews create a story that illustrates reliance on process adjustment. Kevin's mother describes the family as "totally child-centered." The father concurs "I guess we try to do too much for the kids. It's like there is no tomorrow."

Within the context of school, Kevin is seen by his teachers as having social difficulties. One teacher's explanation is that "He is very bright and his interests are so different that somehow he never learned the social skills needed with peers. So it became a cyclical thing. He would be talking about things or be interested in things they weren't, he'd get a bad response, so he'd isolate himself, not pick up the social skills, so even his intellectually similar peers rejected him."

Kevin's lack of achievement adjustment was compensated by his reliance on process adjustment or his appraisal of his peer relationships in a manner that did not cause him emotional distress: "Most people at school I am not good friends with . . . We don't really hate each other, we just sort of live with each other. Occasionally I might talk to them or play a game . . . but we're not like buddies, pals, come over to my house sort of thing. . . . See you can only have so many really good friends anyway."

Kevin sums his story clearly as he describes himself: "I've never been a real social person anyway. I could go off by myself and read a book at recess . . . I said to myself . . . who needs it? . . . . Forget this."

IMPLICATIONS AND CONCLUSIONS

Families and schools should foster a balance between achievement adjustment and process adjustment mechanisms to assist gifted children and adolescents in the development of social and emotional adjustment skills. The means for fostering simultaneous adjustment mechanisms differ based on the reliance of the gifted child or adolescent on one area of adjustment over another. Gifted children or adolescents who are reliant on achievement adjustment need to strengthen their personal identity and feel more comfortable in expressing and abiding by their personal beliefs systems. A stronger sense of personal identity promotes trust in their own cognitive appraisal and helps recreate balance in the simultaneous adjustment mechanism.

In turn, gifted children or adolescents who rely on process adjustment as a means of coping need to incorporate others into their appraisal process. It is important that schools and families help young people learn to understand the views of their peers and others even when they are perceived as dissimilar. The increasing importance of peers in adolescence may facilitate this process and serve as a means of promoting achievement adjustment.

During its development, the applicability of the model was considered for minority populations and both genders. Ethnic, racial, and sexual identity play important roles in both the personal identity of the adolescent and the comparison with similar peers (Boyd-Franklin, 1989). The role ethnicity, race, and gender play in the model is determined by the importance of ethnic, racial, and sexual identity within the family. Therefore, if the family incorporates these issues by employing balanced adjustment mechanisms, the gifted child begins a simultaneous path in regard to ethnic, racial, and sexual identity (see Figure 1). If the family relies on either achievement adjustment or process adjustment approach to incorporate the minority or gender issues into their personal adjustment mechanisms, the gifted child is likely to exhibit such a reliance. Future research is needed on the implications of ethnicity, race, and gender within this model.

Additional research using quantitative techniques also is needed to clarify the relationships within the model of social and emotional adjustment presented. This model is built on the premise that social and emotional adjustment are not the same constructs and rely on separate adjustment mechanisms. This conceptual model of social and emotional adjustment portrays a pictorial representation of gifted children's and adolescents' vulnerability. It is based on the delicate balance of both fitting into the world while being different and understanding one's own uniqueness. This balance is important for all persons living and working with gifted children and adolescents to remember.

REFERENCES

Bandura, A. (1986). *Social foundations of thought and action: A social cognitive theory.* Englewood Cliffs, NJ: Prentice-Hall.

Boyd-Franklin, N. (1989). *Black families in therapy: A multisystems approach.* New York: Guilford Press.

Chan, L. K. S. (1988). The perceived competence of intellectually talented students. *Gifted Child Quarterly, 32*, 310–315.

Collins, W. A. (Ed.). (1984). *Development during middle childhood: The years from six to twelve.* Washington, D.C.: National Academy Press.

Compas, B. E. (1987). Coping with stress during childhood and adolescence. *Psychological Bulletin, 101*, 393–401.

Compas, B. E., Malcarne, V. L., & Fondacaro, K. M. (1988). Coping with stressful events in older children and young adolescents. *Journal of Counseling and Clinical Psychology, 56*, 405–411.

Cornell, D. G., Pelton, G. M., Bassin, L., Landrum, M., Ramsey, S., Cooley, M., Lynch, K., & Hamrick, E. (1990). Self-concept and peer status among gifted program youth. *Journal of Educational Psychology, 3,* 456–463.

Dise-Lewis, J. E. (1988). The Life Events and Coping Inventory: An assessment of stress in children. *Psychosomatic Medicine, 50,* 484–499.

Erikson, E. H. (1963). *Childhood and society* (2nd ed.). New York: Norton.

Goldenberg, H., & Goldenberg, I. (1994). *Counseling today's families* (2nd ed.). Pacific Grove, CA: Brooks/Cole.

Hollingworth, L. S. (1931). The child of very superior intelligence as a special problem in social adjustment. *Mental Hygiene, 15*(1), 1–16.

Hollingsworth, P. L. (1990, May/June). Making it through parenting. *Gifted Child Today,* 2–7.

Lamborn, S. D., Mounts, N. S., & Steinberg, S. M. (1991). Patterns of competence and adjustment among adolescents from authoritative, authoritarian, indulgent, and neglectful families. *Child Development, 62,* 1049–1065.

Lazarus, R. S. (1961). *Adjustment and personality.* New York: McGraw-Hill.

Lazarus, R. S. (1993). From psychological stress to the emotions: A history of changing outlooks. *The Annual Review of Psychology, 44,* 1–21.

Lazarus, R. S., & Folkman, S. (1984). *Stress appraisal and coping.* New York: Springer.

Mathews, F. N., West, J. D., & Hosie, T. W. (1986). Understanding families of academically gifted. *Roeper Review, 9,* 41–42.

Minuchin, S. (1974). *Families and family therapy.* Cambridge, MA: Harvard University Press.

Morelock, M. J. (1992, February). The child of extraordinarily high IQ from a Vygotskian perspective. Paper presented at the Esther Katz Symposium on the Psychological Development of Gifted Children, University of Kansas, Lawrence.

Rathus, S. A., & Nevid, J. S. (1989). *Psychology and the challenges of life: Adjustment and growth* (4th ed.). Fort Worth, TX: Holt, Rinehart, & Winston.

Rimm, S. B. (1990, May/June). Parenting and teaching gifted children: A model of relativity. *Gifted Child Today,* 33–36.

Ryan-Wenger, N. M. (1992). A taxonomy of children's coping strategies: A step toward theory development. *American Journal of Orthopsychiatry; 62,* 256–263.

Torrance, E. P. (1965). *Gifted children in the classroom.* New York: Macmillan.

7

A "Rag Quilt": Social Relationships Among Students in a Special High School

Laurence J. Coleman

University of Toledo

The experience of being a gifted student at a public residential high school was studied from the student perspective using ethnographic and phenomenological inquiry. The social system that emerged, one that the students judged as atypical, is described. Contextual factors are presented in an effort to understand the students' experience.

Editor's Note: From Coleman, L. J. (2001). A "rag quilt": Social relationships among students in a special high school. *Gifted Child Quarterly*, 45(3), 164-173. © 2001 National Association for Gifted Children. Reprinted with permission.

The life of students in special programs from the perspective of the students has not been a frequent subject of study in the field of gifted and talented child education. Students in programs have been studied, but from the perspective of the researcher, not the child. In general, educational studies looking at the perspectives of the participants in a school community have been growing. Public schools (Chang, 1992; Cusick, 1973; Peshkin, 1978, 1986, 1991), as well as private, independent schools (Cookson & Persell, 1985; Henry, 1993), have been studied. Those ethnographic studies reveal a view of schooling that is missing from most accounts because they offer an insider, rather than an outsider, perspective. The participants' views and the school culture are described, not from an expert perspective, but from a living-in-that-world perspective. In the field of gifted education, few ethnographic studies have been published (Kitano, 1985; Story, 1985), although qualitative studies are increasingly appearing (Hébert, 1998a, 1998b; Kitano, 1998a, 1998b, 1998c). This study, like others in the genre, explores meaning from the perspective of the participants. In this particular case, the student experience of living at the school was the centerpiece, and the others in the setting were considered as contextual elements of students' lives. Unlike any other study, this study explores life in a residential, public high school for gifted and talented students.

My purpose is to describe the social system I discovered at a two-year residential public high school. The experience of being there and the resultant social system was reported by students to be different from that found at their local high schools. I came to see the system through their eyes, and it also appeared different to me from what has been generally reported about high schools. Social relationships among the students seemed more open, inclusive, and fluid than those found in other schools (Chang, 1992; Cusick, 1973; Peshkin, 1991). In this article, I describe the social system and end with some observations about what the results mean.

RATIONALE FOR THE STUDY: THEORETICAL AND PRACTICAL

The study has a theoretical and a practical genesis. It is an extension of my concern about the experience of being gifted in American society. The importance of *setting* had been growing in my mind as a way to understand the development of gifted persons (Coleman, 1995, 1997). I had come to believe that research approaches that focus on the individual out of the context in which giftedness grows, or that look at the person before looking at the setting in which giftedness grows, were conceived in a backward fashion. That is, giftedness emerges in supportive conditions. The most advanced examples of giftedness and talents are connected to such settings. Thus, studying special settings filled with bright, promising children before their talents reach fruition is an uncharted way to learn what gifted persons experience and how they develop.

Waiting until later in life to study the individual in isolation from the conditions that nurtured him or her has been a useful strategy for understanding giftedness but one that leaves many questions unanswered (Bloom, 1985; Subotnik & Arnold, 1994).

Putting the Research to Use

This study describes the social system of one special program that seemed to the students in that program to be different from the social system in typical high schools. The nature of any school's social system is a byproduct of the interaction between the community, the institution, and the students. The social system that was created at Greenhouse Institute (GI) happened only there. That system is neither generalizable nor directly exportable to another school. Yet, at the same time, a reader will encounter descriptions of GI's social system and its processes that are evocative of other special programs. By reflecting on those similarities and differences, readers can judge the meaningfulness of these findings for their own situations. The fact that a social system like the one at GI is possible in one setting is an indication that such a system might be created in other places.

This study was also conceived as a practical question. Only 12 public residential high school programs for gifted students exist in the United States. What students experience in such settings has not been well documented. The perspective of the students would be useful to developers thinking of beginning such a program, to administrators who run such programs, to parents and children considering applying to such programs, and to those who question the usefulness of such programs.

METHODOLOGY, SETTING, AND PARTICIPANTS

My intention was to learn about the experience of being gifted in a selective residential program over the course of one academic year. The program, hereafter called the Greenhouse Institute (GI; a pseudonym), was a two-year public residential high school designed to serve 300 gifted and talented juniors and seniors in one state. I got access to GI at the invitation of the director. While discussing his probable appointment and our mutual interest in studying the experience of being gifted, we speculated on the possibility of obtaining funds to support a study of the life of GI students. Six months later, the money became available, and I seized the opportunity.

Methodology

My basic research plan was to use ethnographic and phenomenological techniques to learn about the students' experience. I took fieldnotes as a participant observer, conducted interviews, and collected documents. My notebook accompanied me wherever I went for two purposes: to keep a written record of what I saw and heard and to remind people at all times that I was observing them. I began in the first month making painstakingly detailed entries, including maps, descriptions of the physical environment, and reflections on observations. The fieldnotes became more focused in successive months as aspects of the students' experience, such as friendship and classroom life, became more figural to me. As a participant observer, I hung out in public spaces where I would meet students, and I went to places where they were known to congregate. By living in the dorm, I interacted with students in private spaces. When activities were spontaneously announced or part of the schedule, I attended. I was invited on walks, participated in birthday parties, ate at the same tables in the cafeteria, participated in role-play games in the dorm rooms, watched videos, shared bathroom facilities, and attended club meetings and Conduct Board meetings. On occasion, I would shadow students, with their permission, through their daily routine. I also attended administrative and staff meetings in which students were not present and student meetings where I was the sole adult. Interviews were either informal conversations, which were later entered into my fieldnotes, or scheduled audio-taped interviews that were later transcribed. I collected three file drawers of documents as they were placed in my mailbox. I have official handbooks and forms, copies of e-mail transmissions addressed to the community, as well as signs, journals, poetry, homework, and so forth.

My enthusiasm for the topic and the excitement of living with the students sustained me as the mountain of data accumulated. For 10 months I lived with the students. In the fall semester, I spent three of every four weeks there, and in the spring, when I conducted in-depth interviews, I spent 10 days out of each month there. The time I spent travelling back and forth from home to the GI was used to listen to tapes, generate provisional themes, and reconsider where to focus my attention. I lived in the male dorm for part of the time and was known as "Larry" or "the guy on the second floor." The study began two days before orientation and continued through the afternoon of graduation. Six notebooks (5" × 8") were filled with 100 days of fieldnotes. One side of facing pages was for description and the opposite side for reflections and maps. These, too, were entered into my computer daily. I taped hour-long interviews with 8 students four times and with 13 students one time. My fieldnotes indicated person-specific conversations with 89 students, some multiple times, in various settings around the school, such as the lounge, classrooms, walks, and outside the school on field trips, in a coffee house, and so forth. After four months, a questionnaire was developed for students and another for faculty to corroborate ideas gained from observations and informal conversations. To organize and analyze the fieldnotes and interview data, I used NUD*IST 4, a program for handling nonnumerical data (Qualitative Solutions and Research, 1997). As the study matured, I found my attention drawn toward various dimensions of student experience. Given the wealth of data gathered in an ethnographic undertaking, I have chosen to highlight the social system portion of the story in this paper. All the quotes in the paper are students' words. When names are used, they are fictitious to maintain anonymity. Rarely, I associate incorrect descriptors with a quote for the same purpose.

Setting and Participants

The GI is a two-year public residential high school funded by a state department of education and located on the grounds of a public university. Three hundred is the maximum enrollment. Students are selected on the basis of standardized test scores, four recommendations, and an essay. Many students were identified as gifted and talented in their local schools. The result is an "extremely diverse" group selected from around the state who share an interest in being at the school. The tuition is paid by the state.

The mission of the GI is "to provide a healthy and challenging residential community for eleventh- and twelfth-grade students of high academic ability who are committed to reaching their full potential within a holistic framework" (Greenhouse Institute, 1998, p. 1). At the same time, the GI is to assist "other high schools across the state for quality staff development, distance learning, and support services" (p. 1).

The statement of philosophy in the faculty handbook reads:

> The curriculum of the GI is designed to provide a balance between the study of required subjects from traditional disciplines and the opportunity for individual exploration and personal enrichment. Throughout the curriculum, the processes of critical thinking, creativity, problem solving, research, and decision making are stressed. . . . Established . . . by the legislature, the GI is . . . devoted to the education of students who demonstrate extraordinary intellectual ability and a commitment to scholarship. The philosophy of the GI originates from the proposition that a society in which justice is a prime concern ordinarily tries to provide educational opportunities appropriate to the expressed ability and potential development of as many sorts of citizens as possible. . . . The GI is dedicated to inspiring and challenging highly gifted young adults to reach their full potential within a framework of the common good. (Greenhouse Institute, 1998, p. 6)

The program is structured into Academic Life, Residential Life, and Outreach. Each division regards the mission of the school in its own way. Outreach has an important role, primarily off-campus, so students have limited knowledge of it, and it is not part of ordinary conversation around the school.

The students see the GI as a special place. As some say, "like no place else in the world." As teenagers and as adolescents, all are caught in the conflicting demands between developmental and institutional issues. Some handle the GI adroitly; most come to terms with the place and learn all they can; others trudge through it on the verge of being swallowed up by the experience; still others realize that this is not the place for them; and a few crash. The latter two groups officially leave by "withdrawal."

The basic program is college preparation with rigorous demands determined by each teacher's notion of what is appropriate within the state curricular guidelines. The content is varied, more like a college than a high school. The curriculum is organized into divisions: sciences; mathematics, which includes computers; and humanities. The latter division is the largest and includes history, literature, and foreign languages. Students also attend special courses called colloquia and research. Most classes are on Monday, Wednesday, and Friday, with Tuesday and Thursday reserved for labs in science and foreign languages. In May, a special term is offered with non-standard curricula and opportunity to travel.

Residential life consists loosely of all the time students are not in class. Residence counselors (RCs) supervise dorm life, intramural sports, the wellness program, extracurricular hall-dorm programs, and so forth. Lounges on the ground floor of the adjoining male and female dorms serve as a meeting place for students. Access to mailboxes and sign-in and sign-out take place there. Two or more residence counselors are assigned to each floor of the dorm. The floors of the dorms have different appearances and feeling due to the interaction between each RC and his or her students. A clear difference is evident between the boys' and the girls' side of the dorm in terms of noise (boys are louder), activity level (girls start earlier in morning; boys later into the night), sleeping patterns (girls go to sleep earlier), and conversational topics. Students who are not in class are likely to be in the dorm in their rooms studying, sleeping, or eating. Weekends are a time for "sleeping in, catching up, and hanging out."

Faculty and residential counselors have different roles. Teachers have teaching experience and advanced degrees. Some have taught in the public schools, some in colleges, a few in both. Teachers' average age is early 40s. Residence counselors have experience as counselors and have completed their bachelor's degree. Counselors' average age is mid-20s. Other adult roles are administration, admissions, and career counseling.

Data Analysis

The process of data analysis followed the principles of grounded theory and the constant comparative method (Glazer & Strauss, 1967; Strauss & Corbin, 1990), with insight gained from Peshkin (1986, 1991) and others who have conducted similar kinds of investigations. Permission to conduct the study was granted as the study began. In the next paragraphs, I explain how I modified the method to fit my situation.

As the research study unfolded, I organized my fieldnotes and wrote memos to myself while in the field. Every month during the first semester, I wrote plans for the next month during the week I was away from GI at my university. The ongoing analysis was combined with data collection until I left. I kept files headed "My Subjectivity" and "Reflections by Date" to record my thinking. I also kept a file on possible themes, and I updated this file each month. Months after leaving the GI, I was preoccupied with the data analysis. While rereading my notes, interviews, and memos, I taught myself how to use NUD*IST and began to code the data using a preliminary list of categories that were straightforward and that required minimal interpretation. Some beginning categories and their definitions were:

- *Kids:* students who are my informants;
- *Big people:* adults at the school;
- *Being a researcher:* where my being a researcher is evident to others;
- *Residential life:* anything relevant to residential life;
- *Academic life:* anything that applies to academic life;
- *Parents/family/home:* references to families at any time;
- *Life in classes:* emphasis is on the interactions in the class;
- *First impressions:* expressions of the impact of arrival, expectations;
- *Social relations:* events about social system, status, dating;
- *Friendships:* any mention of friends, "fitting in";
- *Schedule:* personal schedules of kids; and
- *Diversity:* ethnic, racial, sexual orientation, gender variations.

Categories were added, collapsed, and synthesized as I coded the data. NUD*IST has a utility that facilitates memo writing by providing for the attaching of memos to specific codes so one can audit the process. Over the summer and early fall, I created three broad themes that integrated the old and newer categories. These were "Structural and Background Issues," such as developmental issues or who owns the kids; "Dialectics," such as power and autonomy or rule keeping/rule breaking; and "Essences," such as the rhythm of the schedule or learning things the system teaches that may not be intended by the GI. When I returned for a member check with the students and adults at GI four months later, my analysis was greeted with acceptance. In one group setting, an adult commented—trying to be honest and apologetic about it, too—that my efforts had only conveyed a very familiar story to someone with years of experience at the GI. In my talks with students, I also got confirmation for my interpretation of their experience. Both reports spurred me forward toward a more fine-grained analysis. The process continued for a year. During that time, besides the practices mentioned, I made other efforts to ensure credibility and trustworthiness of the study, which are reported in the Discussion section of this article.

THE SOCIAL SYSTEM IN GENERAL

My intention was to learn about the experience of being a student in a residential educational setting. In the course of living at GI, I heard conversations and references by students that compared their local high school to the residential school. As I probed those comments more deeply, I became more aware of the relationships among the students and the social system at the special school. This realization became the topic of convergence for this paper.

Social system is my term to represent the interrelationships among the students. Students would more likely use the term *friends.* However, that latter term is loaded with surplus meaning for everyone and did not fit what I observed and what they experienced. In this paper, I describe the student-to-student relationships, sidestepping the adult–young person relationships until another paper. To capture many of the elements of the school, I quote a student, a female senior, who suggested this simile during a group interview among peers who approved her description. The title of the paper is the student's metaphor:

> The GI is like a quilt [general, warm laughter]. It's like, okay, my mom makes rag quilts, and my grandma does, too. All the pieces of material come from things that she had around the house, like old dresses, bedspreads, sheets, or curtains. . . . That's what I thought GI was like because we all come from very different places, and maybe we're all a little odd. You wouldn't think that if you threw us all together we'd fit together; but, like, I think that we do. And this place is really neat! Like when we're all together, I know that I am nothing like any of these kids in this room, except that somebody somewhere thought that I was gifted and they thought that I should come here. That's neat that we were all thrown together. And now we all get to explore and see what kinds of different groups and friends and ideas we can have when we meet. You know?

GI students are "thrown together," and a social system emerges that students identify as being different from their home schools. Obviously, the program shapes the social system. GI values learning and diversity and recognizes the commitment students make to live there. In response to observations and questions about the meaning of status, being cool, popularity, diversity, racism, and friendship, I learned of a social system that differs from the typical high school. Some characteristics are similar to a local high school, and in some ways the characteristics are different. Was I seeing a social system that reflected many of the values that we claim to honor in our pluralistic, democratic society?

WHAT DOES EMERGE?

On the surface, GI appears to be a typical urban high school. Students of different hues, in varying styles of dress, carrying book bags, walk to class. Conversations can be heard about the previous night (How late were you up?);

about schoolwork (Could you believe those problems he gave us?); about food (I couldn't eat that lunch."). In the classrooms, familiar scenes of one teacher and groups of students sitting at desks are visible. Some students slouch, some are taking notes, a few pass notes, and several look like they are half-asleep. In the lounges, I see students in pairs or larger groups talking, joking, reading, studying, wrestling, making plans for later. In the dining hall, most students eat quickly and leave; few linger to talk, except at dinner. What is happening here? What does this mean to them?

Beneath the obvious, glimpses of the social system were apparent, but the atypicality was less evident. A network of relationships among students emerged that was neither fixed nor hierarchical. Groups were loosely formed with boundaries that were permeable. Indicators of status, coolness, and popularity were minor issues of concern to students. Differentness or being different was recognized, acknowledged, and accepted. Students moved comfortably from group to group. Isolates were present, yet the circumstance was their choice. Being different in this way was accepted, too. Recognizing that these descriptors were in marked contrast to most high schools, I asked, "Is what I am seeing really happening and how does this system get created?" In the next pages, I will try to answer those questions.

HOW DOES THIS SYSTEM GET CREATED?

The "rag quilt" quote, cited earlier, presented the student perspective of being "thrown together." That is not the administrative perspective, nor would their parents accept that possibility. The network of relationships occurred in an organization with a mission and a structure intended to carry out that mission. The students and their parents accepted GI's mission in order to gain entrance.

Essentially, GI was visualized from the student perspective, not the official perspective, as overlapping circles resting on a central point. The students are in the middle, and coursework (Academic Life) and dorm living (Residential Life) overlap, pressing on students. All these circles rest on a small administrative fulcrum. The school has a set of policies and rules governing the students' lives. Students regarded the rules as creating restrictions on the freedom to which they were entitled. "Prison" or similar words denoting control were metaphors used by many students to answer the question, "What is the GI like?" The place is more like "a highly restricted college." (My favorite metaphor was "a dysfunctional family on speed.") Students recognized the need for rules because of their age and because of parental insistence; yet, at the same time, they resisted them. One student, a junior male, echoed a common sentiment in saying, "Like, my ideal environment is that everybody here should be capable of dealing with a dorm and handling their academic life and everything, and they shouldn't need someone to enforce the rules." Students would prefer a system in which they had "complete freedom, where we are responsible for ourselves" and if "you mess up, you leave" (multiple students). The protective tendency of GI, fueled by state politics and parental worry, engenders the rules and policies that constrain student behavior.

When juniors arrived for orientation, social relationships began due to proximity, and friendships started to grow. The newness was unsettling. According to one junior female,

> I don't know how anybody who hasn't gone through it can understand it. In a half semester, I have gone through more stuff than I went through all last year. Just people, things happening, You are exposed to so much, so many new things all at once. It kind of blew my senses.

The seniors and adults treated them in a way that shaped their evolving friendship-relationship system. The values students brought and the values of the school collided. Basically, the values were similar, at least in official terms, because students were voluntarily in this particular setting. The students accepted the restraints and welcomed the apparent freedoms initially. In actuality, there was considerable variation among students. Juniors learned quickly that they were neither in their home nor in the local school. They welcomed the change while being stunned by it. Diversity, official rules, and rigorous academic demands became clearer. As juniors became seniors, their sense of the social relationships remained consistent. The prospect of college entrance became dominant in seniors' thoughts, and the end brought feelings of estrangement, loss, and wistfulness. Visiting alumni told residents that the GI is "more demanding, harder" than the select colleges many of them would attend.

Central to understanding the social system is comprehending the importance of friendships. The development of friendship followed a familiar pattern. Students arrived excited and found it difficult to sleep. Placed in orientation activities run by Residence Counselors and Resident Assistants (RAs) after an official welcome, the students began to interact. Most knew no one. A few already knew one another from summer camps, hometown, or preview visits. Roommates generally were new to each other. People gravitated toward those who resembled them in appearance and demeanor. Initial feelings associated with anxiety among a diverse group of strangers gave way to a sense of "openness" and freedom. At this stage, relatively few groups formed that were reminiscent of the home school. Within a few weeks, students noticed that boundaries had not hardened, cliques had not evolved. Movement in and out of groups was easy. Friends extended in all directions. A junior male said, "What's neat is that you meet strangers and they know what you are talking about [referring to home school] without having to explain it." Roommates were friendly, but they did not necessarily become fast friends. As one junior female put it, "Here you are never far from a friend." Friendships helped students deal with the times when classwork and homework was not going on. "You go through such crazy things here; but, since you're with people who want to learn also, it makes a difference" (junior female). The importance of friendships for juniors and seniors was evident in this provocative metaphor about life at the GI:

I think friendship's very important here because it's just so hard to get through a week. Because a week is just so sectioned off [by being busy doing the academic work] that you're like, okay, next one, next one. It's just like you're standing in the ocean and you're waiting for the next wave to hit and, on the weekend, you crawl back up to the beach, and you rest, and Monday you go out there and stand again. Friends help you keep going and live with it. (junior female)

Friendship also caused stress. Friendships formed quickly. "You form them so fast and they're so strong; and then they can get broken really fast and just go away" (senior female). Friendships were intense because students lived with and saw each other all the time. One student was having a disagreement with another, "And everywhere I go, he's there in the dining hall, in class, in the lounge, in the computer lab. There is no time like I can get away from it and think about it" (junior female). A student presented an intriguing notion of the situation:

I would say that, if there's ever a person you don't, you know, particularly like . . . it's going to be like really bad. Because you are going to see them a lot of the time. And you have to be able to have this self-control to not act on this dislike. Because, you know, when you're living in such a close environment, the relationships are going to be strained. They're either going to, like, go through and be like coal turning into a diamond and being hard core; or else it's going to be crumbled to the dust and you're going to hate them. (male junior)

In his view, students made choices to make their residential world livable. An aspect of physical closeness, privacy, was mentioned by girls as a factor that heightened friendship pressure. "Everyone knows what you are doing. It gets around" (junior female). Among boys, friendship stress seemed related to being attracted to activities away from studying, and toward computer and role-playing games.

Friendships with persons who were different from oneself were more likely at GI than at the home school. Some children noted the heterogeneity of their own friendships. Every student I asked reported being friendly with someone with whom they would not likely be friendly at the home school. "Like, I have some friends that are really different and nothing like anybody I ever hung out with before" (male senior). These statements refer to persons who are "not straight [gay]," as well as persons of a different race.

ENCAPSULATING THE SOCIAL SYSTEM

The system of relationships among the students with all its complexity can be characterized by six terms: *openness, fluidity, acceptance, busy, pressure,* and *shock and amazement*. Some of these terms are direct expressions of the students (*openness, pressure, shock and amazement*); the remaining three terms (*fluidity, busy,* and *acceptance*) were similar to the words students used and are intended to capture what they experience. Each term is described below.

1. *Openness* means that all kinds of ideas are floating around in conversations and classes.

2. *Fluidity* means that relationships, as well as group membership, change, with the boundaries between groups being permeable.

3. *Acceptance* means that it is okay for someone to express various sorts of behaviors, ranging from conforming to idiosyncratic.

4. *Busy* means that scheduled events or activities and deadlines are ever present. Students are usually on the verge of moving on to another activity or class.

5. *Pressure* means that the pace of life is amplified by notions of self and academic requirements. All students feel the pressure, but the intensity of that feeling depends on many factors, such as personality, schedule, luck, previous schooling, and so forth.

6. *Shock and amazement* means the reaction students have when they encounter diversity, official rules, rigorous academic demands, and the limits of residential life. They learn they are in a place that is not the family home, but is their home.

Eventually, the bewilderment gave way to an allegiance to the ways of the place. Much like people who have survived adversity, the students changed into GIs and swapped stories when they returned as alumni. The four student speakers at commencement voiced these six themes.

INCONGRUITIES OF THE SOCIAL SYSTEM

In the network of relationships, some elements seem incongruent to my description up to this point and are indicative of the complexity of the social system. The school's enrollment was small, less than 300 students, yet not everyone was sure who everyone else was by name. Seniors and juniors were aware that they did not know each other by name. Three factors figured into this situation. First, the dorm arrangement was a powerful force. The genders were separated into different buildings, and while choice of roommates and residence counselor was possible for seniors, juniors had few choices. Students tended to know people on their residence floor, especially in their RC group. The schedule was the second variable. Schedules were crammed, and time was at a premium. Students tended to know people who were in their classes. The third factor was the weekend departure of one-third or more of the students.

Those who lived within two hours of the school or had families with the time and money periodically went home for the weekend.

Conflict among people is inevitable in social groups. At GI, people did get annoyed, "on edge," and "pissed off" at each other. Misinterpretations of other's behaviors and words happened. The lack of privacy in a residential school was a constant fact of life. I cannot estimate the actual amount of interpersonal conflict. Rarely did it happen aloud in public places. When it occurred, it happened verbally, mostly in the dorm where the RC and RA helped smooth any incidents. My fieldnotes contain no instances of obvious conflict. Although there was friction, there was no physical violence. GI students reported no stories of fights. Students used words that suggested that it could happen, but it never did during the year I was there. Adults told me fights had never happened in the history of the program.

Some groups of students were identifiable as groups. Two groups were obvious to everyone. The first group was identified by their commonality: They were couples who dated for more than a month. This was a small group at GI, so they were noticeable. Members of some ethnic or racial group formed the second group.

Outsiders might identify these groups as cliques, but very few students did; that would be an incorrect designation in this system. Whenever I heard the term *clique*, I followed up with that student at some later time and tried to find out who constituted the clique. My observations and questions, direct and indirect, yielded similar responses. Students hedged their descriptions, unable to supply a picture that would fit the idea of rigid boundaries implied in the term clique. In fact, my informants moved away from the idea. Students noted two groups, the most obvious being Asian Indian males and African American females, whom I had noticed during meals early on in my stay. Students did point out these groupings, yet did not interpret them as cliques. Interestingly, not all Indian males nor all Black females belonged to those groups. In the dining hall or the lounges, mixed groups were the standard. The boundaries were open. Explanations for this behavior by outsiders who were of the same or different ethnicity had to do with accepting the others' need to be "exclusive" at this time and a chuckle that any group would think themselves to be special. Probing in various ways over the months did not produce statements about clique-like grouping having to do with racism. The students felt that the members of those groups had a need that was viewed as mildly different from other GI students.

American history consists of many stories of racism. In GI, racism exists, too, but apparently not in the usual way. In fact, many students would say it is not present; others would say it is. Diversity stands out as a foundational notion of the school. Students were amazed by the scope of it in their lives. The pervasive presence of diversity required that they make sense of it. For most, it was "not like anything" they had experienced. Most reported that their home school was monocultural. Whites go to school with Whites, Blacks with Blacks. The other ethnic groups were too small in the state to be used in a characterization of the home school. The students found the diversity attractive and bewildering. The variety of ethnic and religious differences was startling, even for members of the same general ethnic group. I recall a meeting of a club at which the members who acted like they shared a subcontinental culture (India) were not able to understand the foods each described.

The meaning of diversity at GI was complex. The term applies to many kinds of variations. Not only were racial, ethnic, and religious differences included, but also urban-rural differences, gender differences, and sexual orientation differences. The first and most common meaning was racial difference, and that means Black-White differences. The other races were recognized, but were seen as tangential to the dialogue when diversity and racism were mentioned. (Of course, members of the group recognize each other.) Members of non-Black racial groups said racism was present. All students downplayed it as an active force in the life of the place. For students, the second and most disturbing notion of diversity was sexual orientation. The presence of gay, lesbian, or bisexual classmates *forced* students to make sense of the disconnection between personal liking for someone and religious training about those others (homosexuals). I used the word *force* because students lived 24 hours a day for 10 months with each other. For example, statements like "I am a Christian, and it is against my religion" were coupled with "Frank is a great person. I like him. He is like me."

Typically, diversity was talked about very positively and was taken for granted. Many stated diversity was the dominant characteristic of the school for them. If there were strong inclinations to be negative about it, I did not hear them voiced. Notwithstanding, conversations about racism were experienced as discomforting. Blacks and Whites saw the situation differently. Both parties acknowledged off-hand comments that hint of racism. "Attempt at humor" was the students' universal descriptor when racist comments appeared. Both parties were hesitant to say that racism was actively present. All were aware that diversity is valued at GI and the environment would not support racist comments. "Every once in a while, there's some people who [make comments] and everybody's like, shut up now, we don't want to hear it, you shouldn't say that" (female junior). Another student noted, "It would not be smart" (male junior), meaning racist comments did not fit in a diverse environment like GI.

How Whites and Blacks reported the frequency of conversations about diversity presents a meaningful dichotomy. Whites stated that diversity was a familiar conversational topic. Blacks said it was not discussed. The split in viewpoints was because the Black students were speaking of racism; Whites were not. The lack of conversation about racism disturbed Black students. A student said it for his peers:

The GI is such an open environment that everything gets talked about, I mean sex, drugs, everything gets talked about except race. Except race. And the thing about it, okay, if we can talk about all those things, why can't we talk about race? Is something so bad? So scary that we can't get people's opinion about the subject? (male senior)

The extent to which students from other racial groups thought about racism was never clear to me. I am certain that they recognized their differences from others in general, as well as their differences from specific other groups such as Koreans or Iranians, yet those groups have mixed memberships. The formation of clubs linked to ethnic groups suggests such an identification. Some of that awareness may have been heightened by being the children of immigrants with traditional culturally relevant values more than by being members of the racial group.

Dating occurs, but it was not a big part of life at GI. A small group of students were referred to as couples. *Stickies* was one term used to denote couples who were physically close to each other, and sex was an ever-present topic of jokes. Friendship was more important than dating. Friendships between the genders could be seen in study sessions in the lounges and in pairs or in groups of threesomes or more leaving the dorm in the evening, in the dining hall, and in the halls of the school. Sometimes a long-term friendship would turn into romance and a couple would develop. According to the students, these seem to be the ones that lasted. My sense is that there was less sexual activity at the school than in most high schools. A questionnaire answered by half the students, comprising a relatively even proportion of males and females, indicated that dating did not occupy a lot of time. There was some intense activity by a few. Stories of sexual activity were available for listeners. My hunch, after four months, was that those stories were largely exaggerations or fabrications that were indicators of wishful interest, rather than real activity. Two students confirmed this on my last day in the field when I asked them point blank to give me percentages and numbers. During a member-checking visit four months later, I shared with seniors my finding and asked for feedback. What I received were explanations that were familiar from my fieldnotes, including "We know each other so well it is like dating your sibling"; "We see so much of each other that relationships arise and end rapidly"; "We have other priorities at this time" or "This is a transition time in our lives with nothing permanent"; and "Many of us have relationships with friends outside the school."

Indicators of status were present in the school, although they did not seem to exert much pressure on the social relationships. I suspect that some students were concerned about their place in the school. A few adults expressed concerns about this point, but rarely did students express any to me. I was never able to determine anything resembling a consensus about what made someone cool or popular or attractive. Some points that may relate to thoughts of status included taking hard courses, the college a student got into, science over humanities, and clothing. How such thoughts affected social interaction was unclear. I have little evidence on the subtleties of this point, and I believe that this is one of the weakest areas of my analysis. For seniors, the college to which they are admitted was a concern. At the same time, it was also an unpredictable process. Students acknowledged by others as bright did not always get into the prestigious schools, and size of scholarships could influence the final choice. Of course, college admission becomes public in the last semester of the senior year, rather late in the life of the students at GI and in the formation of the social system. Because I spread my attention between juniors and seniors, I may have missed some changes in the system.

DISCUSSION AND IMPLICATIONS

The person doing the study is the prime research instrument in interpretive scholarship. All data are comprehended through the researcher's mind as he or she constructs the meaning of the participants from the data. Understanding who has conducted the research becomes important in order to determine the trustworthiness of the findings (Denzin & Lincoln, 1994). Throughout this paper, I have provided theoretical and methodological information relevant to the issues of trustworthiness and credibility, such as evidence of prolonged engagement, thick description, and member checking. In this last section of the paper, I add a description of my background to help readers make sense of the findings and the inferences in the discussion.

I am an advocate for programs for the gifted. My experience in such programs includes direct teaching, organizing, administering, and evaluating day and residential programs. These skills and knowledge have resulted in a written record of my experiences. Cognizant of my established views and wary of their potential influence, before I began I wrote a statement clarifying what I expected to see at GI and a statement detailing the limits of my role to the director of the institute who is a colleague and a friend. Also, I reported only themes that were supported by multiple sources (students, documents, and adults) and multiple methods (participant observation, documents, and interviews) that have been shared with the participants in person or by e-mail and that have been presented for critique to colleagues in the field and in a research group.

Students at GI constructed a social system that they identified as different from their home high schools and different from the literature on high schools (Chang, 1992; Cusick, 1973). A group of diverse students from the same state who share a serious interest in learning enter a selective program designed to promote academic excellence. A social system emerges in that high school that values diversity and advanced learning. In this system, differences of many kinds are accepted and appreciated, cliques do not form, boundaries among groups are permeable, movement is fluid, and academic accomplishment is valued. In my fieldnotes, the frequent variance of who was with whom at different times and places emphasizes these facts.

The picture of the social system seems almost idyllic. How can the divisions within society not be manifested here? Differences based on gender, socioeconomic status, sexual orientation, race, and ethnicity exist at GI. Recognition of difference is evident, yet conflict based on them is almost invisible. The historical divisions based on those differences in our larger society exert insufficient strength to reproduce the typical high school society as produced and experienced by these students in their reports of home schools. Instead, the students see the differences among themselves; students belong to multiple, loosely formed groups; they like the diversity, as well as recognize some groups reminiscent of the larger societal divisions; they interpret the presence of such groups as inappropriate at the GI, yet understandable; and students create a fictitious group of insiders—the GIs—representing the whole.

The social system is no accident. The participants (students, faculty, staff, and administrators) make it happen. In this paper, I have concentrated on how the students reported their experience, and I downplayed the adults in the story. I wanted to bring to the surface the students' lives. Actually, the students, their families, and the program influence the creation of a social system. GI, circumscribed by its mission, its academic life, its residential life, and its administration, clearly contributes to the development of the social system by constraining what happens there. GI is almost a total institution, a term coined by Goffman (1961) to describe places where all the elements of life are controlled or influenced. Unlike a total institution, GI students can decide to leave. Student choices are within a limited range, set by the adults. Students participate in discussion of policy and of the enforcement of rules in some cases, but the power rests with the adults. Students do circumnavigate obstacles and negotiate rules with adults to get their needs met.

The institution is not trying to create the precise social system that emerges, although many of GI's values are consonant with it. I believe GI unwittingly creates a climate of pressure and pace that pushes the students toward the creation of the social system that emerges in order for the students to sustain themselves at the school. In this way, the situation reminds me of Sherif's (1966) notion of a superordinate goal that diverse groups need to bridge racial and ethnic differences. I doubt that GI could prevent the emergence of a more typical social system unless the students were willing to exchange their experience in the home school for that of GI (Cusick, 1973). I see the students tacitly agreeing to ignore the forces that could divide their social relationships and to buy into the culture of the school. This picture has some elements similar to Peshkin's (1991) description of how high school students at a multiethnic community school dealt with difference.

Two additional stories need to be told from my data about the student experience in reference to the social system. The first has to do with the students, and the second with the research process. As one student informant told me when I asked for advice on writing about his and others' experiences one week before graduation, "Do not forget we are adolescents, teenagers, okay?" (male junior). The point is so obvious, readers may have missed it. GI students must grapple with issues of identity, now and in the future, as well as thoughts about sexuality, drugs, career, and so forth, as all adolescents do (Chang, 1992). Those issues are evident in the conversations among students and adults.

The second story that should be mentioned is the way I conducted the investigation. I might have focused on instances of friction among students and spent more time than I did investigating what they mean. My decision to not explore those frictions was because participant observation showed that the few instances I encountered were inconsequential to the bigger story of the adaptation to the program and the emergence of the social system. I simply neither witnessed nor heard much about friction among students. What I did hear had little heat. The students' conversations were mostly about coming to terms with the rigorous academic and residential demands of GI.

The story I have chosen to tell in this paper was not obvious to me for a year after leaving the field. My fieldnotes and my reflections during that period reveal multiple entries on students adapting to the constraints of the institute. I wanted to understand social relationships, but my choice to concentrate on the social system occurred after I recognized that my spontaneous reaction to questions like "So, what have you learned?" was about the social system. I interpret my slow realization as an indication of my effort to not see what was there because I feared my values might be pushing me in that direction.

My findings are about the student experience in one residential high school during one year. To a lesser extent, my findings may transfer to what might happen in subsequent years at GI. The findings suggest that it is possible to have a social system that differs from that found in most high schools. Whether the system I have described is feasible or desirable in another program is something to ponder. Those who have designs on starting such a school or those who are considering participating as a student, parent, teacher, or counselor should recognize that GI is an exciting and demanding place. Not everyone would want to stay in that environment, and who fits in that environment depends on many factors that are beyond the scope of this paper. Finally, for those who want to understand more about the experience of being gifted in any setting, I recommend listening to the students because they have much to share with us about their own development and we have much to learn.

REFERENCES

Bloom, B. S. (1985). *Developing talent in young people.* New York: Ballantine.

Chang, H. (1992). *Adolescent life and ethos: An ethnography of a U.S. high school.* London: Falmer.

Coleman, L. J. (1995). The power of specialized environments in the development of giftedness: The need for research on social context. *Gifted Child Quarterly, 39,* 171–176.

Coleman, L. J. (1997). Studying ordinary events in a field devoted to the extraordinary. *Peabody Journal of Education, 72,* 117–132.

Cookson, P., & Persell, C. (1985). *Preparing for power: America's elite boarding schools.* New York: Basic Books.

Cusick, P. A. (1973). *Inside high school: The student's world.* New York: Holt, Rinehart, & Winston.

Denzin, N., & Lincoln, Y. (Eds.). (1994). *Handbook of qualitative research.* Thousand Oaks, CA: Sage.

Glazer, B., & Strauss, A. (1967). *The discovery of grounded theory: Strategies for qualitative research.* New York: Aldine de Gruyter.

Goffman, E. (1961). *Asylums: Essays on the social situation of mental patients and other inmates.* Garden City, NY: Anchor.

Hébert, T. (1998a). Gifted Black males in an urban high school: Factors that influence achievement and underachievement. *Journal for the Education of the Gifted, 21,* 385–414.

Hébert, T. (1998b). DeShea's dream deferred: A case study of a talented urban artist. *Journal for the Education of the Gifted, 22,* 56–79.

Henry, M. (1993). *School cultures: Universes of meaning in private schools.* Norwood, NJ: Ablex.

Kitano, M. (1985). Ethnography of a preschool for the gifted: What gifted young children actually do. *Gifted Child Quarterly, 29,* 67–71.

Kitano, M. (1998a). Gifted Asian American women. *Journal for the Education of the Gifted, 21, 3*–37.

Kitano, M. (1998b). Gifted Latina women. *Journal for the Education of the Gifted, 21,* 131–159.

Kitano, M. (1998c). Gifted African American women. *Journal for the Education of the Gifted, 21,* 254–287.

Peshkin, A. (1978). *Growing up American: Schooling and the survival of community.* Chicago: University of Chicago Press.

Peshkin, A. (1986). *God's choice: The total world of a fundamentalist Christian school.* Chicago: University of Chicago Press.

Peshkin, A. (1991). *The color of strangers, the color of friends: The play of ethnicity in school and community.* Chicago: University of Chicago Press.

Qualitative Solutions and Research. (1997). *QSR NUDIST 4 user guide.* Thousand Oaks, CA: Sage.

Sherif, M. (1966). *In common predicament: Social psychology of intergroup conflict and cooperation.* Boston: Houghton-Mifflin.

Story, C. (1985). Facilitator of learning: A micro-ethnographic study of the teacher of the gifted. *Gifted Child Quarterly, 29,* 155–59.

Strauss, A., & Corbin, J. (1990). *Basics of qualitative research: Grounded theory procedures and techniques.* Newbury Park, CA: Sage.

Subotnik, R., & Arnold. K. (Eds.). (1994). *Beyond Terman: Contemporary longitudinal studies of giftedness and talent.* Norwood, NJ: Ablex.

8

Family Factors Associated With High Academic Competence in Former Head Start Children at Third Grade

Nancy M. Robinson

University of Washington

Robin Gaines Lanzi

University of Alabama at Birmingham

Richard A. Weinberg

University of Minnesota

Sharon Landesman Ramey

Craig T. Ramey

Georgetown University

Most studies of gifted students have looked at already identified groups, often convenience samples. This study takes a more epidemiological

Editor's Note: From Robinson, N. M., Lanzi, R. G., Weinberg, R. A., Ramey, S. L., & Ramey, C. T. (2002). Family factors associated with high academic competence in former head start children at third grade. *Gifted Child Quarterly*, 46(4), 278-290. © 2002 National Association for Gifted Children. Reprinted with permission.

approach. Of the 5,400 children in the National Head Start/Public School Early Childhood Transition Demonstration Project tested at the end of third grade, the highest achieving 3% (N = 162) were selected by conducting a principal components analysis on their scores on the vocabulary and achievement measures. Compared with the remaining children, the high-achieving children were thriving both socially and academically, and, although as a group they were not enamoured of school, fewer were strongly disaffected. On the whole, the families of these children had somewhat more resources on which to call and somewhat fewer stresses with which to deal than the families of the remaining children, although their mean income was only 1.26 times the Poverty Index. Compared to caretakers of the remaining children, caretakers of high achievers ascribed to more positive parenting attitudes and were seen by teachers as more strongly encouraging their children's progress. Of the 113 third-grade high achievers with test scores at grades 1, 2, and 3, 52 had met the 3% criterion in at least 2 grades, and 37 had done so in all 3. Years of high achievement correlated with family resources. These findings demonstrate that even families sorely stressed by life circumstances can support very positive intellectual and social competence in their children.

Children identified as high achieving tend to come from homes that are relatively rich in resources—psychological and educational resources, socioeconomic resources, and parental time (e.g., Bloom, 1985; Karnes, Shwedel, & Steinberg, 1984; Kulieke & Olszewski-Kubilius, 1989; Moon, Jurich, & Feldhusen, 1998; Moss, 1992; Terman, 1925). Parents of high-achieving young children tend to devote more time to child-rearing than do other parents; to engage the children in stimulating, playful, and child-centered interactions; to provide language-rich environments and to read to them even after they can read to themselves; and to promote metacognitive thinking and independent problem solving. More propitious home environments increase the ability of children to profit from early educational programs in the area of problem solving and reasoning (Bryant, Burchinal, Lau, & Sparling, 1994). Although differing somewhat across ethnic groups, parental beliefs also relate significantly to children's school achievement (Okagaki & Frensch, 1998).

Putting the Research to Use

Identifying and nurturing high ability wherever it is found is clearly one of our field's highest priorities. This study shows that some families in the income group that qualifies for Project Head Start are able to support, very effectively, the development of high academic and social competence in their children. Whether all these children would be designated *gifted* is beside the point; they are achieving well above grade level to the point that most of them need differentiation of the curriculum in order to be challenged in school. We need to be particularly alert to identifying and serving these children, many of whom are not identified by their teachers as doing so well. It is somewhat worrisome that more than a third of these very successful children say they only like school *sort of* or *not at all*. Continuing success in school is, for these children, their (and our) best hope for the future. Therefore, they need and deserve our attention. Despite the good job they are trying to do, the families also experience barriers to success. One in five of the families of high-achieving children is on public assistance; the average family in this group is living at only 1.26 times the poverty level; nearly a third of the fathers are uninvolved in the families; and a quarter of the caretakers (mostly mothers) have been depressed at least two years in their lives. What if members of the school community who had more resources reached out to these families, recognized and supported their successes, and made available help where it may be needed? What, indeed, might be the positive long-term outcomes for their competent children? Is it not clearly worth a try?

This family picture is clearly not characteristic of all gifted children, however. Numerous projects funded by the only federal research resources earmarked for the gifted population, the Javits grants, have identified many gifted children living in poverty and coming from families facing difficult conditions. Money is certainly not the most important variable here. Far more important are resources such as the organization and stability of the home and the existence of someone who cares very much and who monitors, supports, and focuses the child's efforts (VanTassel-Baska, 1989a).

Investigators of high-achieving children and their families are, however, generally hampered by the fact that available populations have been selected in ways that are likely to limit generalization. For example, in his quest for a large group of gifted children to follow longitudinally, Terman (1925) was unable to test large, unselected populations and had to resort to several shortcuts, such as teacher nominations and a focus on California middle-class urban schools.

These procedures probably reduced the likelihood of including children of color, children from homes of poverty, and children whose problem behaviors or learning disabilities masked their cognitive strengths. In his sample, the percentages of grandparents reported as "Negro" were 0.1%; "Indian," 0.1%; and "Mexican," 0.1% (p. 55). Of the fathers, 10 times as many were professionals as in the population as a whole, and only one father reported his occupation as a "laborer" compared with 15% in the 1920 census report (p. 63). Since Terman's time, almost all other investigators of highly capable students have also dealt with convenience samples, which often include students already identified for special school classes or students participating in talent searches or summer programs.

The opportunity to take a more "epidemiological" approach to the study of giftedness was presented by a comprehensive follow-up of a large national sample of children whose eligibility was determined only by the fact that they had been served by Project Head Start as 4-year-olds. This 4-year longitudinal study offered a rich database representing responses of caregivers, teachers, and the children themselves. Head Start participants constitute a group of special interest in the field of giftedness because there is clear national interest in nurturing the development of talent in children who might otherwise be overlooked. It is for this reason that the single source of federal funds earmarked for educational projects with gifted children, under the Jacob K. Javits Gifted and Talented Students Act of 1988, is directed at underserved groups (Ross, 1994).

This report is the third-grade sequel to a similar study conducted when the children were in first grade (Robinson, Weinberg, Redden, Ramey, & Ramey, 1998). The earlier study found that the highest achieving first graders were successful not only academically, but socially, as well. They tended to have somewhat fewer siblings, they came from homes with more educational and monetary resources, and their parents tended to engage in more supportive child-rearing practices than did the parents of the remaining 97% of the sample. Even so, these families were by no means "well off," and, indeed, many were faced with significant challenges.

METHOD

The overall plan and methodology of the multi-site study known as the National Head Start/Public School Early Childhood Transition Demonstration Project has been described in detail elsewhere (Ramey & Ramey, 1992; Ramey, Ramey, & Phillips, 1996; Ramey et al., 2000). This project, initiated in 1990 by Congressional mandate and with the sponsorship of the Administration on Children, Youth, and Families, was designed to enable Head Start agencies and local education agencies to work together to assist low-income children and their families in making successful transitions from Head Start through the primary grades of public schools. Although local projects were free to design the programs to fit local priorities and goals, all were required to continue supportive social and health services for the child and family throughout the early elementary school years. In addition, a strong focus was placed on welcoming low-income parents into school activities and classrooms, appreciating cultural and linguistic diversity, encouraging the active involvement of parents in the education of their children, improving the quality of classroom instruction through the use of developmentally appropriate educational practices, and creating strong community-based partnerships to streamline and enhance health and social support services. Transition Demonstration projects were implemented in 31 distinct sites located in 30 states and the Navajo Nation. More than 450 schools in some 85 school districts participated in the effort. Approximately half the schools, randomly selected, served as comparison schools, while the target schools were involved in services such as those mentioned above. Even in the comparison schools in many states, however, comprehensive social, health, and educational services were also offered through other initiatives. Few overall differences have been found in the outcomes for demonstration and comparison groups. It is important to note, moreover, that on four of the five achievement tests administered yearly to the children (see Table 1) the scores for the total group of child participants were approximately at the national average. For reports of the Transition Demonstration study, see Ramey, Ramey, and Phillips (1996) and Ramey et al. (2000).

The Transition Demonstration effort was evaluated by a consortium of investigators working locally in the 31 sites in collaboration with a National Research Coordinating Team based at the Civitan International Research Center at the University of Alabama at Birmingham (UAB). The longitudinal study included a total of approximately 8,400 former Head Start children, approximately half entering kindergarten in the fall of 1992 and the other half entering kindergarten in the fall of 1993. These children and families were followed and assessed annually through third grade. Data collection procedures involved: (1) interviews with family caregivers, (2) direct assessments of and dialogues with children, (3) standardized ratings completed by teachers concerning individual children and school environments, (4) reports by principals on school climate and use of transition supports, (5) direct observation of classrooms, (6) reviews of permanent school records, and (7) content analysis and coding of open-ended and qualitative information collected during family interviews. The data utilized for the current investigation are necessarily a fraction of the total database and were selected a priori to represent family variables most likely to exert an impact on student academic performance and social skills. We report data concerning the students' academic achievement and social behavior from parent, teacher, and student points of view, as well as family variables found in previous research to relate to children's school achievement.

Assessment Procedures

The assessment procedures reported here parallel those used in the study of high-achieving children at the end of first grade (Robinson et al., 1998). The

Table I   Standardized Test Scores: Means (Standard Deviations) of Each Measure

	Highest 3%	Others	Eff. Size[a]
N	162	5,238	
PPVT-R	118.3 (13.8)	87.4 (17.3)	1.79
Woodcock-Johnson—Revised			
Letter-Word Identification	127.0 (13.0)	95.0 (15.6)	2.05
Reading Comprehension	129.7 (7.8)	101.0 (16.4)	1.75
Calculation	124.6 (14.1)	99.6 (18.6)	1.34
Applied Problems	129.8 (9.5)	101.0 (15.2)	1.89

Note: [a] Effect size (d) = difference between means divided by standard deviation of the comparison group.

current data were all collected at the end of the children's third-grade year, with the exception of the academic test scores gathered in earlier grades. All assessors were carefully trained and supervised, and protocols were checked not only at the local site, but also at UAB's Civitan International Research Center.

Assessment Instruments

Caretakers participated in individual interviews, and children were tested individually in their schools. In addition, questionnaires describing the children's behavior and competence were completed by their classroom teachers.

Interview. Demographic information and life circumstances were described by the child's primary caregiver during a structured interview. Questions were included about family routines; how often the caregiver interacted with the child in conversations, reading, television, and the like; and caretakers' participation in school communication and activities. Poverty status was calculated for each family according to its reported size and income range.

Woodcock-Johnson Tests of Achievement, Revised (WJ-R; Woodcock & Johnson, 1989). These tests are widely known and will not be further described here. Only the standard reading and mathematics subtests were administered.

Peabody Picture Vocabulary Test, Revised (PPVT-R; Dunn & Dunn, 1981). This widely used, nationally standardized measure assesses receptive vocabulary by asking the child which of four pictures corresponds to a spoken word. Re-test reliability of standard scores over a period of up to a year is reported by the authors as $r = .72$, as well as a median correlation of .71 with other vocabulary tests. When necessary, the PPVT-R was administered in Spanish.

Parenting Dimensions Inventory (Slater & Power, 1987). A 26-item short form of this measure assesses parenting practices in the areas of nurturance, responsiveness to child input, nonrestrictive attitude, and consistency of parenting practices. The inventory has been found to work well with parents of preschoolers and school-aged children from a variety of ethnic groups. A replication study (Slater & Power) with 140 parents of children ages 6–11 yielded goodness-of-fit indices of .97–.98, indicating that each scale represented a single, independent dimension closely fitting the model. Cronbach's alphas of .76 (nurturance), .54 (responsiveness), .70 (nonrestrictiveness), and .79 (consistency) suggest reasonable internal consistency of the scales. Scores from all scales of the inventory are reported by the authors to predict children's psychosocial adjustment as measured by other standardized tools.

Parent Health and Depression Questionnaire. Items on this questionnaire were drawn from the Mental Health Battery of the RAND Health Insurance Survey (Brook et al., 1987). This brief screening tool yields a sensitivity (proportion of truly depressed persons detected) of 82%, a specificity (proportion of truly nondepressed persons detected) of 88%, and a positive predictive value (probability that an identified person is truly depressed) of 61% (Kemper & Babonis, 1992).

Social Skills Rating System, Elementary Level (Gresham & Elliott, 1990). This questionnaire, consisting of 38 items for parents and 30 for teachers, assesses adult perceptions of the children's social skills and problem behaviors. An additional section for teachers consists of nine items that compare a child's academic competence with that of classroom peers and an item about parental encouragement for the child to succeed academically. The instrument also gathers information on the importance of each skill or behavior to the adult respondent. The questionnaire was developed on a national sample of 4,170 children, and separate norms for boys and girls at each grade level are available. The reliability for the teacher version for social skills is reported to be .94 and .82 for problem behaviors. Internal consistency alpha coefficients exceed .90 for teacher and parent forms on social skills and .72 for problem behaviors. Standard scores for the teacher ratings were derived from the manual on the basis of the original standardization sample.

Your Child's Adjustment to School (Reid & Landesman, 1988b). This eight-item interview, consisting of open-ended questions and ratings (on a 10-point scale) was administered as part of the caretaker interview and is designed to elicit information about parents' perceptions of their children's school adaptation: how well the child is doing academically, how well the child gets along with teachers and peers, how important school is to the child, how hard the child tries to do well in school, and the child's overall adjustment to school.

What I Think of School (Reid & Landesman, 1988a). This instrument consists of dialogues with the children that yield information on how much they like school, how hard they try in school, how well they get along with teachers and peers, how important it is to them and to their parents that they do well in school, how well they are doing academically, and how much the teacher helps them learn new things. Children indicate their responses on a 3-point scale. With a sample of 337 children, the authors reported a retest reliability of .84 and an internal consistency Cronbach's alpha of .69 for this instrument.

Sample

The children who constituted the high-achieving group for this investigation were participants in both cohorts with the highest performance on standardized academic measures administered at the end of third grade. Aside from those scores, it was not required that every item of data be available for each child included in this study.

The standardized scores attained on the PPVT-R and on the four standard reading and mathematics scales (Letter-Word Identification, Passage Comprehension, Calculation, and Applied Problems) of the WJ-R were entered into a principal components analysis (PCA), a form of factor analysis. The first principal component was taken as the index of achievement, on which all five of these measures loaded significantly. Of the 5,400 children meeting the criteria described in the previous paragraph, 162 children, the 3% with the highest first principal component scores, were designated as high achieving. The eigenvalue of the first principal component was 3.227, accounting for 64% of the variance. Table 1 shows, for each of the standardized measures, the means and standard deviations of the scores attained by the target group and the remainder of the sample, as well as effect sizes of the differences.

There exists no widely accepted cut-off of scores indicating "giftedness" (Gagné, 1996) nor, for that matter, any consensus of what constitutes high academic achievement. A cut-off of 3% was selected both because it constitutes a common guideline for defining eligibility for special programs (such as the various talent searches for highly capable adolescents) and because that proportion would yield a group of sufficient size to permit interpretable statistical analyses.

The high-achieving children's scores were clearly advanced over the group as a whole, with mean nationally standardized scores ranging from the 88th percentile (PPVT-R) to the 98th percentile (Reading Comprehension and Applied Problems). Slightly lower calculation scores than those on math reasoning skills are to be expected for children who are advanced in mathematical reasoning (Robinson, Abbott, Berninger, Busse, & Mukhopadhyay, 1997) because procedural knowledge is dependent on specific instruction.

Of the 162 high-achieving children, 56% were male, compared with 52% in the remaining sample, c^2 (1) = 1.20, p = NS. The mean age of the high-achieving children when they were tested was 8.75 years, virtually identical to that of the other children (8.74 years). Of the 162 children, 52% were in the demonstration group and 48% in the comparison group, a nonsignificant difference. For a report covering group treatment effects for all the post-Head Start children, see Ramey et al. (2000).

Table 2   Children's Academic Competence: Additional Evidence

	Highest 3%		Others		Analyses[a]
N	162		5, 238		
Teacher standardized rating	106.8	(10.1)	89.4	(14.9)	$t\,(143) = 8.67,$ $p < .001, d = 1.17$
Reading (top 10%)		58%		14%	
Math (top 10%)		55%		14%	
Intellectual functioning (top 10%)		65%		10%	
Parent: School performance (0–10)	8.77	(1.2)	7.39	(2.0)	$t\,(177) = 3.26,$ $p < .001, d = .69$
Child: How well I do in school (1–3)					
"Great"		64%		43%	
"Sort of good"		36%		51%	
"Not good"		0%		6%	$\chi^2\,(2) = 32.76, p < .00$
Current Individual Education Plan (IEP)		6%		17%	

Note: [a]Effect size (d) = difference between means divided by standard deviation of the comparison group.

As an additional way of looking at achievement, Table 2 reports the parents', teachers', and children's assessment of academic performance. The responses of teachers and parents clearly reflected the differences in school achievement in the two groups, although the comparison-group parents also tended to see their children as doing well. Of the 9 high-achieving children with IEP's, 2 were speech/language impaired, 3 were hearing impaired, and 4 were listed as "other." The high-achieving children also recognized their own school competence. In particular, not one reported him- or herself as doing "not good," as did 6% of the other children, one predictor of particularly poor outcomes (Ramey, Gaines, Phillips, & Ramey, 1998). It is of interest that, while the teachers clearly recognized this group as advanced over the remaining children, the standard score derived from teacher ratings was not as high as the children's actual achievement on the nationally standardized measures.

RESULTS

In the following findings, specific probability values are reported at the level of .10 or lower.

Family Variables

Table 3 reports descriptive demographic information about the families. Although the families of high achievers had fewer children and had access to somewhat greater monetary resources than the other families, 64% still

Table 3   Family Resources

	Highest 3%	Others	Analyses[a]
N	162	5,238	
Family % Poverty Index	1.26 (.81)	.95 (.69)	$t(2104) = 3.77, p < .001, d = .45$
Number of children	2.58 (1.21)	2.96 (1.47)	$t(4588) = 3.11, p = .002, d = .26$
Number of adults	1.95 (.74)	1.89 (.88)	$t(4589) = .85, p = NS$
Family challenges	1.54 (1.45)	2.53 (1.77)	$t(151) = 8.01, p < .001, d = .56$
Family strengths	1.77 (1.33)	1.19 (1.04)	$t(157) = 5.14, p < .001, d = .58$
Father involved	69%	59%	$\chi^2(1) = 4.47, p = .035$
Lived in house 4 + years	62%	45%	$\chi^2(1) = 7.65, p = .006$
Family Type			
Most resourceful	64%	44%	
AFDC/SSI/Single	18%	32%	
Homeless	0%	3%	$\chi^2(6) = 31.72, p < .001$
Current AFDC or SSI	21%	36%	$\chi^2(1) = 13.80, p < .001$
Ethnicity			
White	66%	44%	
African American	19%	34%	
Hispanic	8%	14%	
Asian	3%	4%	
Native American/	1%	3%	
Alaskan Native			
Other	4%	2%	$\chi^2(3) = 28.69[b], p < .001$
English not primary home lang.	4%	10%	$\chi^2(1) = 6.08, p = .014$
Grad. High school or GED	87%	68%	$\chi^2(1) = 22.19, p < .001$
Parent depressed 2 yr.[c]	25%	23%	$\chi^2(1) = .34, p = NS$
High depression index	23%	29%	$\chi^2(1) = 2.60, p = NS$

Note. [a]Effect size (d) = difference between means divided by standard deviation of the comparison group.
[b]Asian, Native American, and Other collapsed into one category because of small expected cell sizes.
[c]Significant at first grade, not third grade.

reported monthly incomes no higher than \$1,500 per month. Fewer families of children in the target group were on public assistance. There were not significantly more adults in the homes of these children, and only a marginal trend existed for more fathers of the high achievers living in the home. On the other hand, educational levels of parents were higher and English was more often the primary language of the home. Of a summary list derived from the caretaker interviews of up to 12 family "challenges" (e.g., income < 50% poverty level, homelessness, chronic health problems of caretaker) and up to 6 strengths (e.g., income = 150% poverty level, caretaker having college degree, highly organized family routines), the families of high achievers exhibited significantly more favorable circumstances. Overall, although these families were by no means well off, they could call on somewhat more resources, had faced fewer challenges, and had somewhat fewer children among whom they spread those assets.

One of the secondary analyses conducted by Ramey, Ramey, and Lanzi (1998) on the overall sample used a form of cluster analysis to designate six

Table 4   Parenting Behavior and Involvement

	Top 3%	Others	Analyses
N	162	5,238	
Parenting Dimensions Inventory			
(Slater & Power, 1987)			
Nurturance	−31.63 (4.09)	31.24 (4.40)	t (4571) = 1.06, p = ns
Responsiveness	23.61 (4.49)	21.48 (4.51)	t (4570) = 5.70, p = .001, d = .47
Nonrestrictive	28.26 (6.82)	24.49 (6.85)	t (4571) = 6.64, p < .001, d = .55
Consistency	35.05 (6.88)	34.83 (7.24)	t (4571) = .36, p = ns
Parent Report of Frequency of			
School Involvement			
Volunteer in school			χ^2 (3) = 9,28, p = .026
Discuss child's school day			χ^2 (3) = 3.41, p = ns
Participate parent activities			χ^2 (3) = 2.47, p = ns
at school			
Keep in touch with teacher			χ^2 (3) = 2.13, p = ns
Teacher Report of Parental			χ^2 (4) = 61.94, p = .001
Encouragement to Succeed			
Child Report How Important to			χ^2 (2) = .59, p = ns
Parents that I Do Well[a]			

Note. [a]Significant at first grade. By third grade, 92% of both groups say very important.

family types, which included most resourceful families, single-parent families on public assistance, mother-absent families, homeless families, ESL families (in which English was a second language if spoken at all), high-mobility families, and families in which the caretaker had a chronic health problem. The cluster analysis used the correlation coefficient as the measure of similarity and Ward's method as the clustering criterion. As seen in Table 3, compared with the rest of the participants, more families of high achievers fell into the category of most-resourceful families (higher education, higher employment), and fewer were homeless or dependent on public assistance. A higher proportion of families of high achievers were White/non-Hispanic and, in a higher proportion of homes, English was the primary language.

In response to structured interview questions about how often caregivers interacted with the children, read to them, played with them, worked on things the child was learning in school, discussed television programs the child had watched, or talked about community happenings, no clear pattern differentiated the caregivers of high-achieving children from those of the rest of the group. Indeed, when suggestive chi-square comparisons emerged, none was significant at the .05 level except reading, χ^2 = 13.24 (5), p = .02. Differences tended to be in the direction of the caregivers of high achievers reporting less often they did an activity "every day." The apparent social desirability of positive responses leads us to caution conservatism in interpreting these findings.

A depression index derived from several questions also failed to reveal more than a slight trend toward lower depression in parents of high achievers (Fisher's Exact Test, 2-tailed $p = .12$). Interestingly, in these third-grade interviews, there was no significant difference in the proportion of caretakers reporting that they had ever experienced depression of at least 2 years in duration and a nonsignificant difference in a multi-item depression index not previously calculated. Such a difference had in fact been reported when the children were in first grade (23% in the target group vs. 34% in the larger group), with the third-grade reports by the larger group having now dropped to the level of the target group. The disparity suggests that, for the larger group, positive changes had occurred in the interim that had reduced their memories of protracted periods of depression, while, for the caretakers of the high-achieving group, no comparable change had occurred.

As shown in Table 4, parents' responses to the Parenting Dimensions Inventory, as at first grade, yielded significant differences in responsiveness and nonrestrictive attitudes; but, as before, no significant differences in either nurturance or consistency were found. Parents of high achievers did not report discussing school with their children, being in touch with the teacher, or participating in planned parent activities at school more often than the other group, but they did report volunteering more often at their child's school. Despite the fact that the parents did not so describe themselves, teachers saw parents of high achievers as more strongly encouraging their children to succeed in school than other parents.

Perceptions of and by the Children

These high-achieving children tended to thrive not only academically, but socially. As shown in Table 5, using the scales' standardized norms, teachers rated the high-achieving children as significantly more socially competent, as more motivated to succeed academically, and as exhibiting more positive overall classroom behavior than the teachers of the remaining children. Parents, too, saw their high-achieving children as more socially skilled, although (as at first grade) not necessarily more cooperative than did parents of the remaining children, and saw them as better adjusted to school in an overall sense than did the parents of their peers.

The children's responses to the instrument What I Think of School revealed that, in general, these highly successful children were not invariably positive about their school experience, but fewer of them found it to be truly negative than did children in the remainder of the sample. Except for a strong difference between the groups in their perceptions of how well they do in school, reported in Table 2, there were nonsignificant differences between the groups in how important the children reported it was to them that they do well in school, how hard they try in school, how important it is to their parents that they do well in school (unlike first grade, almost all children in both groups now reported it to

Table 5   Child Outcomes

	Top 3%		Others		Analyses
N	162		5,238		
Teacher Report of Social Skills and Behavior					
Social Skills Rating System (factor scores, Gresham & Elliott, 1990)					
Cooperation	15.8	(4.2)	13.5	(5.0)	$t(138) = 5.93, p < .001, d = .46$
Assertiveness	13.8	(3.5)	12.0	(4.4)	$t(138) = 5.60, p < .001, d = .41$
Self-control	14.4	(4.4)	13.4	(4.9)	$t(4071) = 2.39, p < .017, d = .20$
Sum (standard score)	104.5	(15.2)	97.1	(16.8)	$t(4143) = 4.93, p = .001, d = .44$
Academic Competence Ratings					
Motivation to succeed					$\chi^2(4) = 118.04, p < .001$
Overall classroom behavior					$\chi^2(4) = 32.14, p < .001$
Parent Report of Social Skills and Adjustments					
Social Skills Rating System (factor scores, Gresham & Elliott, 1990)					
Cooperation	12.2	(3.5)	12.0	(3.6)	$t(4608) = .66, p = NS$
Assertiveness	17.0	(2.5)	16.0	(2.9)	$t(4597) = 4.07, p < .001, d = .34$
Responsibility	15.1	(2.7)	13.9	(3.0)	$t(4562) = 4.63, p < .001, d = .40$
Self-control	12.6	(3.3)	12.0	(3.5)	$t(4603) = 2.06, p = .040, d = .17$
Sum (standard score)	100.6	(14.5)	95.8	(16.1)	$t(4620) = 3.55, p < .001, d = .30$
Your Child's Adjustment To School (0-10)					
How well likes school	8.31	(1.7)	8.00	(2.0)	$t(4620) = 1.85, p = .065, d = .15$
How hard tries in school	8.11	(1.9)	7.83	(2.0)	$t(4620) = 1.77, p = .076, d = .14$
Overall adjustment	8.45	(1.5)	8.03	(1.9)	$t(4612) = 2.66, p = .008, d = .18$

be *very important*), or how much the teacher helps them learn new things. Marginal findings emerged for how well the children reported liking school, $\chi^2(2) = 7.52$, $p = .02$, how well they get along with the teacher, $\chi^2(2) = 10.08$, $p = .006$, and how well they get along with other children, $\chi^2(2) = 7.68$, $p = .02$. In each of these last three comparisons, the essential differences between the groups were in a reduction of the most negative alternative. For example, in reporting how well they like school, about two-thirds of both groups said they like school *a lot*, while 35% of the high-achieving children versus 29% of the other group said they *sort of* liked school, and only 2.5% of the high achievers versus 7.5% of the other children said they do not like school. Similarly, more of the higher achieving children endorsed *sort of* and fewer endorsed *not much* as to how well they get along with their teacher.

Table 6   Previous Standardized Test Scores for the 162 Third-Grade
High-Achieving Students

	N	Mean	SD	Grade Equiv[a]
Kindergarten				
PPVT-R	157	102	15.74	
WJ-R Letter-Word Identification	162	102	14.75	K.7
WJ-R Reading Comprehension	162	106	14.94	K.9
WJ-R Calculation	162	100	18.04	K.3
WJ-R Applied Problems	162	111	13.85	1.1
First Grade				
PPVT-R	144	112	14.79	
WJ-R Letter-Word Identification	144	119	15.30	2.6
WJ-R Reading Comprehension	144	124	11.42	3.2
WJ-R Calculation	144	114	12.17	2.1
WJ-R Applied Problems	144	115	14.43	2.4
Second Grade				
PPVT-R	121	111	14.15	
WJ-R Letter-Word Identification	151	124	14.68	4.4
WJ-R Reading Comprehension	151	126	11.68	5.1
WJ-R Calculation	151	117	14.70	3.3
WJ-R Applied problems	151	125	13.11	4.0
Third Grade				
PPVT-R	162	118	13.81	
WJ-R Letter-Word Identification	162	127	12.96	7.1
WJ-R Reading Comprehension	162	130	7.76	7.6
WJ-R Calculation	162	125	14.10	5.0
WJ-R Applied Problems	162	130	9.53	6.8

Note: [a] e.g., K.7 = seventh month of kindergarten.

Previous Test Performance

Previous test performance for the 162 high-achieving third-grade students
was examined to assess if such scores provided early indicators of their future
high-achieving performance (see Table 6). There were different numbers of
children in the various grades because some data were not available on all
children. As early as kindergarten, the third-grade high-achieving children
were already performing well. In terms of mathematical reasoning (Applied
Problems), they were performing at the first-grade level. Consistently from first
through third grade, the children were performing at least one to two standard
deviations above the mean and one to four grade levels higher than their current grade level. Over the years, the children's school achievement showed a
steady increase, with children performing at the fifth- to seventh-grade level in
the third grade.

Figure 1   Longitudinal analysis of the number of children who scored in the top 3% on the WJ-R and PPVT-R at each grade level. Diagram displays overlap in children scoring this high in 1 or more years.

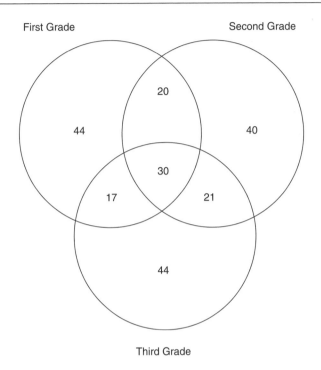

Longitudinal Analyses of Children With Test Scores Available in First, Second, and Third Grades

Of the 5,400 children who were tested at the end of third grade, WJ-R and PPVT-R scores were also available on 3,742 children in all grades. PCA analyses were conducted on the 3,742 children's scores to obtain the top 3% ($n = 113$) at first, second, and third grade. In this analysis, the eigenvalue of the first principal component and the variance accounted for at first grade was 3.05 (61%); at second grade, 3.06 (61%); and, at third grade, 3.20 (64%).

Figure 1 displays the overlap in membership of the top 3% group during the three grade levels. Kindergarten was not included in this analysis because the scores at that age were not considered sufficiently reliable. Of the 113 third-grade high achievers with complete test scores at grades 1, 2, and 3, 61% had met the 3% criterion in at least two grades. Of the 3,742 children who had test scores available in all three grades, 217 (or 5.8% of the children) were in the top 3% at least once between first and third grades. Of this group, 128 (3.4%) did so in one grade only, 52 (1.4%) did so in two grades, and only 37 (1%) did so in all three.

Correlations were calculated between earlier test scores and those at third grade for the 69 third-grade high achievers with high scores in at least two grades. For this group, correlations between first-grade and third-grade scores were .48 for PPVT-R, .53 for both reading scores and Calculation, and .60 for Applied Problems. Correlations between second-grade and third-grade scores on PPVT-R were .55; on both reading scores, .57; on Calculation .52; and on Applied Problems, .56. These correlations were not corrected for attenuation.

Further analyses were conducted to explore the relationship between the number of years that the children had been in the top 3% and their academic achievement. Table 7 presents the children's PPVT-R and WJ-R scores in each grade. By third grade, there was a 34-point mean difference in PPVT-R scores between those who were in the top 3% for 3 years versus those who were never in the top 3%. Similar patterns were evidenced for WJ-R scores. Interestingly, children who were in the top 3% at least 1 year were at least one standard deviation above the mean every year after kindergarten on all four WJ-R tests of achievement.

As indicated in Table 8, the majority of students scoring in the top 3% were White/non-Hispanic. Almost all of their primary caregivers had at least a high school diploma or GED, although it is intriguing to note that 15% of the children who scored in the top 3% for either 1 or 2 years had primary caregivers with less than a high school diploma or a GED. Further, there was a tendency for children who scored in the top 3% at any time to come from families with more economic resources. Particularly intriguing is the fact that, in comparing the children scoring in the top 3% for all 3 years to all other groups, a higher percentage (13%) came from families in which English was not the primary language.

DISCUSSION

These third-grade high achievers, with mean WJ-R standard scores in the 95th to 98th percentiles, came from homes characterized by fewer family challenges and more family strengths and resourcefulness than the remainder of the sample. This is in keeping with the previous literature about the families of gifted children (Robinson, 1998; Simonton, 1994; VanTassel-Baska, 1989a). Even among families of the gifted, and especially among those of the eminent, however, there is often stress and deprivation (Goertzel, Goertzel, & Goertzel, 1978; VanTassel-Baska, 1989b). Among low-income groups, conditions favoring high achievement echo those described in the general population: supportive families that value education and work (VanTassel-Baska, 1989a), relatively favorable educational and financial resources and more optimal parenting practices (Robinson et al., 1998; Steinberg, Lamborn, Dornbusch, & Darling, 1992), and a higher degree of stimulation (Bryant, Burchinal, Lau, & Sparling, 1994).

The present study and its first-grade predecessor (Robinson et al., 1998) are unique in the wide perspective they afford of a large-scale, low-income population unbiased by identification procedures. The children in the target group were identified by their outstanding academic performance, but all the information available about them was equally available about the children who were not

Table 7 Test Data for Children at Each Grade Level by Number of Years in the Top 3%

	Kindergarten Top 3%				1st Grade Top 3%				2nd Grade Top 3%				3rd Grade Top 3%			
	Never	1 yr.	2 yrs.	3 yrs.	Never	1 yr.	2 yrs.	3 yrs.	Never	1 yr.	2 yrs.	3 yrs.	Never	1 yr.	2 yrs.	3 yrs.
PPVT-R	84.19 (14.92)	98.16 (12.88)	102.27 (15.55)	106.78 (19.78)	89.19 (15.41)	106.89 (13.19)	112.61 (13.39)	117.46 (14.27)	86.90 (16.69)	105.01 (12.93)	112.02 (9.20)	117.22 (15.08)	88.13 (16.62)	108.74 (14.03)	116.96 (11.59)	122.51 (15.82)
WJ-R																
• Letter Word	85.67 (12.68)	97.60 (12.32)	100.67 (13.80)	107.92 (17.01)	96.63 (15.05)	115.26 (13.33)	121.00 (14.20)	129.38 (13.47)	97.66 (16.07)	122.09 (13.78)	125.23 (14.87)	132.86 (13.80)	95.01 (15.44)	117.09 (12.06)	122.38 (20.95)	126.71 (10.12)
• Reading Comp.	100.21 (13.06)	103.42 (12.71)	104.48 (14.57)	110.89 (19.53)	98.66 (16.34)	119.98 (11.24)	126.29 (9.22)	131.76 (8.74)	101.41 (16.72)	122.96 (10.99)	126.98 (9.47)	133.81 (10.75)	101.61 (16.27)	122.87 (11.27)	126.54 (8.56)	130.51 (7.72)
• Calculation	89.00 (11.26)	98.05 (17.69)	102.56 (16.90)	102.86 (18.31)	99.11 (15.04)	114.01 (11.28)	113.94 (13.29)	123.08 (12.44)	98.20 (16.51)	115.23 (15.24)	116.54 (14.22)	126.22 (14.99)	99.71 (18.31)	118.30 (14.67)	119.79 (12.30)	122.02 (15.93)
• Applied Problems	91.10 (15.96)	107.08 (13.12)	110.97 (14.62)	116.24 (11.87)	95.50 (14.57)	113.18 (14.05)	118.44 (15.13)	125.73 (13.45)	101.09 (15.75)	122.33 (12.88)	126.61 (11.12)	134.30 (11.50)	100.73 (14.70)	123.03 (11.85)	125.58 (9.26)	132.04 (11.45)

Table 8   Demographic Data at Kindergarten for Children by Subsequent
Number of Years in the Top 3%

	Years			
	Never	*1*	*2*	*3*
N	3,525	128	52	37
Ethnicity				
White	48	70	77	85
African American	35	19	9	6
Hispanic	11	7	4	0
Asian	1	1	4	3
Native American/ Alaskan Native	2	2	2	0
Other	2	1	2	7
English Not Primary Home Language	9	6	2	13
Caretaker Education				
Less than high school	27	15	15	8
High school or higher	73	85	85	92
Percent of Poverty Index				
≤ 125%	83	69	60	78
≥ 125%	17	31	40	22

Note. Demographic data reported by percentage, except for N.

as academically successful. By no means, furthermore, could the families of the high-achieving children be characterized as advantaged when compared with the U.S. population as a whole. Indeed, their mean income fell at only 1.26 times the Poverty Index even when the children were completing third grade, at least 4 years after the families had qualified to enroll the children in Head Start. In the interim, indeed, in a generally improving economy, there had been considerable opportunity for upward mobility to have taken place. Some families had "made it," but many others were still facing significant barriers of circumstance. Their child-rearing practices, their support of the children's school achievement, and their management of their own family resources appear in large part to relate to the children's high achievement. It is particularly interesting that, although only 4% of the children who were high-scoring in grade 3 came from homes in which English was not the primary language, a surprising 13% who had scored high in all 3 years came from such homes. Perhaps we are seeing here the effects of the high value placed on school achievement by at least some immigrant families.

The high-achieving children were starting school with not only academic, but motivational and social assets as seen by their teachers and parents. In this respect, too, the current findings are congruent with research on groups of gifted children identified through other means (Janos & Robinson, 1985; Robinson & Noble, 1991) and substantiate the generally favorable social adjustment of children of advanced ability (National Association for Gifted Children, 2000).

There is considerable concern that high-ability children who come from families of limited means and marginal social status may be overlooked by school personnel. Teachers of these children identified only about half of them as scoring in the top 10% academically, and about two-thirds as represented in the top 10% intellectually. This finding is suggestive of the possibility that teachers tend to overlook high ability in children from economically disadvantaged homes, but it is difficult to interpret in the absence of ratings on other students in the same classes who had not attended Head Start and were not participating in the study. Furthermore, it is of concern that more than a third (35%) of these academically successful children reported only liking school *sort of* and a few of them (2.5%) *not at all.*

The pattern of high performance for children who ultimately do very well was seen in their scores as early as kindergarten, in comparison with the rest of the sample. By first grade, it had emerged more strongly. The families of those who did well in multiple grades were relatively more advantaged within the families whose children had ever been in the top 3%, but were by no means an "elite."

The story evident in the data on these high-achieving children should reinforce our efforts to identify and encourage high capability wherever it emerges. With parents whose child-rearing attitudes and personal resources are conducive to children's optimal development and with the assets the children themselves bring to the picture in intellectual and social domains, these third-graders are clearly a success story. Their achievement was such that, in fact, they will probably need adaptations of the regular curricula through advancement and enrichment to maintain their forward momentum.

As they enter an era in which peer pressure to be "just like everyone else" becomes stronger and stronger, it is even more essential that children who are not just like everyone else have the strong support of parents and teachers and access to high-achieving friends who can help them maintain their motivation to succeed and their pace of development. The responses of the children indicate that they are not necessarily fond of school, even at this age. As a nation, we need to take note and participate with both enthusiasm and resources in giving these children and their families the encouragement and opportunities to develop and maintain this valuable reservoir of talent.

REFERENCES

Bloom, B. (Ed.). (1985). *Developing talent in young people.* New York: Ballantine.

Brook, R., Ware, J., Davies-Avery, A., Stewart, A., Donald, C., Rogers, W., & Johnston, S. (1987). *Conceptualization and measurement of health for adults in the Health Insurance Study. Vol. VII: Overview* (8-HEW). Santa Monica, CA: Rand.

Bryant, D. M., Burchinal, M., Lau, L. B., & Sparling, J. J. (1994). Family and classroom correlates of Head Start children's developmental outcomes. *Early Childhood Research Quarterly, 9,* 289–309.

Dunn, L. M., & Dunn, L. M. (1981). *Peabody Picture Vocabulary Test-Revised.* Circle Pines, MN: American Guidance Service.

Gagné, F. (1998). A proposal for subcategories within gifted or talented populations. *Gifted Child Quarterly, 42,* 87–95.

Goertzel, M. G., Goertzel, V., & Goertzel, T. G. (1978). *Three hundred eminent personalities.* San Francisco: Jossey-Bass.

Gresham, F. M., & Elliott, S. N. (1990). *Social skills rating system.* Circle Pines, MN: American Guidance Service.

Janos, P. M., & Robinson, N. M. (1985). Social and personality development. In F. D. Horowitz & M. O'Brien (Eds.), *The gifted and talented: A developmental perspective* (pp. 149–195). Washington, DC: American Psychological Association.

Karnes, M. B., Shwedel, A. M., & Steinberg, D. (1984). Styles of parenting among parents of young, gifted children. *Roeper Review, 6,* 232–235.

Kemper, K., & Babonis, T. (1992). Screening for maternal depression in pediatric clinics. *American Journal of Diseases of Children, 146,* 876–878.

Kulieke, M. J., & Olszewski-Kubilius, P. (1989). The influence of family values and climate on the development of gifted children. In J. L. VanTassel-Baska & P. Olszewski-Kubilius (Eds.), *Patterns of influence on gifted learners: The home, the self, and the school* (pp. 40–59). New York: Teachers College Press.

Moon, S. M., Jurich, J. A., & Feldhusen, J. F. (1998). Families of gifted children: Cradles of development. In R. C. Friedman & K. B. Rogers (Eds.), *Talent in context: Historical and social perspectives on giftedness* (pp. 81–99). Washington, DC: American Psychological Association.

Moss, E. (1992). Early interactions and metacognitive development of gifted preschoolers. In P. S. Klein & A. Tannenbaum (Eds.), *To be young and gifted* (pp. 278–318). Norwood, NJ: Ablex.

National Association for Gifted Children. (2000). *Task force report on social-emotional issues of gifted students.* Washington, DC: Author.

Okagaki, L., & Frensch, P. A. (1998). Parenting and children's school achievement: A multiethnic perspective. *American Educational Research Journal, 35,* 123–144.

Ramey, S. L., Gaines, R., Phillips, M., & Ramey, C. T. (1998). Perspectives of former Head Start children and their parents on the transition to school. *Elementary School Journal, 98,* 311–328.

Ramey, S. L., & Ramey, C. T. (1992). *The National Head Start/Public School Early Childhood Transition Study: An overview.* Washington, DC: Administration on Children, Youth, and Families.

Ramey, C. T., Ramey, S. L., & Lanzi, R. G. (1998). Differentiating developmental risk levels for families in poverty: Creating a family typology. In M. Lewis & C. Feiring (Eds.), *Families, risks, and competence* (pp. 187–205). Mahway, NJ: Erlbaum.

Ramey, S. L., Ramey, C. T., & Phillips, M. M. (1996). *Head Start children's entry into public school: An interim report on the National Head Start/Public School Early Childhood Transition Demonstration Study* (Research Report Number 1997–02). Washington, DC: U.S. Department of Health and Human Services.

Ramey, S. L., Ramey, C. T. Phillips, M. M., Lanzi, R. G., Brezausek, C., Katholi, C. R., Snyder, S., & Lawrence, F. (2000, November). *Head Start children's entry into public school: A report on the National Head Start/Public School Early Childhood Transition Demonstration Study (Executive Summary).* Available at http://www2.acf.dhhs.gov/programs/hsb/exesummary/summary.htm.

Reid, M., & Landesman, S. (1988a). *What I think of school.* Seattle: University of Washington.

Reid, M., & Landesman, S. (1988b). *Your child's adjustment to school.* Seattle: University of Washington

Robinson, N. M. (1998). Synergies in families of gifted children. In M. Lewis & C. Feiring (Eds.), *Families, risk, and competence* (pp. 309–324). Rahway, NJ: Erlbaum.

Robinson, N. M., Abbott, R. D., Berninger, V. W., Busse, J., & Mukhopadhyay, S. (1997). Developmental changes in mathematically precocious young children: Longitudinal and gender effects. *Gifted Child Quarterly, 41,* 13–27.

Robinson, N. M., & Noble, K. D. (1991). Social-emotional development and adjustment of gifted children. In M. G. Wang, M. C. Reynolds, & H. J. Walberg (Eds.), *Handbook of special education: Research and practice* (Vol. 4, pp. 23–36). New York: Pergamon.

Robinson, N. M., Weinberg, R. A., Redden, D., Ramey, S. L., & Ramey, C. T. (1998). Family factors associated with high academic competence among former Head Start children. *Gifted Child Quarterly, 42,* 148–156.

Ross, P. O. (1994). Introduction to descriptions of Javits grant projects. *Gifted Child Quarterly, 38,* 64.

Simonton, D. K. (1994). *Greatness: Who makes history and why.* New York: Guilford.

Slater, M. A., & Power, T. G. (1987). Multidimensional assessment of parenting in single-parent families. In J. P. Vincent (Ed.), *Advances in family intervention, assessment, and theory* (pp. 197–228). Greenwich, CT: JAI Press.

Steinberg, L., Lamborn, S. D., Dornbusch, S. M., & Darling, N. (1992). Impact of parenting practices on adolescent achievement: Authoritative parenting, school involvement, and encouragement to succeed. *Child Development, 63,* 1266–1281.

Terman, L. M. (1925). Mental and physical traits of a thousand gifted children. *Genetic Studies of Genius: Vol. I. Mental and physical traits of a thousand gifted children.* Stanford, CA: Stanford University Press.

VanTassel-Baska, J. L. (1989a). The role of the family in the success of disadvantaged gifted learners. In J. L. VanTassel-Baska & P. Olszewski-Kubilius (Eds.), *Patterns of influence on gifted learners: The home, the self, and the school* (pp. 60–80). New York: Teachers College Press.

VanTassel-Baska, J. L. (1989b). Characteristics of the developmental path of eminent and gifted adults, ln J. L. VanTassel-Baska & P. Olszewski-Kubilius (Eds.), *Patterns of influence on gifted learners: The home, the self, and the school* (pp. 146–162). New York: Teachers College Press.

Woodcock, R. W., & Johnson, M. B. (1989). *Woodcock-Johnson Tests of Achievement: Standard Battery–Revised.* Allen, TX: DLM Teaching Resources.

9

Academic Underachievement Among the Gifted: Students' Perceptions of Factors That Reverse the Pattern

Linda J. Emerick

University of St. Thomas

Underachievement among the gifted has been a focus of research for over 35 years. With few exceptions, studies of interventions for gifted under-achievers have demonstrated only limited success. This study investigated factors which had influenced the reversal of the underachievement pattern in 10 gifted students, ages 14 to 20, who moved from chronic underachieve-ment to academic success. Results indicated six factors were influential in

Editor's Note: From Emerick, L. J. (1992). Academic underachievement among the gifted: Students' perceptions of factors that reverse the pattern. *Gifted Child Quarterly*, 36(3), 140-146. © 1992 National Association for Gifted Children. Reprinted with permission.

reversing poor school performance. There was evidence that some gifted underachievers may respond well to interventions incorporating educational modifications which focus on individual strengths and interests.

A cademic underachievement has been a persistent area of concern for educators, parents, and students for at least the past 35 years. The gifted underachiever has been described as "one of the greatest social wastes of our culture" (Gowan, 1955, p. 247). Beyond the social cost, however, there are personal wastes as well—opportunities for advanced educational experiences and personal development are thwarted by academic underachievement. Today, there is no problem more perplexing or frustrating than the situation in which a bright child cannot or will not perform at an academic level commensurate with his or her intellectual ability.

The gifted child who is an academic underachiever may suffer from more than poor grades and the disapproval of parents and teachers. Unfortunately, if performance in school is deemed inadequate, the child may also perceive himself or herself as inadequate in other kinds of learning experiences. As these unpleasant experiences continue, a negative attitude toward school, self, and learning in general may result, and poor motivation habits may develop (Covington, 1984). According to Bloom (1977), "There is considerable empirical support for relating the individual's perception of his inadequacy in school learning to the development of related interests, attitudes, and academic self-concept" (p. 197). The strengths and potential of gifted underachievers are often ignored or go unrecognized. As a result, the student may be denied appropriate educational opportunities and his/her curiosity and love of learning may be extinguished.

Considerable research has been devoted to understanding and helping the gifted underachiever. Studies have focused on identifying characteristics unique to this group, isolating causal factors, and developing effective interventions to reverse the underachievement pattern. In spite of the number of studies conducted in these areas, the picture of the underachiever which emerges is complex and often contradictory and inconclusive. With few exceptions, interventions reported by researchers have failed or have had limited success (Dowdall & Colangelo, 1982). It has been suggested that reversing the underachievement pattern among the gifted has not progressed because researchers failed to understand the individual sufficiently and failed to investigate systematically all aspects of the problem (Lowenstein, 1977).

One area of academic underachievement not investigated previously is the gifted student with a record of chronic underachievement who has been able to reverse the pattern without apparent attempts at intervention by parents or educators. Although experts such as Bricklin and Bricklin (1967) have confirmed the existence of such students, no studies have focused specifically on identifying characteristics of this group and understanding the factors that brought about academic success.

In order to understand the process of the reversal of the underachievement pattern, it is necessary to gain some understanding of the meaning the individual attaches to achievement-oriented behaviors or to the factors contributing to such behaviors. Discovering those factors that may contribute to above-average performance in school entails investigating bright children and young adults who have moved from patterns of underachievement to academic achievement. The purpose of this study, therefore, was to identify those factors the gifted underachiever perceived as contributing to the reversal of the academic underachievement pattern.

Putting the Research to Use

Parents and teachers working with students to reverse the underachievement pattern may wish to consider a number of factors. Results from this study indicate that it is important to identify the underachiever's areas of strength and talent. Personal interests can motivate the student to learn and provide an avenue for learning various skills related to school success. Providing appropriately challenging curriculum *during* the period of underachievement also appears to be important. School personnel should consider gifted underachievers candidates for gifted education services and/or advanced classes. The underachievers in this study also seemed to respond well to parents and teachers who had high expectations, provided calm and consistent guidance, and maintained a positive, objective regard for the student. The study's findings indicate that academic underachievement can be reversed as a result of modifications on the part of both the student and the school.

METHOD

Subjects

The subjects who participated in the study were selected using purposeful sampling. Notices were sent to state and district coordinators of gifted education asking them to nominate students who met the following criteria:

1. The student demonstrated intellectual giftedness as evidenced by any of the following: standardized achievement test scores (90th+ percentile),

scores on tests of general aptitude (125+ IQ), or other objective and subjective indicators of potential for well-above-average academic performance.

2. The student demonstrated a sustained period of general academic underachievement (2 years or longer) as supported by evidence of average or below-average academic performance. Evidence included test scores, grades, and observations by education professionals.

3. The student demonstrated a sustained reversal of the academic underachievement pattern (1 year or longer) as evidenced by above-average academic performance. Indicators of academic achievement included test scores, grades, academic awards and honors, and observations of education professionals.

The age range of students who were nominated for the study was carefully determined in order to (a) ensure that students were "close" in time to the period of academic underachievement and the subsequent reversal of the underachievement pattern and (b) increase the probability that, developmentally, the students would be able to reflect upon and articulate their perceptions of various aspects of these events (Harris & Liebert, 1987).

Once a group of students had been nominated, 10 individuals were selected. Variability among the participants helped to strengthen the explanatory power of the data gathered. The students were 10 young adults, ages 14 to 20, from northern New England, the Northeast, and the Southeast regions of the United States. The group was made up of 2 females and 8 males and included 2 Afro-Americans and 8 Caucasians of varying socioeconomic backgrounds. The subjects came from urban, suburban, and rural settings. Table 1 summarizes the general demographic and achievement history of the subjects.

Data Collection

There were two phases in the collection of data. Phase one involved gathering information about each subject regarding biographical background, evidence of above-average intellectual ability, and history of academic performance. This phase was accomplished by the use of questionnaires for parents, nominating educators, and the subjects; follow-up written and telephone communication; and the collection of related school records for each participant. The data collected in this phase were used to verify that criteria for participation in the study were met and to aid in the development of the questionnaire and interview guide used in phase two.

Phase two of data collection involved gathering information directly from the 10 subjects. Two methods were used: written responses to an open-ended questionnaire and in-depth interviews with each subject. The written questionnaire provided information that aided in the development of interview questions

Table 1   Subject Information and Achievement Pattern

Subject	Gender	Race	Age	Residence	Period of Underachievement	Period of Reversal
Emily	Female	Caucasian	14	suburban Southeast	5th–8th grade	9th grade
Michael	Male	African American	19	urban Northeast	5th–9th grade	10th–1st year college
Steven	Male	Caucasian	20	rural New England	5th–9th grade	10th–2nd year college
Laura	Female	Caucasian	17	rural New England	4th–8th grade	9th–12th grade
James	Male	Caucasian	19	urban Northeast	4th–7th grade	8th–1st year college
Alan	Male	Caucasian	15	suburban Northeast	2nd–8th grade	9th–11th grade
Nathan	Male	Caucasian	15	suburban Northeast	2nd–3rd grade 7th–8th grade	4th–6th grade 9th–10th grade
Jason	Male	African American	16	suburban Northeast	1st–3rd grade 6th–7th grade	4th–5th grade 8th–11th grade
David	Male	Caucasian	18	suburban Northeast	6th–9th grade	10th–12th grade
Chris	Male	Caucasian	19	suburban Northeast	4th–7th grade 12th–1st year college	8th–11th grade 2nd year college

and provided between-method triangulation of subjective perceptions when used in conjunction with interview data. The interview guide approach (Patton, 1987) was used in conducting interviews with each subject. Interviews were conducted over a 4-month period with individual sessions averaging 2 to 3 hours per subject. One to three sessions with each student were conducted. The number of sessions was determined by the point at which data saturation was attained.

Data Analysis

The goal of the analysis was to discover common themes in the written and oral responses of the subjects, to organize this information, and to draw conclusions about this population which could be verified and lead to further action. The data from the questionnaires and interviews were analyzed using a three-step data reduction process to code perceptions, organize the codes into themes, and identify themes held in common by the 10 subjects.

RESULTS

Analysis of questionnaire responses and interview data revealed six themes or factors consistently addressed by all 10 subjects in relation to reversal of the academic underachievement pattern. These factors were labeled as: (a) out-of-school interests/activities, (b) parents, (c) the class, (d) goals associated with grades, (e) the teacher, and (f) self. Although all six factors were perceived as important to the 10 subjects, there were different opinions regarding the level of importance except for factors 5 and 6. These two factors were identified by all the subjects as primary in importance. All six factors and the perceived role of each in helping the subjects achieve academic success are described below. Names of the subjects have been changed to ensure anonymity.

Out-of-School Interests/Activities

All 10 students had long-standing out-of-school interests and activities of a decidedly intellectual or creatively productive nature. For example, Alan had constructed a science laboratory in the basement of his parents' home at age 8 and had added to it and continued to use it extensively for 7 years. Jason wrote musicals in fifth grade which were produced and performed by the high school drama club. He had also organized a dance troupe of teenagers who performed professionally. David started his own computer business in junior high, designing software and netting $3,000 his first year. Laura had a wide range of interests and conducted her own investigations into various topics out of school. In every instance, the students were engaged in these and similar types of activities during and after the periods of chronic academic underachievement in school. The students believed that their interests and hobbies helped them achieve academic success in four ways:

1. The outside interest provided an "escape" from what the students determined to be less-than-favorable school situations. As Nathan explained, "[The area of interest] is an outlet for your frustrations . . . you can't just focus on school. There is more to life than school . . . I mean, when I started getting into [photography, computers], I think that helped my school [performance], too, 'cause it gave me something to concentrate on *besides* school."

2. The area of interest or activity provided the subject with a sense of self-worth and success in the face of academic failure. According to Chris, this was something he sometimes believed "was the only thing I knew how to do well. It kept me going." He believed performing in the school band and creating his own jazz group corresponded with academic improvements in school because it allowed him some degree of control over his life as well as being a constructive, creative endeavor.

3. Out-of-school interests were seen as an avenue for maintaining a love of learning and increasing the skills necessary to become an independent

learner. Steven believed his educational program did not always provide a challenge, as a result of both the curriculum and his own in-school difficulties. His interests in reading, math, and computer science filled the gap he thought existed— "I could find my own enrichment. School does not need to be particularly enriching to me now."

4. Out-of-school interests and activities helped the subjects identify in-school learning experiences which were meaningful to them. In other words, school and academic achievement became relevant because of its usefulness in the area of personal interest. For example, Jason saw his strong interest in drama, "aspects of feelings and people," and reading as enabling him to perform well in an English class and experience academic success. He had always seen himself as a "people person" and found himself interested in this class because he enjoyed discussing the literary characters and what motivated their actions, topics which related directly to his own playwriting activities.

Parents

The students perceived that their parents had a positive effect on their academic performance. Parental impact appeared to have been primarily of a psychological nature, relating to the students' feelings of self-worth. Parents were perceived as contributing to their academic success in three ways:

1. The parents had directly or indirectly approved of and supported the children's out-of-school interest. In general, the students' regarded this support as an indication that their parents valued them for more than their achievements in school. They also believed their parents hesitated to use these interests as a means of changing their behavior. Although a student might have to spend less time on his or her out-of-school interest area in order to catch up on assignments or to study more, the interest area was never withheld as a form of punishment for poor performance in school.

2. The students indicated that their parents had maintained a positive attitude toward them, even in the face of academic failure. When Nathan found himself in academic trouble "that was really discouraging . . . [my parents] really helped me get through some tough times . . . helped me keep it in perspective." Nathan and the other students believed their parents had not been discouraged and had not seen the underachievement pattern as a permanent situation.

3. Parents were perceived as having remained calm, consistent in behavior, and objective during the underachievement situation. The students also believed the parents had eventually placed the responsibility for performance in school directly on them. The students reported initially resisting their parents' attempts to remain calm and objective.

Eventually, however, they felt the shifting of responsibility had had a positive effect on their academic performance.

The Class

All of the subjects in this study identified specific characteristics of academic classes as contributing to the reversal of academic underachievement. These characteristics included the following:

1. The class that had a positive influence on the student provided opportunities for intellectual challenge and advanced studies. This type of class was frequently described as "fun." For many of the students, the "fun" classes were more difficult and often eliminated basic course content that the students had previously mastered. They were encouraged to progress through material at a faster rate than in classes where they did not perform as well. Alan described finally being successful academically when he was allowed to "skip right over [basic science] and take college prep Biology. That part of high school worked really well for me." In addition, these classes were perceived as providing intellectual and creative challenges by "going just over the students' heads academically." All of the students described successful classes as more complex. It was in these classes that the gifted underachieving students began to strive to improve academic performance.

2. The class that provided opportunities for independent study in areas of interest was believed to promote academic excellence. The students perceived assignments as "easier to complete" when they were part of a project the student had selected. Laura became excited about learning while in a high school science class "because you were expected to go on your own a bit [in learning] . . . I liked going off and working on something that way." Other students found the opportunity to participate in independent studies invaluable since many of the skills related to their projects and interests outside the school setting.

3. Classes that included opportunities for student discussion as part of instruction were important to these students. All 10 expressed a need for the personal involvement that discussions provided, and they believed the discussions made the content more interesting and relevant.

4. Class activities and assignments motivated the students to excel when they were "real" or relevant to the student. The subjects believed they exerted more effort in their studies when they had the opportunity to apply skills and content they had learned. Emily had failed science courses on a regular basis until she enrolled in a class that emphasized hands-on experiments. She believed she performed at a higher level because she was "doing what real scientists do . . . not just answering questions in a book and taking a test."

5. Classes in which the students were successful academically focused on the process of learning as well as the final product in the assessment of achievement. The subjects were especially delighted with classes in which traditional methods of grading were minimized. In turn, they believed they learned more and were more successful in classes where opportunities for feedback and revision were provided.

Goals

The students agreed that grades and similar indicators of academic achievement held little or no meaning and importance for them. Most remembered earlier efforts to succeed academically as motivated primarily by a desire to please their parents and win general approval. One way in which the students perceived themselves as able to reverse the underachievement pattern was through developing goals the attainment of which was both personally motivating and directly related to academic success.

The goals chosen to be paired with academic achievement varied from one student to another. Entry into a particular field of study such as engineering or into a specific college or university was selected by some; more global aspirations were chosen by others. Michael, a young Afro-American, chose to succeed academically because his "goal was to break the stereotype of the Black teenage male who can't make good grades. And I succeeded." Other students believed they could improve their self-image or increase the amount of time they had for their other interests by improving their classroom performance: "You put a bit more time into school, you see. Otherwise, it creates lots of friction, you're tense, and it's counterproductive. Now I actually have more time to work on my own because there's no more hassle."

The Teacher

The students who participated in this study believed a specific teacher was the single most influential factor in the reversal of the underachievement pattern. All the subjects thought that although the previous four factors were crucial to their academic turnaround, it was the actions of and respect for a particular teacher that had the greatest positive impact. According to them, the teacher who motivated each of them to learn and excel in school displayed the following characteristics:

1. He or she cared for and sincerely liked the student as an individual. Interestingly, "caring" teachers were described by the students as displaying a wide variety of characteristics. Some caring teachers were described as soft-spoken and able to empathize with the student who was performing poorly in class. Others described gruff, abrupt, nononsense individuals as equally caring. According to James, his influential teacher was "very callous, really; but he just drove us to learn. I think

his callousness was just an exterior. I know he really liked us." The common factor in the descriptions of the teacher among all subjects was the *belief* that he or she was concerned about the individual.

2. The teacher was willing to communicate with the student as a peer. The students described instances in which they "could really talk" to the teacher about ideas, topics of interest, and personal concerns. The teacher was viewed as an equal as well as a facilitator for learning.

3. The teacher was believed to be enthusiastic and knowledgeable about the topic taught and demonstrated a personal desire to learn more. All students reported instances in which they were motivated by a teacher's love for a subject and as a result, performed at above-average levels in subjects they did not like. As one student stated, "If the teacher is enthusiastic enough and knows her stuff, it's just contagious."

4. The influential teacher was perceived as not being "mechanical" in methods of instruction. Usually, the student reported being directly involved with the teacher during the learning process. Student participation was seen as a top priority of the teacher. In addition, the teachers incorporated a wide range of resources and strategies beyond the textbook and lecture. One teacher was described as being a positive influence because she used videotapes to help bring the study of Irish poetry to life. The students analyzed the poems and the films. Another teacher was remembered for the unique items he brought from home and his travels to illustrate concepts in a science class. The students believed these behaviors indicated flexibility on the part of the teacher.

5. The teacher was perceived as having high but realistic expectations for the academically underachieving student. The students reported the influential teachers knew the students well enough to be able "to go over my head academically and make me climb the rope to that higher level."

Self

Although it was not selected by the students as the most influential factor, a significant change in the individual's concept of self was viewed as necessary for the reversal of the underachievement pattern. In particular, each student believed he or she had undergone such a change and that without this change, the other factors would have had little or no personal impact. The perceived changes in attitude toward self included the following:

1. The student believed he or she developed more self-confidence and a positive attitude toward the underachievement situation. Some believed their confidence grew from a series of small successes experienced in and out of school. Other students believed they had overcome

the detrimental effects of perfectionism in order to gain the confidence to succeed.

2. The student began to perceive academic success in school as a source of personal satisfaction and a matter of personal responsibility. The students expressed the belief that they had previously seen academic achievement as a way to please others. Once the process of learning in school became a personal matter, they believed they were ready to reverse the underachievement pattern. In turn, the sense of personal pride in their success led to the perception that responsibility for improved performance rested with the student.

3. The students believed they had gained the ability to reflect on and understand factors that may have contributed to the underachievement pattern. They were not certain what had brought about the ability to "see the whole picture" but viewed this as very important.

CONCLUSIONS AND DISCUSSION

This study examined gifted students' perceptions of factors which contributed to the reversal of academic underachievement. Six factors were identified by the students as having a positive impact on their academic performance: out-of-school interests, parents, goals associated with academic achievement, classroom instruction and curriculum, the teacher, and changes in self. Although the factors differed to some degree from those found by other studies, the number and nature of them support the idea that underachievement and its reversal is complex and unique to each child (Rimm, 1986; Whitmore, 1980).

The gifted underachiever who had reversed patterns of academic underachievement in this study exhibited characteristics also associated with the highly creative and gifted individual: independence of thought and judgment, willingness to take risks, perseverance, above-average intellectual ability, creative ability, and an intense love for what they were doing (Renzulli, 1978; Torrance, 1981). The level of achievement occurring outside the classroom indicated that school was frequently the only place academic and creative achievement were not taking place. The students also expressed a need for personal involvement with and respect for the abilities of those directing their education.

This study suggests that reversing the underachievement pattern may mean taking a long, hard look at the underachiever's curriculum and classroom situation. The responses and actions of the students in this study indicate that when appropriate educational opportunities are present, gifted underachievers can respond positively. This supports the findings of Whitmore (1980) and Butler-Por (1987) who discovered that when the gifted child is educated in the "least restrictive environment" in the school setting, underachievement is minimized. Attempts should be made continually to upgrade content and skills, minimize repetitive and redundant lessons, and provide educational challenges in the regular classroom, even when it appears remediation is necessary.

The educational experiences in which the students improved or performed well were related to their out-of-school interests and were characteristic of learning situations deemed appropriate for the gifted: "real world" application of learning, minimal repetitive assignments, use of higher levels of critical thinking, and opportunities for self-initiated and self-directed learning, to name a few (Betts, 1991; Renzulli & Reis, 1985; Treffinger, 1986). While not all the classes in which the students began to improve academically were labeled "classes for the gifted," they bore the characteristics of those in which the curriculum and instruction had been differentiated to meet the needs of the gifted learner.

Factors not previously researched as contributing to the reversal of the underachievement pattern were revealed in the study. The students' out-of-school interests and the role of particular teachers were regarded as major factors in the improvement of academic performance and increase in appreciation for learning in the school setting. Few interventions described in the literature have attributed academic success among underachievers to having very strong interests in other areas. Although it has been widely assumed that the teacher plays a crucial role in the reversal of underachievement, few research studies have examined the specific role of the teacher and his or her personal characteristics as the basis for developing effective interventions. This study suggests that the role of the teacher and the effort to link the underachiever's areas of interest to academic pursuits need to be investigated further. The studies of effective role models and mentors, many of whom are teachers, may be especially helpful as a guide to further study.

The in-school performance pattern of the students in this study suggests that the reversal of underachievement may be lengthy and marked by uneven progress. The students expressed the expectation that there would be "steps backward" as they moved toward academic success, and records of school performance supported their perceptions.

IMPLICATIONS

The findings reported here reflect the perceptions of one group of students who moved from patterns of academic failure to academic success. Although the results should not be generalized widely, this study does suggest steps that may be taken to help gifted underachievers with strong creative interests and involvement. These include the following:

1. Identify the underachiever's strengths and interests as well as areas that need improvement Through recognizing and emphasizing the characteristics of the child that relate to his or her giftedness, educators and parents can see the child as more than a problem waiting to be "fixed." This approach focuses on the positive behaviors of such students and communicates positive expectations about behavior in the academic setting. Knowledge of the underachiever's

strengths and interests can also help pinpoint abilities which may not be evident from the student's test scores or school performance. The experiences of the subjects in this study indicate that schools may fail to investigate these indicators of potential or may identify these indicators solely as problems rather than examples of motivation and ability to learn.

2. Integrate the strengths and interests of the child with academic performance in school. The students in this study believed that when they could perceive a relationship between their own interests and learning experiences in the classroom, they were motivated to perform well.

3. Provide opportunities for gifted underachievers to receive special educational programming in gifted education. The students in this study were often denied access to gifted programs which might have been beneficial in the development of their abilities as independent learners. Those students who were able to participate in such programs found the advanced opportunities for independent studies valuable in maintaining their desire to learn.

4. Include parents of gifted underachievers in determining the educational needs of their children. The importance of parental support and the need for positive action and attitudes makes it imperative that parents be informed of the unique needs of their child, particularly as related to gifted behaviors, and the role they can play in the reversal process.

5. Teachers of gifted underachievers should be encouraged to advocate for the underachiever. In fact, according to these students, teachers at all grade levels play a major role in reversing underachievement. It appears that teachers who are seen as the most willing to help and are perceived as the most effective in learning situations exhibit many of the same characteristics as the subjects— love of learning, task commitment, personal involvement with the subject matter and the students.

6. Be patient. It will take time to reverse the patterns of underachievement. Hopes for the development of an intervention which offers immediate and permanent reversal of the underachievement pattern may be unrealistic and may inhibit the search for effective measures.

Because of the many factors which can influence the onset and the reversal of underachievement, we must expect uneven progress and periodic setbacks when helping the gifted underachiever. What is heartening about this study, however, is the evidence that some forms of academic underachievement can indeed be reversed.

REFERENCES

Betts, G. T. (1991). The autonomous learner model for the gifted and talented. In N. Colangelo & G. A. Davis (Eds.), *Handbook of gifted education* (pp. 142–153), Boston, MA: Allyn and Bacon.

Bloom, B. (1977). Affective outcomes of school learning. *Phi Delta Kappan, 32,* 193–198.

Bricklin, B., & Bricklin, P. (1967). *Bright child, poor grades.* New York: Delacorte.

Butler-Por, N. (1987). *Underachievers in schools: Issues and intervention.* New York: John Wiley and Sons.

Covington, M. V. (1984). The self-worth theory of achievement motivation: Findings and applications. *Elementary School Journal, 85,* 5–20.

Dowdall, C. B., & Colangelo, N. (1982). Underachieving gifted students: Review and implications. *Gifted Child Quarterly, 26,* 179–184.

Gowan, J. C. (1955). The underachieving child: A problem for everyone. *Exceptional Children, 21,* 247–249, 270–271.

Harris, J. R., & Liebert, R. M. (1987). *The child: Development from birth through adolescence.* Englewood Cliffs, NJ: Prentice Hall.

Lowenstein, L. F. (1977). *An empirical study concerning the incidence, diagnosis, treatments, and follow-up of academically underachieving children.* Khartoum, Sudan: University of Khartoum. (Eric Document Reproduction Service No. ED 166 922).

Patton, M. Q. (1987). *Qualitative evaluation methods.* Beverly Hills, CA: Sage.

Renzulli, J. S. (1978). *What makes giftedness? Re-examining a definition.* Ventura, CA: N/S-LTI G/T.

Renzulli, J. S., & Reis, S. M. (1985). *The schoolwide enrichment model.* Mansfield Center, CT: Creative Learning Press.

Rimm, S. (1986). *Underachievement syndrome: Causes and cures.* Watertown, WI: Apple Publishing.

Torrance, E. P. (1981). Emerging concepts of giftedness. In W. B. Barbe & J. S. Renzulli (Eds.), *Psychology and Education of the Gifted* (3rd ed.) (pp. 47–54). New York: lrvington.

Treffinger, D. J. (1986). Fostering effective, independent learning through individualized programming. In J. S. Renzulli (Ed.), *Systems and models for developing programs for the gifted and talented* (pp. 429–460), Mansfield Center, CT: Creative Learning Press.

Whitmore, J. R. (1980). *Giftedness, conflict, and underachievement.* Boston, MA: Allyn and Bacon.

10

A Comparison of Gifted Underachievers and Gifted High Achievers

Nicholas Colangelo

University of Iowa

Barbara Kerr

Arizona State University

Paula Christensen

Northwestern State University of Louisiana

James Maxey

American College Testing Program

The purpose of this study was to compare a national sample of gifted underachievers and gifted high achievers on a number of characteristics.

Editor's Note: From Colangelo, N., Kerr, B., Christensen, P., & Maxey, J. (1993). A comparison of gifted underachievers and gifted high achievers. *Gifted Child Quarterly, 37*(4), 155-160. © 1993 National Association for Gifted Children. Reprinted with permission.

Giftedness was measured as a composite score at or above the 95th percentile on the American College Testing Program (ACT). Underachievement was defined as reporting a high school grade-point average of = 2.25 (on a 4.00 scale), and high achievement was defined as reporting a grade-point average of = 3.75 (on a 4.00 scale). Participants for this study were 30,604 high school juniors and seniors: gifted underachievers $n = 257$; gifted high achievers $n = 30,347$. The underachievers generally had lower scores on the ACT and less extensive out-of-class accomplishments. Over 90% of the underachievers were Caucasian males. Comparisons are provided on a number of nonacademic variables between underachievers and high achievers.

Gifted underachievers have been a source of controversy for educational researchers and a source of frustration for classroom teachers. Educational researchers disagree about the nature and even the existence, of gifted underachievers (see Behrens & Vernon, 1978). Anastasi (1976) questioned the legitimacy of underachievement as a category of academic behavior, particularly when discrepancies between intelligence test scores and achievement test scores are the only evidence of underachievement. Most underachievement, according to Anastasi, is simply test error: a statistical artifact of imperfect methods of measurement. Other authors are concerned that too many definitions exist for underachievement (Dowdall & Colangelo, 1982; Lukasic, Gorski, Lea, & Culross, 1992; Whitmore, 1980). Dowdall and Colangelo (1982) found at least three different categories of definitions in their review of the literature; the difference between two standardized measures, the difference between a standardized measure and performance on some nonstandardized measures, and the difference between two nonstandardized measures. The many definitions of underachievement within these categories led the authors to conclude that the variability of definitions was of a magnitude that made the concept of underachieving gifted almost meaningless.

Nevertheless, most classroom teachers can quickly recall a student whose classroom performance seemed far below the evidence of high ability. The multiplicity of definitions and confusion about the construct of underachievement has done little to dissuade clinicians and researchers from attempting to understand underachieving gifted students, to draw conclusions about their behavior, and to develop remedial interventions (Bricklin & Bricklin, 1967; Fine & Pitts, 1980; Lukasic et al., 1992; Rimm, 1986; Whitmore, 1980). Clear commonalities emerge in the observations of practitioners and the findings of researchers about the characteristics of gifted underachievers. Compared to achievers, gifted underachievers seem to be more socially immature (Hecht, 1975), to have more emotional problems (Pringle, 1970), to engage in more antisocial behavior (Bricklin & Bricklin, 1967), and to have lower social self-concepts (Colangelo & Pfleger, 1979; Whitmore, 1980).

Putting the Research to Use

The findings in this study provide some new perspectives on under-achievement. First, gifted underachievers are not necessarily from poverty or at-risk backgrounds. There is a middle class background to our sample. Also, the underachievers in our study did not seem antagonistic toward school. Their evaluation of the school experience was fairly positive and balanced. Our suspicion is that these students may not demonstrate behavior and attitude problems and thus are "overlooked" by educators. It is our recommendation that counselors pay attention to the folders of high-scoring students. If classroom performance is low but standardized test scores are high, there is cause for concern.

The gender imbalance in this study is striking. The males are the underachievers when there is a comparison of classroom performance and standardized test scores. If a school has a number of boys who fit the def-inition, it may be a good opportunity for group discussions with a coun-selor. These boys could learn from one another and perhaps gain insight into why classroom performance is low and what effects such performance has on them. A caution needs to be made about girls. The standard for being an underachiever in this study was fairly extreme. We think there may be a considerable number of gifted girls who are performing well below ability in class but who do not cross the line that would get them noticed. We think when it comes to being "invisible" in schools, girls are more adept than boys. Again, it would be important for counselors to check on high-ability girls who perform below expectations in the class-room since their tendency to be cooperative may keep them from receiv-ing the attention they need.

In most ways, gifted underachievers are more similar to low achievers in general than to gifted achievers (see Dowdall & Colangelo, 1982). Arceneaux (1990) found one intriguing difference: gifted underachievers scored high on the need for understanding, a measure of general intellectuality, on the Personality Research Form (Jackson, 1974).

Perhaps the most puzzling group of gifted underachievers are those students who have high scores on standardized achievement tests but perform poorly in the classroom. Achievement tests are usually tests of knowledge and are closely tied to curriculum; therefore, the student who receives high scores on achievement tests is likely to possess the precise knowledge that is needed in the classroom. For some reason, the student does not, or will not, display that knowledge. Kerr (1991) proposed three hypotheses to explain this form of underachievement. The first, in keeping with Anastasi's hypothesis, is simply that the test score is wrong and that measurement error is the problem. The second hypothesis is that the student is a "closet learner" who is motivated to learn at home but does not perform within the structure of the school. The third hypothesis is that the student is bored: too angry or depressed about the dullness of repetitive material to perform in class but happy to have an opportunity on a challenging achievement test to show the extent of his or her knowledge.

It may be helpful to explore this type of underachievement further because high performance on achievement tests usually indicates that the student possesses the content knowledge necessary for high academic performance. In addition, it might be useful to study extreme cases, that is, students whose achievement test scores and grades are so discrepant that measurement error is not a likely explanation of the difference.

The purpose of this study was to examine just such a group: students who scored at the 95th percentile and above on the American College Testing Program (ACT) composite score and who obtained a 2.25 grade-point average (GPA) (4.00 scale) or below in their high school coursework. In previous studies of high-ability students, those students scoring at the 95th percentile have been defined as *gifted* (Colangelo & Kerr, 1990; Kerr & Colangelo, 1988). In order better to understand the characteristics of these underachievers, comparisons were made to a group of gifted high achievers. These are students who scored at the 95th percentile and above on the ACT composite and obtained a 3.75 or above GPA (4.00 scale). A profile of these two groups of students may lend insight into the characteristics of talented students who achieve and underachieve.

METHOD

Participants

The participant pool in this study consisted of 58,180 high school juniors and seniors ($n = 35{,}701$ males; $n = 22{,}479$ females) who scored at or above the 95th percentile on the composite score on the American College Testing Program (ACT) in the spring of 1988; this was equivalent to a composite score of $= 28$. The ACT composite ranges from 1 to 35. For the purposes of this study, two groups of students were selected from the participant pool: the gifted underachievers were made up of the entire group of students ($n = 257$) at this percentile level (95th) and above who had achieved a grade-point average (GPA) of $= 2.25$ (4.00 scale) in high school coursework, and the gifted high achievers ($n = 30{,}347$) were those at the same percentile level who had achieved a grade-point average $= 3.75$.

Instrument

The American College Testing Program (ACT) (*ACT Technical Manual*, 1988) is the second most widely used college admissions exam in the United States, with more than 1,000,000 students taking the test every year. The ACT has four subtests: English, Mathematics, Social Studies, and Natural Sciences. Scores on each of these subtests are averaged to create the ACT composite score, which can range from 1 to 35 (*ACT Technical Manual*, 1988). Besides the academic tests, all students are administered the Student Profile Section (SPS) of the ACT and an interest inventory, the Unisex Edition of the ACT Interest Inventory (UNI-ACT). The SPS contains questions on demographics, high school coursework and activities, educational and career plans, needs for services, and questions pertaining to academic attitudes and concerns. Only responses to the SPS were used for the purposes of this study. As part of SPS, students are asked to report their grades received in high school courses. The accuracy with which high school students report courses taken and grades received was studied by Valiga (1987), who reported a correlation of .93 between noncertified self-reported grades and grades from students' transcripts. The GPA for each student was computed from the reported grades.

Procedure

The data tape for this study included the responses to the SPS by all students at the 95th percentile and above who earned high school grade-point averages = 2.25 (4.00 scale) and all students at the 95th percentile and above who achieved grade-point averages = 3.75 (4.00 scale). Items were selected based on their relevance to generating a useful descriptive profile of high achievers and underachievers. Items selected for analysis included demographics (gender, ethnicity, income, community size, high school size and type); students attitudes toward their high school (evaluation of instruction, guidance, and overall adequacy of high school education); out-of-class accomplishments; academic and career plans (major, certainty about major, career choice, confidence about career choice, highest level of intended education, type of institution chosen); needs for services (help with educational and occupational planning, help with personal concerns, study skills, independent study, and honors work).

For the ACT scores and out-of-class accomplishment scores, t-tests were computed. In order to control for inflated alpha, a significance level of $p = .01$ was used. Differences on all other items were computed by chi-square analyses. The percentages for underachievers were compared to those of high achievers for these items and as a decision-rule, differences of 5 percentage points or more were considered of practical importance and worthy of discussion. (Chi-square analyses were computed on the frequencies in the cross-tabulation tables. Chi-square totals are depicted in the appropriate tables.)

Table 1   Comparisons Between Gifted Underachievers and Gifted High Achievers on ACT Means

ACT Test	Underachievers		High Achievers		
	Mean	SD	Mean	SD	t
English	25.837	2.501	26.611	2.579	4.74**
Mathematics	26.949	3.244	29.874	3.354	13.80**
Social Studies	28.961	2.342	28.723	2.389	1.58
Natural Sciences	31.588	1.567	31.268	1.893	2.68**
Composite	28.514	.839	29.276	1.349	8.96**

$**p \leq .01$

RESULTS

ACT Scores

Although all the students in this study received a composite score of = 28 on the ACT, there was still a difference by composite with high achievers earning a higher composite (see Table 1). There were significant differences between the groups on three subtests. High achievers scored higher than underachievers on English and Mathematics; surprisingly, underachievers earned a higher score on Natural Sciences. No difference was found on Social Studies. The Mathematics subtest indicated the most disparity between the two groups. It may be that mathematics ability among able students is a key variable between underachievers and high achievers.

Demographics

There were significant gender differences between high achievers and underachievers. Male high achievers (n = 16,539) outnumbered female high achievers (n = 13,808) (54.5% to 45.5%); however, male underachievers (n = 232) outnumbered female underachievers (n = 25) by a far greater proportion (90.3% to 9.7%). With regard to ethnicity, there was little difference between high achievers and underachievers in proportions of ethnic groups. There were too few underachievers in any ethnic group other than Caucasian to make generalizations. The population of underachievers was overwhelmingly Caucasian (91.2%), as was the population of high achievers (91%).

Although there was a significant difference by income levels, both underachievers and high achievers came from more affluent families. The majority of underachievers (60.1%) and high achievers (58.2%) came from families with incomes over $36,000 a year and more than a third in each group came from families with incomes over $50,000.

Chi-square analyses indicated significant differences between the two achievement groups by community size. There did seem to be a tendency for underachievers to reside in urban areas: they were twice as likely as achievers to live in cities over 250,000, and half as likely as achievers to live in towns or suburbs of 2,000 to 9,999 population. Underachievers were also more likely to attend high schools with over 200 students (73.5% vs. 63.1%). There were no differences in type of high school attended, with public schools being the place of learning for 84.1% of underachievers and 87.4% of high achievers. Demographic characteristics of underachievers and high achievers are shown in Table 2.

Attitudes Toward School

Chi-square analyses indicated significant differences between underachievers and high achievers in their attitudes toward their high school education. Underachievers were less likely to be satisfied with high school class instruction (52% vs. 68%); more likely to have "No feelings in either direction" (30% vs. 20.3%); and more likely to be dissatisfied (17.0% vs. 11.5%). They were less likely to be satisfied with overall guidance services in their schools than high achievers (44.4% vs. 51.5%), although it should perhaps be noted that over half of both groups were less than satisfied with guidance. More than twice as many high achievers as underachievers rated their high school education as excellent (38.8% vs. 17.0%), although a surprisingly large proportion of underachievers rated their high school education as good (44.5%). Table 3 contains information about attitudes toward high school education.

Out-of-Class Accomplishments

The out-of-class accomplishments provide a ranking of 1–7 on a number of activities outside the classroom. These activities are delineated in Table 4. The rankings 1–7 indicate the extent of involvement and the level of accomplishment related to an activity. The ranking of 1 is the lowest (e.g., participation at an entry level); the ranking of 7 is the highest (e.g., a major award or recognition in the activity). In a t-test comparison of means, high achievers had higher rankings in six activities and there were no differences in three activities. The high achievers were more active and accomplished outside the classroom.

Academic and Career Plans

Chi-square analyses indicated significant differences between underachievers and high achievers in college majors and occupational choice. Differences of approximately 5% emerged in 3 of the 20 possible education majors; these are reported in Table 5. (The category *Other* represents the combination of the remaining 14 choices grouped together for chi-square analysis.) High achievers more often chose health professions and engineering than underachievers; underachievers more often chose fine and applied arts, letters, social sciences or undecided. Underachievers were as certain about their chosen majors as high

Table 2   Demographic Characteristics of Gifted Underachievers and Gifted High
Achievers

Demographics	Underachievers Pct.	High Achievers Pct.	Chi-Square Totals
Gender			
Male	90.3	54.5	
Female	9.7	45.5	131.6500*
Ethnicity			
Black American	1.2	0.6	
American Indian	0.4	0.2	
Caucasian	91.2	91.0	
Mexican American	0.8	0.8	
Asian American	1.2	4.5	
Hispanic American	0.8	0.6	
Other	1.2	0.7	
No Response	3.2	1.6	12.7778
Income Ranges			
$0 – 11,999	8.0	14.2	
$12,000 – 23,999	10.5	13.8	
$24,000 – 35,999	21.4	23.8	
$36,000 – 49,999	23.1	24.8	
$50,000 – 59,999	14.3	12.4	
$60,000 – above	22.7	21.0	16.4890*
Community Size			
Farm-open country	7.6	10.7	
less than 500	1.6	2.0	
500–1,999	1.6	6.3	
2,000–9,999	7.6	16.7	
10,000-49,999	30.4	29.4	
50,000-249,999	20.0	18.8	
Over 250,000	31.2	16.2	59.3700*
High School Size			
<25	0.0	2.6	
25-99	9.8	16.1	
100-199	16.7	18.2	
200-399	40.2	33.0	
400-599	22.0	19.4	
600-899	8.9	8.6	
>900	2.4	2.1	11.4352
Type of High School			
Public	84.1	87.4	
Catholic	10.7	7.8	
Private (independent)	3.2	2.3	
Private (denominational)	1.2	2.2	
Military	0.0	0.1	
Other	0.8	0.2	8.9180

*p ≤ .05

Table 3   The Attitudes Toward High School Education of Gifted Underachievers and Gifted High Achievers

Rating	Underachievers (pct.)	High Achievers (pct).	Chi-Square Totals
Evaluation of High School Classroom Instruction			
Satisfied, no change	52.0	68.0	
No feelings in either direction	30.0	20.3	
Dissatisfied, need improvement	17.0	11.5	
No experience with this aspect of school	1.0	0.3	37.9700*
Evaluation of Overall Guidance Services			
Satisfied, no change	44.4	51.5	
No feelings in either direction	25.8	23.7	
Dissatisfied, need improvement	25.8	23.4	
No experience with this aspect of school	4.0	1.4	16.9830*
Evaluation of Adequacy of High School Education			
Excellent	17.0	38.8	
Good	44.5	42.2	
Average	25.1	9.6	
Below average	8.1	1.8	
Very inadequate	5.3	7.6	144.4300*

*$p \leq .05$

achievers. Occupational choice followed the same patterns as academic majors, and underachievers were as confident in their career choices as high achievers.

There were strong differences in educational aspirations. Almost half of the high achievers aspired to a professional degree (49.4%) whereas only 33.7% of underachievers aspired to such a degree. The proportions of students aspiring to a master's degree, however, were equal (32.9% vs. 32.2%). More underachievers than high achievers planned to stop after a bachelor's degree (30.9% vs. 17.7%). Underachievers also chose public institutions of higher education more often than high achievers, and high achievers chose private institutions more often than underachievers. Academic and career plans are displayed in Table 5.

Needs for Services

As Table 6 indicates, the needs for services between high achievers and underachievers are significantly different. Underachievers claimed less of a

Table 4 Comparisons Between Gifted Underachievers and Gifted High Achievers on Out-of-Class Accomplishments

| | Underachievers | | High Achievers | | |
Activity	Mean	SD	Mean	SD	t
Leadership	.992	1.237	2.238	1.797	10.98**
Music	1.437	1.904	2.264	2.180	6.00**
Speech	1.060	1.409	1.126	1.421	0.73
Arts	.861	1.250	.854	1.389	0.08
Writing	1.369	1.355	1.621	1.521	2.62**
Science	.655	1.162	1.179	1.504	5.52**
Athletics	2.142	1.853	3.118	1.987	7.77**
Community Service	.857	1.225	1.435	1.499	6.05**
Work Experience	1.964	1.337	1.879	1.370	0.98

**$p \leq .01$

need for help with educational plans than high achievers (46.6% vs. 54.1%), although they claimed slightly more need for help with personal concerns (12.3% vs. 7.7%). The differences were much more extreme when asked about the need for study skills: 60.9% of underachievers felt the need for study skills; only 14.8% of high achievers indicated this need. Many more high achievers desired honors courses (80.7% vs 36.2%) and independent study (69.3% vs. 51.2%) than underachievers.

DISCUSSION

The picture of the typical gifted underachiever that emerges from this study is a Caucasian male from a moderately affluent family. He lives in an urban area and attends a large public high school. Unlike many gifted males, math is not his strongest area of achievement (although his scores are still quite high). His major and career choices are likely to be somewhat less traditional than those of high-achieving males. It is difficult to make generalizations about the gifted underachiever's attitude toward school because the data are conflicted (as perhaps are the underachievers). On the one hand, many underachievers think their school is good; however, they are less likely than high achievers to be satisfied with their classroom instruction and the guidance they have received. Underachievers display a certain amount of realism in their educational aspirations and choices: they seem to be aware that private colleges may be out of their reach; the doctorate may also seem unattainable given their low performance. However, the vast majority seem to expect to go to college somewhere, and many expect to earn a master's degree.

Underachievers also have some notion of the kind of help they need. Surprisingly, they are fairly confident about educational plans and resist the idea of help. It is as though they have determined what kind of major and

Table 5   The Academic and Career Plans of Gifted Underachievers and Gifted High Achievers

Response	Underachievers (pct.)	High Achievers (pct.)	Chi-Square Totals
Education Major			
Engineering	14.6	22.7	
Fine & Applied Arts	8.3	2.7	
Health Professions	5.9	14.2	
Letters	5.1	2.3	
Social Sciences	16.6	10.9	
Undecided	9.1	6.8	
Other	40.4	40.4	67.2120*
Occupational Choice			
Engineering	12.7	21.3	
Fine & Applied Arts	10.0	2.8	
Health Professions	6.4	17.2	
Letters	6.4	1.6	
Social Sciences	12.4	11.3	
Undecided	10.4	7.7	
Other	41.7	38.1	108.2770*
Confidence about Proposed Educational Major			
Very sure	29.6	26.7	
Fairly sure	44.7	47.2	
Not sure	25.7	26.1	1.1682
Confidence about Occupational Choice			
Very sure	25.1	21.0	
Fairly sure	45.8	46.3	
Not sure	29.1	32.7	2.9611
Planned Highest Level of Education			
Two years	1.2	0.3	
Bachelor's Degree	30.9	17.7	
Master's Degree	32.9	32.2	
Professional Degree	33.7	49.4	
Other	1.2	0.4	48.0900*
Choice of Type of Institution			
Public 4	67.5	54.9	
Private 4	27.2	44.2	
Public 2	4.1	0.5	
Private 2	1.2	0.4	90.4610*

*$p \leq .05$

college is within their grasp or appropriate to their needs and do not wish to discuss it. They do not wish to be involved in honors or independent study, an unusual stance for gifted students. Only in the area of study skills do they wish

Table 6   The Needs for Services of Gifted Underachievers and Gifted High
Achievers

Response	Underachievers (pct.)	High Achievers (pct.)	Chi-Square Totals
Need for Help with Educational Plans			
Yes	46.6	54.1	
No	53.4	45.9	5.5960*
Need for Help with Personal Concerns			
Yes	12.3	7.7	
No	87.7	92.3	7.5190*
Need to Improve Study Skills			
Yes	60.9	14.8	
No	39.1	85.2	414.8700*
Interest in Freshman Honors Courses			
Yes	36.2	80.7	
No	63.8	19.3	308.6040*
Interest in Independent Study			
Yes	51.2	69.3	
No	48.8	30.7	37.8240*

*$p \leq .05$

to have help. The gifted female underachiever seems to differ little from her male counterpart on any of these items; but the fact that she is female in a predominantly male group sets her apart as worthy of further study.

In many ways, this was an unusual study with puzzling findings. We chose an extreme group, a group of young people whose classroom performance was extraordinarily discrepant with their ability and acquired knowledge as measured by a standardized achievement test. However, after considering the results, we believe that they have much in common with the gifted underachievers who exist in almost every classroom and who have been described in the literature. Like the underachievers described in some literature (e.g., Rimm, 1986; Whitmore, 1980), they are, for the most part, white, male, middle-class young people with some dissatisfactions about their school and some concerns about their own behavior. Unlike the underachievers in the literature who are portrayed as rebellious and antisocial (e.g., Bricklin & Bricklin, 1967), these students do not seem to be rebelling in any typical way; they do not seem to blame the system, and they are making educational and occupational plans that conform to the usual model of anticipating college and career entry of other middle-class young people. They may not be aware of the fact that their performance is closing doors.

Counselors and teachers working with underachievers may draw some implications from this study. Although these students probably need personal counseling and career planning, they are most willing to accept help with study skills; therefore, concrete help must be offered for low grades, perhaps combined with individual counseling. Although they eschew honors and independent study, there is clinical evidence that more rigorous academic challenge may actually have a positive impact on underachievement (Kerr, 1991; Whitmore, 1980). Therefore, the evidence of high standardized achievement scores may need to be used to persuade the student of his or her capability to do more difficult rather than less difficult work.

It may be difficult for educators and counselors to work up concern for this group. As white, middle-class males of high ability, they fit none of the categories considered to be at risk. Nevertheless, we and they may be losing the opportunity to see the fulfillment of their potential, and further work seems warranted to understand the nature and needs of the gifted underachiever.

REFERENCES

ACT Technical Manual. (1988). Iowa City, IA: American College Testing Program.

Anastasi, A. (1976). *Psychological testing.* New York: Macmillan.

Arceneaux, C. (1990). *Personality characteristics, interests, and values of differentially achieving able college students.* Unpublished doctoral dissertation, The University of Iowa, Iowa City, IA.

Behrens, L. T., & Vernon, I. E. (1978). Personality correlates of overachievement and underachievement. *British Journal of Educational Psychology, 48,* 290–297.

Bricklin, B., & Bricklin, P. (1967). *Bright child, poor grades.* New York: Delacorte.

Colangelo, N., & Kerr, B. A. (1990). Extreme academic talent: Profiles of perfect scorers. *Journal of Educational Psychology, 82*(3), 404–409.

Colangelo, N., & Pfleger, L. R. (1979). Academic self-concept of gifted high school students. In N. Colangelo & R. Zaffrann (Eds.), *New voices in counseling the gifted* (pp. 188–193). Dubuque, IA: Kendall-Hunt.

Dowdall, C. B., & Colangelo, N. (1982). Underachieving gifted students: Review and implications. *Gifted Child Quarterly, 26,* 179–184.

Fine, M., & Pitts, R. (1980). Intervention with underachieving gifted children: Rationale and strategies. *Gifted Child Quarterly, 24,* 51–55.

Hecht, K. A. (1975). Teacher ratings of potential dropouts and academically gifted children: Are they related? *Journal of Teacher Education, 26,* 172–175.

Jackson, D. (1974). *Personality Research Form manual.* Menlo Park, CA: Research Psychologists Press.

Kerr, B. A. (1991). *Handbook for counseling gifted and talented.* Alexandria, VA: American Association for Counseling and Development.

Kerr, B. A., & Colangelo, N. (1988). The college plans of academically talented students. *Journal of Counseling and Development, 67*(1), 42–48.

Lukasic, M., Gorski, V., Lea, M., & Culross, R. (1992). *Underachievement among gifted/talented students: What we really know.* Unpublished manuscript.

Pringle, M. L. (1970). *Able misfits.* London: Longman Group.

Rimm, S. (1986). *The underachievement syndrome.* Watertown, WI: Apple.

Valiga, M. J. (1987). The accuracy of self-reported high school courses and grade information. *Educational and Psychological Measurement, 42,* 575–583.

Whitmore. J. R. (1980). *Giftedness, conflict, and underachievement.* Boston: Allyn and Bacon.

11

Reversing Underachievement: Creative Productivity as a Systematic Intervention

Susan M. Baum

College of New Rochelle

Joseph S. Renzulli

The University of Connecticut

Thomas P. Hébert

The University of Alabama

This study combined qualitative and quantitative methodology in a multiple case study to examine the phenomenon of underachievement and the effect of using creative productivity (Type III) enrichment as a systematic

Editor's Note: From Baum, S. M., Renzulli, J. S., & Hébert, T. P. (1995). Reversing underachievement: Creative productivity as a systematic intervention. *Gifted Child Quarterly*, 39(4), 224-235. © 1995 National Association for Gifted Children. Reprinted with permission.

intervention in reversing the pattern. Twelve teachers who received training in the *Enrichment Triad Model* selected 17 students identified as gifted who were also underachieving in their school performance. The 17 students, ages 8–13, included five girls and twelve boys. All students were guided through a Type III study by their referring teacher during one school year. Questionnaires, interest surveys, interviews, product evaluation, and participant observations provided information about individual students in the context of pursuing Type III investigations.

The findings regarding the use of creative productivity to address underachievement were numerous. First, a variety of factors contributed to the underachievement of students with high academic potential including: emotional issues (dysfunctional families); social and behavioral issues (the influence of an inappropriate peer group); the lack of an appropriate curriculum (students not motivated by the regular curriculum); and a suspected learning disability or poor self-regulation.

The most compelling finding of this research study was the positive gains made by the students through their involvement in the Type III intervention. Eighty-two percent of the students made positive gains during the course of the year and in the year following the intervention. Most were no longer underachieving in their school settings at the end of the intervention. Five aspects of the process evolved as important foci for different groups of students: 1) the relationship with the teacher; 2) presentation of self-regulation strategies; 3) opportunity to investigate their own issue of underachievement; 4) the opportunity to work on an area of interest in their preferred learning style; and 5) the opportunity to interact with an appropriate peer group.

Nothing may be as frustrating to educators and parents as a bright young mind that seems to be wasted. In fact, concern over the problem of underachievement, especially among potentially high-achieving students, has increased substantially in recent years (Reid, 1991). Professionals have agreed for decades that the phenomenon of underachievement is complex, baffling, and challenging (Passow and Goldberg, 1958; Rimm, 1986; Whitmore, 1980). Although there is considerable research on underachievement among students with high academic potential (HAP), the only consensus of researchers concerns the factors that contribute to the problem. Evidence about effective intervention strategies is inconsistent and inconclusive.

Two major approaches underlie attempts at intervention—counseling and education. While some evidence points to positive gains using family counseling (Colangelo, 1984; Rimm, 1986), psychological interventions often depend upon a long-term commitment by the family, the availability of appropriate psychological services and the assumption that the primary causes of underachievement lie within the student and/or the home. The role of educators in contributing both to the causes and possible solutions to the problem are often ignored in the counseling approach. Likewise, educational intervention strategies have not enjoyed widespread success in reversing underachievement (Emerick, 1992). Several explanations have been offered for lack of success in reversing the underachievement pattern. For instance, Passow and Goldberg (1958) argued that *one* common intervention is unrealistic because no one common cause for underachievement exists. Interventions should be individually designed to address the unique situation of the underachiever. Another claim is that appropriate strategies will remain elusive until a holistic knowledge of the underachievement syndrome emerges (Lowenstein, 1977). Complementing these concerns is the hypothesis that the most typically used approaches focus on the negative behaviors of these students. Some of these efforts include enrolling underachieving students in study skills courses (Crittenden, Kaplan, & Helm, 1984; Hastings, 1982; Scruggs & Cohn, 1983), providing full-time special classes (Whitmore, 1980; Butler-Por, 1987) or using behavior management techniques (Rimm, 1986). The "learn-how-to-get organized-and you-will-achieve" or "work-hard-and-you-will-be-rewarded" philosophy implies that underachieving students consciously want to improve and are willing to work hard and become self-disciplined in order to reverse their pattern of underachievement. According to Kaufman (1991), this is not the usual case. She defines these learners as discouraged and argues that they need encouragement, not discipline or more time on task to overcome their failure.

Putting the Research to Use

The problem of underachievement among high ability students has been a challenge to educators and parents alike. Understanding what factors may contribute to the problem and finding an approach that has enjoyed widespread success in reversing the pattern of underachievement have remained somewhat elusive. The findings of this study offer an explanation of possible causes that underlie the problem and alert professionals to watch for telling symptoms of these factors such as an undiagnosed learning disability or emotional problems. In addition, their research offers a strategy found to be highly effective in reversing underachievement regardless of the underlying problems individual students experience. The strategy consists of engaging the student in an investigation of a real problem (Renzulli's Type III Enrichment) guided by an encouraging teacher. Analysis of the process revealed specific teacher behaviors felt to be integral to the success of the intervention. These strategies can serve as a guide to professionals interested in helping students to achieve success. Most importantly, the study provides support for the notion that more is gained by developing and respecting students' individual gifts, talents, and interests than by efforts aimed at remediation of weaknesses and elimination of inappropriate behavior.

The few studies that have examined various curricular approaches effective with HAP students who are underachieving have several important points in common. Unlike the remedial approaches mentioned above, the successful approaches tend to be child-centered, accentuate student strengths and value student interests. These approaches stress the process of learning as well as the final product. Learning is seen as an active process in which students choose to learn instead of passively taking notes and taking tests. Several of these studies report that when underachieving students complete a meaningful project, positive gains in self-esteem, academic self-efficacy and overall motivation have been noted (Baum & Owen, 1988; Baum, Emerick, Herman, & Dixon, 1989; Emerick, 1992; Whitmore, 1980). Likewise, research on high ability students in general, has indicated that the highest levels of student productivity often result when students are engaged in self-selected investigations. In other words, allowing students to pursue topics of strong and sometimes even passionate interest often results in high levels of achievement (Delcourt, 1993; Reis and Hébert, 1985; Reis and Cellerino, 1983).

In essence, what schools need is a better understanding of the complexity of the problem and knowledge of strategies educators can use that are likely to succeed for the greatest number of underachievers regardless of contributing factors. Observing selected HAP underachievers when they are committed to pursuing an area of interest may reveal those environmental, psychological, and cognitive factors contributing to success and others impeding progress.

Much has been learned about procedures for applying this type of learning experience to bright youngsters and providing them with the guidance necessary for carrying out advanced level projects. This technology has been incorporated into a major dimension of the *Enrichment Triad Model* (Renzulli, 1977a; Renzulli & Reis, 1985) entitled Type III enrichment. The goal of Type III Enrichment is to provide opportunities for students to become actual investigators of real problems through suitable means of inquiry and to bring their findings to bear on realistic audiences. In Type III enrichment, students become producers of creative products through the collection of raw data, advanced level problem-solving techniques, and the application of research strategies or artistic procedures used by firsthand investigators within various fields of study. Detailed procedures and resources for teacher use in the guidance of Type III Enrichment have been developed and widely field-tested over the past several years (Reis, 1981; Delisle, 1981; Gubbins, 1982; Burns, 1987; Karafellis, 1986). These procedures and materials provide teachers with a systematic set of strategies for guiding students through a Type III investigation.

Purpose of the Study

The purpose of this study was to examine the dynamics of underachievement through a systematic intervention program using Type III investigations. The second purpose of the study was to describe and analyze the effect of the intervention on participating students. Finally, the study sought to examine the successful teacher/facilitator strategies for working with HAP underachievers.

The following specific research questions guided the study:

1. What factors contribute to underachievement?

2. What effect does pursuing a Type III investigation have on particular underachievement patterns?

3. Are there specific strategies that enhance the probability of positive gains resulting from the Type III process?

METHODS

Subjects

Eleven teachers from throughout the United States and one teacher from Singapore volunteered to participate in this study. All teachers were enrolled in a master's degree program at The University of Connecticut and all had training in the *Enrichment Triad Model* ranging from entry level to advanced experiences. Some had previous experience in guiding high ability students through Type III investigations. Teachers were asked to select students who qualified for the gifted and talented program in their respective school districts, but who also were judged to be underachievers by special program and regular classroom teachers. In some cases, the targeted students who would otherwise be eligible for services were currently excluded from the gifted program because they were underachieving.

Seventeen underachieving HAP students from 12 districts throughout the United States and Singapore were selected to participate in the study. None of the students had been involved in previous Type III investigations. Five girls and 12 boys ranging in age from 8 to 12 worked intensively with participating teachers who guided them through a Type III investigation. Column 8 of Table 1 summarizes the project outcomes.

Research Design

This research used a multiple case study design deemed powerful in developing and testing theory when methods based on sampling logic are difficult or

Table I   Summary of Selected Students

Students	Age	Grade	IQ	Interests	Primary Contributors	Focus of Intervention	Product	Results
A	9	4	135	Science (Animals)	Emotional	Relationship with teacher	Bird house in space	Grades improved
B	9	3	144	Science (Animals)	Emotional	Relationship with teacher	Math game	Grades and work habits
C	8	3	120	Science/Technology	Curriculum	Project of interest to student	Rocket launching	Minimal change
D	8	3	117	Science/Technology	Learning Self-regulation	No structure given	Electronic car (not completed)	No change
E	9	3	128	Science/Technology	Emotional Social	Felt needed by peer group	Drama/Video Production	Grades improved to B average
F	9	4	121	Science/Technology	Self-regulation	Investigated own underachievement	Model of brain – How does brain control movement?	Grades improved
G	9	4	123	Science/Technology	Curriculum/Learning Styles	Allowed to build a project	Topographic map	Grades improved
H	11	7	140	Fine Arts	Curriculum/Learning Styles	Teacher oversaw project from a distance	Planetarium group project	Student of month award No gain
I	14	8	NA	Performing Arts	Ld/Self-regulation	Teacher gave strategies	Law simulation to be role played in Social Studies	Improved grades, attitude, self-esteem, more appropriate peer group
J	15	9	99 %ile	NA	Social issues	Investigation own issue	Choose your own adventure pen + ink book about under + over achievement	Improved grades and motivation

Table 1 (Continued)

Students	Age	Grade	IQ	Interests	Primary Contributors	Focus of Intervention	Product	Results
K	9	4	120	Performing Arts	Emotional-dysfunctional family	Relationship with teacher	Researched rumor that he was related to A. Lincoln	Grades improved Behavior improved somewhat
L	13	8	97 %ile	Science/Technology	Emotional, shy, lack of confidence	Relationship with teacher	Designed a solar car	Grades improved Social skills improved
M	10	5	98 %ile	Fine and Performing	Poor self-regulation	Teacher provides organization strategies	Cartoon strip	Improved confidence about better work habits
N	10	5	NA	Performing Arts	Emotional issues	Relationship with teacher	Book about ballet	Grades improved Happier and more social Won contest – Arbor Day poster
O	12	8	99 %ile	Performing Arts/Psychology	Social-behavior issues	Interaction and respect of new peer group	Photo essay of feeling of classmates	Grades improved More appropriate peer group More positive attitude
P	9	4	142	Science/Technology	Social-behavior	Relationship with teacher	Experiment research of behavior of hamsters	Improved behavior
Q	9	4	131	Performing Arts/History	Curriculum	Allowed to change math groups and work on real world problems	Campaign to change lunch problem	Improved grades and attitude

impossible to use. The case study design is recommended when the focus of the study is holistic, that is intended to examine the complex dynamics of a system that cause the phenomenon (Moon, 1991). Thus, by using a case study approach, it was hypothesized that the researchers would be able to consider rich descriptions of HAP underachieving students within a contextual frame where various aspects of the problems are identified and studied over the time of the intervention.

Triangulation of data methods and sources (Jick, 1979; Mitchell, 1986) was employed to overcome the weaknesses and biases of a single-method design. This technique demands more than two sources or methods of data to provide checks for both reliability and validity (Smith, 1975). The sources of information were the student, the facilitating teacher, and the products.

The Intervention

The study was carried out during an academic year and proceeded through four phases. Phase I involved identifying HAP underachieving students by documenting evidence of high intellectual potential and average or below average achievement. The evidence included scores on ability and achievement tests, grades, classroom records, work samples, and anecdotal information supplied by teachers and obtained from permanent records. In Phase II, a high degree of familiarity with the students' academic record and personal life was obtained through the use of document review, interest surveys and questionnaires completed by both teachers and students.

In Phase III, teachers worked closely with the students on a Type III investigation. The steps included focusing the problem to be investigated, setting up a management plan with the students, providing necessary resources and strategies for students, and helping students share the completed investigation with interested audiences. The activities during this phase concluded with teacher interviews about their insights on their individual learning strategies and how the students felt about their investigations.

Phase IV consisted of in-depth interviews by the researchers with the teachers about their reactions to the treatment, the effect the treatment had on the students, and their general perception about the overall experience. The principal investigators conducted interviews during which the teachers shared experiences and insights, made suggestions, and discussed how they planned to interact with the students during the next academic year. Site visitations by principal investigators and interviews with the students in person were conducted when possible, and telephone interviews were used when visitations could not be made.

Data Collection

To gain an understanding of the complex issues involved in the phenomenon of underachievement, the quantitative and qualitative methods reviewed below were used.

Quantitative surveys and questionnaires. To collect information about student interests, academic self-efficacy and creative characteristics, several surveys and questionnaires were administered to the students. Teachers also completed questionnaires about their perceptions of the students' creative characteristics. Students were given the *Interest-a-Lyzer* (Renzulli, 1977b) in order to gain information about their students' current or potential areas of interest. This self-report student survey revealed patterns of interests including fine arts, science and technology, literature, mathematics, athletics, politics, management, performing arts, and history.

To measure the academic self-efficacy of the students, the teachers administered the *Self-Efficacy for Academic Tasks* (SEAT) (Owen & Baum, 1991). This 34-item self-report questionnaire measures the students' confidence in their ability to organize and carry out typical actions in school. (A full description of the SEAT is given in Baum, 1985.)

Characteristics of Creative Productivity (Renzulli & Baum, 1989) sought information about the creative productive characteristics of the students. The scale consists of 27 items and was derived from the *Scales for Rating the Behavioral Characteristics of Superior Students* (Renzulli et al., 1977). The items on the original scale were derived from extensive review of characteristics deemed to describe gifts and talents in 10 areas. The items used in this version were selected from the Learning, Leadership, Motivation, and Creativity Scales and were thought to exemplify the behaviors necessary for creative production. Two parallel forms were devised, a student self-rating form and a form for rating students by adults, and were examined for content validity through a review process based on ratings by experienced teachers of gifted students and leaders in gifted education. The Alpha reliability rating for internal consistency was .91 and the test-retest stability coefficient measured .88.

Qualitative procedures. Student essays, teacher observation, interviews and product assessment were used to collect information about the process of the intervention and the perceived impact of the intervention. The teachers kept logs documenting the process and information they were gaining about the cognitive and affective characteristics of the students. Figure 1 is a sample entry from these logs.

Data Analyses

This investigation used both quantitative and qualitative analyses. Information from the various checklists and surveys completed by the students prior to the intervention were tabulated. Qualitative methods revealed common categories (Strauss, 1987) from logs, interviews and student products from which conclusions about the intervention were drawn. Information from interviews, logs, student essays, and products were coded and analyzed to identify underlying categories. To assure reliability of the coding process and the resulting categories, the researchers assessed the data independently.

Figure I   Teacher's Log

February 6th

Met with Eric to discuss what he is interested in pursuing as a topic. He was enthusiastic about the possibility of gardening. He seemed surprised that he would be able to work on a topic that he had chosen! We did a web to develop other avenues; he narrowed in on exotic plants and building a greenhouse right away! For our next meeting he has set the goal of getting information on greenhouses and will complete the student essay.

February 27th

We discussed the management plan, and Eric filled one out—said he enjoyed it because it helped him to see the "bigger picture" of what he will be doing. We talked a little about setting goals—short term and long term. For our next meeting he chose to have the following goals:

1. Go to several libraries to find information about greenhouses.
2. Contact the county cooperative extension for materials.
3. Visit the Garden Way Store for information.
4. A school goal: finish a pencil sketch for art.

The meeting was positive—Eric was more confident in sharing his ideas, and he seemed more excited about the project.

The coding paradigm suggested by Strauss (1987) which involves three types of coding, was used in this study. The initial type of coding, known as open coding, is unrestricted coding of all data involved by the close scrutiny of transcribed interviews, logs, student products, or any other pertinent documents. In open coding the researcher tries to identify concepts that seem to fit the data and "open up" the inquiry (Strauss, 1987, p. 29). While involved in open coding, the researcher consistently analyzes whether the data are pertinent and what category various incidents indicate. In open coding, data are analyzed minutely and coded in order to verify and qualify the theory that is emerging.

After initial categories are determined, axial coding enables the researcher to intensely analyze one category at a time. Axial coding enables the researcher to specify relationships among the categories that emerge in open coding and ultimately results in the conceptualization of one or more categories selected as the "core."

In the third stage of coding, selective coding, the researcher codes systematically and purposefully for the core category. In the development of theory, a goal is the generation of an explanation that accounts for behaviors. A core category accounts for most of the variation in a pattern of behavior. Researchers using this method of data analysis consciously attempt to identify a core

Table 2   *t*-Test Analysis of differences Between Adult and Student Perceptions of Student Creativity

Groups	M	SD	t
Students	79.12	13.29	
Adults	56.29	19.89	3.93*

* p = 0.001

category while coding data for "the generation of theory . . . around a core category" (Strauss, 1987, p. 34).

RESULTS

Findings Prior to the Intervention

The information collected during Phases I and II of the study was tabulated and descriptive and inferential quantitative methods were used to report characteristics of the students. These initial analyses provided information about interests, student academic self-efficacy, student perception of their creative characteristics, adult perceptions of these students' creative characteristics, and the students' feelings about school. Analyses of frequencies of responses on the *Interest-a-Lyzer* revealed that most students had interests in science and technology (Sum = 99), performing arts (Sum = 77), and fine arts (Sum = 64). Student essays about school also revealed student preferences for projects and arts-related activities as ways of learning.

Analysis of student ratings and teacher ratings of the students (see Table 2.) on the Characteristics of Creativity Scale indicated that the students had a significantly higher perception of their creative abilities than did their teachers ($t = 3.93$, $p < .001$).

Although these students viewed themselves as creative, they were less confident in their ability to perform academic tasks as shown on the SEAT. Their mean score (75.2) more closely resembled the mean score of learning disabled students ($M = 78$) than that of the high ability students ($M = 91.2$) as reported in a validity study of the SEAT (Owen and Baum, 1991).

Post-Intervention Findings

While working with the students on the Type III investigations, the teachers learned about the home, school, and motivation patterns of individual students. Although specific details were often idiosyncratic to individual students, qualitative analysis of information gleaned from logs, student interviews, and products across cases led to the emergence of specific patterns of underachievement. These patterns suggested tentative answers to the three research questions posed earlier. The conclusions and supportive documentation drawn from the data for each question are described below.

Factors Contributing to Underachievement

The first research question explored possible factors and combinations of factors contributing to each student's pattern of underachievement. Through analysis of the emerging categories, it became increasingly evident that four factors contributed to underachievement of the students in the sample: emotional issues, social/behavioral issues, curricular issues and learning disabilities/poor self-regulation concerns. Although the students may display behaviors in more than one factor, a primary (P) factor and several supporting factors (s) generally emerged for each student. A profile of factors contributing to underachievement that existed for each student is provided in Table 3 as is a summary of the frequencies of both primary and secondary factors contributing to underachievement in this sample of students. Emotional issues were the most frequent primary factor, curriculum issues and learning disabilities/poor self-regulation tied for second, and social/behavioral concerns was the least frequent factor.

Emotional issues. This was the primary factor for six students. This factor included dysfunctional families, the students' extraordinary need for attention, perfectionism, and depression. For example, Student K, a fourth grade student, came from a dysfunctional family stricken with divorce, alcohol problems, and accusations of child abuse. His teacher claimed that he was neglected at home: "He never has a haircut, nor does he comb his hair or brush his teeth. He is frequently alone and has been seen riding his bike all over town with no adult supervision." Even his mother claimed "that school is his escape from our rocky home life . . . his older brother, a high school dropout, is currently in trouble with the law."

Student E, a male high school freshman, also came from a family with problems. All four siblings were also HAP underachievers. The parents appear to have few effective strategies for dealing with any of the children. The school psychologist blames the student's home life for his underachievement. The student, himself, spoke of finding a hideout in the woods where he could just be by himself. He claimed that he worries about failing because his teachers and parents would be disappointed in him. On the other hand, he asserted, "I'm not used to doing well. I don't think my life would change greatly if l did well."

Perfectionism and depression also explained some students' underachievement. Student A, a fourth grader, complained of migraine headaches in school. "I worry a lot, especially about writing and taking state tests. My mother says I should get all As. She never lets me do my projects on my own." When asked

Table 3   Student Profiles of Factors Contributing to Underachievement

Factors	Students																	Primary	Secondary	Combined
	A	B	C	D	E	F	G	H	I	J	K	L	M	N	O	P	Q			
Curriculum/Learning Style		P	s	s			P	P	s			s				s	P	4	5	9
Social/Behavioral				s		s		P	s				s	s	P	P	S	3	5	8
Emotional	P	P	s		P	s				P	P		P					6	2	8
Learning Disabilities/Poor Self-Regulation				P	s	P	s		P	s	s	P	s				s	4	6	10

P – Primary Contributor
s – Secondary Contributor

when she gets her headaches, she explained when she had to read or write. Surprisingly, when asked what her hobbies were at home, she replied, "I love to write stories and poems that don't rhyme . . . No, I don't get a headache when I am writing on my computer at home." Her mother reported that her daughter "is acutely aware that with very little effort she can accomplish what others struggle to achieve. I need to keep prompting her or she will never work hard."

Student N, a fifth grader, felt the pressure of parental high expectations. She revealed that her father had told her never to tell anyone when she made a mistake or didn't know something. She learned to treat life seriously. When she finished her Type III investigation, she admitted that she was excited about her book on ballet and hoped others would be, but added "It may not be as important as their schoolwork . . . I do hope that people appreciate the work I put into it." In both cases, parental expectations seem to have taken the fun out of learning and had a profound impact on inhibiting their children's achievement.

Social and behavioral issues. These concerns contributed to underachievement as a primary factor in three of the students and as a secondary factor in 6 additional students in the sample. The specific concerns included in this category were the influence of an inappropriate peer group, questioning of social values, and lack of behavioral controls and social skills. Student Q, a seventh grader, dressed for school every day in black clothing, wore paste white makeup and shredded jeans to gain the approval of a group of students who were reported to be involved with drugs. Members of this group prided themselves on their negative attitude about school. In fact, when she became part of the study she had to miss the choir to meet with the teacher of the gifted. Her negative attitude and flippant remarks made the choir teacher reluctant to allow her to leave. "To let me know," the special program teacher reported, "the choir teacher called saying that the student had just flipped her hall pass in front of her face and said, 'I'm leavin'.'"

Student E, previously described as coming from a dysfunctional family, admitted that he got into trouble in school because he had an image to uphold in front of his peers. He attempted to hide his interest in learning when his friends were present. For example, he never responded in mathematics class when the teacher asked if anyone had a question. The teacher, in turn was resentful when this same student approached her privately to ask for a mathematics tutor. The teacher of the gifted reported that he acted very different with her when they were alone than he did if one of his friends was present: "He seemed shy around [his friend] when discussing his interest. In fact, when I wanted him to do an evaluation of a computer program, he avoided agreeing when [his friend] was present."

Some students, especially during adolescence, question prevailing social ideals. Student J, a 16-year-old Malaysian girl living in Singapore questioned the fast-paced learning and pressure to achieve and compete. Her teacher explained that "she feels out of touch with the majority. Her friends in class are the Chinese girls. She is the only Malaysian girl in class. The Malay culture is very easy-going, so it may be a conflict for her to be part of the rat race." While confronting this conflict, the student put forth minimal effort in her studies and in fact appeared lethargic and tired.

For other students, obeying school rules was problematic. Student P, a fourth grader, was described by his teacher "as a very bright student who has a difficult time achieving in the classroom because he was a severe behavior problem." The problem worsened as the year progressed, and in February he was referred to the special education staff for a complete psycho-educational evaluation. He was subsequently diagnosed as behavior disordered with a lack of appropriate social skills and behavioral controls.

The lack of an appropriate curriculum. Many students were simply not motivated by the regular curriculum. Some believed there was no challenge offered in the curriculum while others preferred different styles of learning. Student I, for instance, saw his participation in the study as a way to be excused from social studies, a course he disliked. He argued that if he could test out of the class he would write a new court case for the eighth grade court drama. "I don't like the old one, it's got some stupid character like Candy Cane in it, and I think we could do a better job."

Student J also complained that too many subjects were "too content based." He indicated that he preferred chemistry "because it is more interrelated and requires the application of skills. I think students should be allowed to study what they like and have an interest in."

Many of the students in their essays on their views of school believed there should be more time made for projects. In fact, Student G, a fourth grader, revealed that he learned much better when he was allowed to make things. "Projects are neat because I am good at [them]. l would like to make projects all day to help me learn." Student H, a seventh grader concurred, "I think homework should be more projects and a lot more oral things. By that, I mean maybe they should have learning tapes instead of writing and reading. I think they should show more movies and have more trips. I really like working in a group especially with the top kids." He is not in the top group in his classroom and is angry about it. "For me, I'm in a situation where I can't move up in a group to the group level that I should be in because of the situation of crowding."

Learning disabilities and poor self-regulation. The final contributor to under-achievement, and the factor that appeared most often, was the presence or suspicion of a learning disability or poor student self-regulation—"command and application of appropriate learning strategies" (Baum, Owen, & Dixon, 1991). These two areas overlap greatly. In fact, the major difference between the underachieving students and the students with learning disabilities may be simply that one can receive special education by law and the other cannot. The students may have been diagnosed as learning disabled or have been referred for poor reading, handwriting or spelling skills. Other typical complaints included disorganization, failure to complete assignments, forgetfulness, and lack of time management skills or attending skills. Student I demonstrated behaviors that could easily fall into either category. According to the teacher of the gifted,

> In sixth grade this student was a basket case—a behavior problem always in trouble on the playground. ADD (attention deficit disorder) was suspected but ultimately ruled out. He was then assessed for the presence of a learning disability or behavior disorder. However, I think the hardest thing for this young man was learning how to edit, organize and attend to his work.

Another subject, Student M, was described as a sensitive fifth grader by his teacher. "Everyone wants to teach him until they get him. He drives them crazy. He cannot focus his attention on anything. He's the proverbial space cadet. He's very bright and very disorganized. When I looked at his grades, they were really good. His regular education teachers had no knowledge that they had given him those grades or how he could possibly have earned them!" The teachers predicted that if his deplorable work habits did not improve, his grades eventually would suffer.

EFFECT OF INTERVENTION ON MANIFESTATION OF UNDERACHIEVEMENT IN INDIVIDUAL STUDENTS

The second research question examined the effects of the Type III process on individual students. Eighty-two percent of the students made positive gains during the course of the year and in the year following the Type III intervention. These changes were documented by report cards (grades and teacher comments), achievement test scores, teacher and parent informal interviews with enrichment teachers, student interviews and a group interview with the enrichment teachers. Improvement was noted in achievement, effort and attitude regarding school, self-regulated behavior, and classroom behavior. Even though the reasons for each student's underachievement were vastly different, most eventually completed their investigations and made positive gains in self-esteem and academics. Table 1 presents an overview of the students' patterns of under-achievement, Type III investigations and changes in behavior in columns 6 through 9.

Analysis of the dynamics that occurred during the course of the intervention as recorded in the teacher logs and interviews with both students and enrichment teachers revealed a possible explanation for the success of the intervention across students whose problems and patterns varied. The Type III experience is a multi-faceted intervention. It provides an authentic problem-based curriculum, allows students to work in an area of interest and strength, and supplies a caring adult with whom to work. A management plan helps to organize the project into manageable parts and offers students the opportunities to interact with others with similar interest or talents. The cross-case comparisons appeared to indicate that the intervention served different purposes or fulfilled different needs depending on the factors contributing to each student's pattern of underachievement.

For different groups of students, different features of the Type III process were most compelling. For instance, if a student tended to underachievement to gain attention from an adult, the relationship with the teacher-mentor was the most important feature of the intervention process. On the other hand, if the student was bored with her regular curriculum the opportunity to work on a self-selected project stimulated her achievement. Five features embedded in the Type III process evolved as a major focus of the intervention for different groups of students.

1. the relationship with the teacher

2. presentation of self-regulation strategies

3. opportunity to investigate issues related to their underachievement

4. the opportunity to work on an area of interest in their preferred learning style

5. the opportunity to interact with an appropriate peer group

Relationship with teacher. In the cases where students had a need for positive attention from an adult, relationships with teachers became the most important aspect of the Type III process. One example was the case of Student K whose home life was described earlier. As the year progressed, the youngster became more and more attached to the teacher of the gifted who was facilitating the Type III investigation. He would gladly do extra work for her and would behave in the regular classroom to be with her. He even began to call her "mom" on occasion. The following excerpt from the teacher's log reveals this emerging bond.

During the past few days, he has said or done something every day to let me know that he likes me and/or to be reassured that I like him. He gave me the name Mom in a computer game we played. When he found my immediate family in my genealogy booklet he said, "Gee, I wish my name was there." I laughed and said I would pencil his name in as my part-time adopted son. After school today he made a gift for me, a heart, and inscribed within was "Mrs. M is a good teacher."

At times the teacher went home feeling emotionally drained by their relationship: "I don't want to sound callous, but I found that by the end of the year I was so emotionally drained that it was almost a relief to not have that with me day in and day out." At the end of his project, which took him time that exceeded the academic year to complete, his teacher commented,

This child has so many strikes against him that I can't predict whether or not he'll be a dropout like his brother. But right now I know that his project was important to him. He finally followed through to the end. But most important, he and I have formed a bond that will hopefully give him needed support and encouragement. He can't wait to start another Type III investigation.

Presentation of learning strategies or compensation techniques. For the students who seemed to have poor learning or organizational skills, completing a Type III helped them to become aware of strategies that facilitate learning. While the students were pursuing their Type III investigations, teachers discovered learning obstacles like poor time management, inability to keep track of their belongings, and poor concentration. When these problems surfaced, the teacher would suggest strategies or the students would invent their own ways of solving the problem.

Student I had difficulty with organization. The teacher gave him a box labeled "R.J.'s Stuff" to keep in the resource room and a file folder next to the computer to store work in progress. To assist him in organizing the steps to complete his project, the teacher and the student prepared a management plan with a time line. She also gave him strategies for editing his work. "When he showed me his schedule-of-events sheet for his simulation, I asked him several questions about how it worked. This helped the student figure out the sections that needed revisions." During the course of the study, he discovered that he could concentrate best when writing on the computer and "plugged into music." Once aware of this strategy, he applied it to other areas. His teacher explained in her log, "He explained to his English teacher that it was more difficult to concentrate on his writing when other students were conferencing around him, and that he could compose much better at a computer. He initiated this [compensation strategy] on his own. Hurray, he has learned to advocate for his learning needs."

When asked at the completion of his investigation what learning skills he had used that would be useful in the classroom, he replied. "Probably the best thing that I have learned from writing this trial simulation is just to keep going. And no matter if it bogs down; just stick with it. Eventually it will be done and then you can go on to something else. You just keep looking forward, not like thank God, it's over, but to see that my simulation will actually be put to use is just overwhelming."

Opportunity to investigate issues related to their own underachievement. Sometimes the student used the Type III process to investigate an area relating to his/her underachievement. Student F, for example, had conducted a comparative study of brain functioning in humans and rats. He built models of each brain and described how the physical brain allowed for advances in human activity. His original research question was "how can the brain tell muscles what to do?" When interviewed at the end of the year, he was asked if he was still underachieving. He answered, "No." When asked to explain why he had been underachieving and what had happened to cause the change, he explained,

> I used to never get my work done. My classroom teachers told me that I take too long in getting started. But I told him that I needed to think about things for a long time. He told me that I could actually think and write at the same time. I wondered how that was possible. Then about a month ago I was thinking about something and looked at my hand and saw that it was writing!

His study of the brain was his way of exploring the issue of thinking and writing at the same time. Another student used her Type III investigation to investigate the notion of overachievement and underachievement. Student J was questioning the extensive drive to achieve she witnessed in her peers in Singapore while she, herself, frowned upon such pressure. To understand both points of view she designed a "choose your own adventure book" in which she characterized the plight of the overachiever and underachiever. This format allows the reader to follow the path of one or the other depending on which behaviors the reader selects. The Type III product for both of these youngsters became an outlet through which they were able to confront their feelings about underachievement and resolve the conflict.

Opportunity to work in an area of interest in their preferred learning style. For many participants in this study, the Type III investigation provided an opportunity to choose a topic of interest and create new knowledge in a preferred style of learning. As mentioned earlier, science and technology were popular areas of interest, and projects and hands-on learning were the favored styles of learning for a majority of this sample of students.

Student G expressed a love for project work and became animated at the mere mention of doing science experiments. He had become interested in geography and maps in social studies that year. He wanted to combine his interest in geology with his interest in maps. When the teacher asked him to read more on the topic he rebelled: "He was unwilling to do any sort of research into his interest in maps. He immediately wanted to start making a model of the earth showing the continents and the inner layer of the earth." He did consent, however to do background research when it entailed visiting the local university's extensive map library and conferring with an expert in cartography. This kind of research and product reflected his style preference. Based on the success that this student experienced pursuing his own strengths and interest, his fifth grade teacher allowed him to do more projects and use the computer in class the following year. As a result, his grades improved and he was selected as Student of the Month. After receiving his last report card, he commented to his teacher, "This is the first time I can remember feeling good about my grades and school."

The opportunity to interact with appropriate peer group. The final focus of the Type III process was that for some students it provided access to a peer group more involved in advanced academic activities. Acceptance by students who valued achievement was powerful in reversing the pattern of underachievement in several of the students. When Student O, who had been associating with an undesirable peer group, began the Type III process, she became more involved with the students in the gifted program who were working on environmental issues. She began associating with other young women on an Earth Day project and spent increasingly more time with them. In addition, her own Type III investigation focused on photographic interpretation of student emotions to be used as part of a formal introduction to the middle school. As her photography project evolved, this creative young woman gained considerable attention among her new peer group and the subjects of her photographs. By the time this student was ready to display her work at the conclusion of the school year, her tendency to wear black clothing and white makeup had changed. Her teacher noted that:

> She really opened up and became very chatty during the final stages of the Type III process. She beamed as many of her eighth grade friends saw her collage. One of the members of the G/T staff commented on how pretty she had become this year. Her hair is clean and shiny; she wears light makeup and her clothes, pastel in color, are neat and clean.

As demonstrated by these examples, the Type III process had different impacts on students, depending on the issues contributing to their pattern of underachievement. The process also had a greater impact on some students than it did on others.

Successful Teacher Strategies

The third research question focused on teacher strategies that influenced the degree to which positive change occurred in the students. Because the intervention had a greater impact on some students that it did on others, the question emerged as to whether or not particular teacher behaviors affected the results. An analysis comparing the methods of the enrichment teachers whose students made the most gains with those whose students gained the least sought to discover differences in teacher strategies. Information was obtained through teacher log entries, records of phone conversations with the research team, and focus group sessions. The students who made the largest gains in reversing their underachievement worked with teachers who

1. Took time to get to know the student before initiating a Type III investigation. When the teacher tried to identify an interest in the student too quickly and force immediate productivity, the students did not seem to be engaged in the process. In some cases it wasn't until year two that the real passion was discovered and the intervention became relevant.

2. Accepted the student. These teachers often ignored the fact that the student was an underachiever and focused on the development of the Type III investigation. In the cases where the teacher spent time trying to convince the student to achieve in the classroom, the student was resistant to the intervention.

3. Saw their roles as facilitators of the process, providing resources and meeting with the student several times a week. Some managed to see the students daily. They did not expect independence or require that the majority of the project be completed at home. They made suggestions when the project seemed to be at a standstill but did not assume control.

4. Understood the Type III process. These teachers recognized that students were to act as the practicing professional, using methods of inquiry and tools of the discipline. They comprehended that the investigation should have real world purposes and audiences rather than simply be considered a project to be graded and taken home. They did not confuse the concept of hands-on inquiry and creative productivity with independent study or library research.

5. Were able to see the dynamic nature of the underachievement problem and provide strategies as needed. They were not afraid to discuss with the researchers their interpretation and frustration. They were open to suggestions and alternate ways of examining the problem.

6. They consistently believed in the student! When days went poorly or the student seemed to regress, the successful teachers consistently demonstrated their belief in the student and their patience in allowing the process to unfold.

CONCLUSION AND DISCUSSION: THE PRISM METAPHOR FOR REVERSING UNDERACHIEVEMENT

The results of the study provide insight into the multiple causes of under-achievement, the dynamic and idiosyncratic effects of the Type III intervention process, and specific teacher behaviors that have a positive impact on student motivation, self-efficacy, self-esteem, and achievement.

These results also suggest a new metaphor for addressing the complex dynamics of the underachievement syndrome. Past efforts to reverse the underachievement problem used the wrong type of lens to focus the problem. Typically telescopic in nature, this approach targeted traditional steps to achievement—study hard, do your homework, get good grades and please your teachers. Rather than a telescopic approach, this metaphor uses a prism to redirect the focus. Just as a prism takes in nondescript light and transforms it into colors, so does the Type III unleash the hidden potential of underachieving students with high academic ability. The Type III experience accomplishes this by capitalizing on the potential for positive interaction among student abilities, interests, learning styles, and supportive student-teacher relationships. The metaphor, as pictured in Figure 2, illustrates the transformation from under-achievement to achievement. As seen in the figure, the underachievement is based on the interrelationship of a variety of factors. These factors, based on existing literature and confirmed by this study are: emotional issues, social and behavioral problems, inappropriate curriculum, and learning deficits. What is interesting is the precipitating factors for some of the underachieving students in this study were not apparent until the student was well into the intervention process.

In this metaphor, the majority of the time, energy and resources of teachers are allocated to *enabling* the underachieving student to experience success rather than exhorting them to do so. The success factors were demonstrated in this study during the process of completing the Type III enrichment. The interaction of five factors—positive relationships with adults, self-regulation strategies, self-understanding, interest-based curriculum and the influence of a positive peer group constitute the ecology of achievement. While it would be premature to assume a cause and effect relationship, desirable behaviors not ordinarily displayed by these students emerged as a direct result of participation in the Type III process. Based on these data, the intervention appears to offer a practical educational strategy that meets the various needs of HAP underachieving students across individual etiologies.

The prism metaphor was selected to help explain the transformation that takes place when underachievers "turn around" because of the complex blending of effects that occur within the context of a Type III experience. Whereas real images are formed when rays of light are reflected in a mirror, something quite different happens when a ray of light is passed through a prism. Not only does it change direction, which was the goal of reversing the underachievement of students in this study, but it also takes on qualitative differences that result in a spectrum of color that is critically different from the light energy that originally entered this special environment. Scientists understand and can explain what happens within a prism only to a certain extent. There is also a "mysterious phenomenon" that happens within the special prism environment that is read-ily observable (the dispersion of white light into a spectrum of color). A similar

Figure 2   The Prism Metaphor for Reversing Underachievement

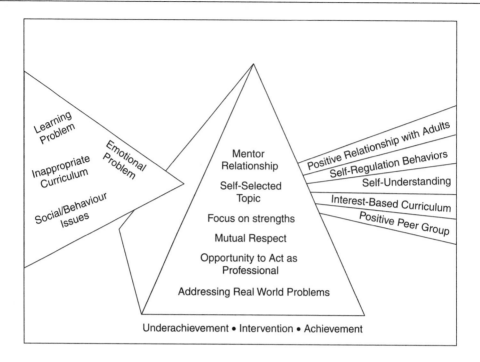

phenomenon was observed as the students pursued Type III experiences. We can only speculate about the combination of ingredients that caused a turn-around within the Type III environment. Because of the uniqueness of each student, and the equally unique interaction between teacher and student, these reversals may remain something of a mystery. No prescription or formula can be written that is appropriate for all underachieving students. However, we believe that the prism metaphor may provide for the beginnings of a grounded theory about the dynamics of underachievement and for specific procedures and guidelines for reversing the patterns of underachievement.

REFERENCES

Baum, S. M. (1985). *Learning disabled students with superior cognitive abilities: A validation study of descriptive behaviors.* Unpublished doctoral dissertation. University of Connecticut, Storrs.

Baum, S. M., Owen, S.V., & Dixon, J. (1991). *To be gifted and learning disabled: From identification to practical intervention strategies.* Mansfield Center, Connecticut: Creative Learning Press.

Baum, S.M., Emerick, L.J., Herman, G.N. & Dixon, J. (1989). Identification, programs and enrichment strategies for gifted learning disabled youth. *Roeper Review, 12,* 48–53.

Baum, S. M. & Owen, S.V. (1988). High ability learning disabled students: How are they different? *Gifted Child Quarterly, 32,* 321–326.

Burns, D. E. (1990). *Pathways to investigative skills: Instructional lessons for guiding students from problem finding to final product.* Mansfield Center, Connecticut: Creative Learning Press.

Burns, D.E. (1987). *The effects of group training activities on students' creative productivity.* Unpublished doctoral dissertation. University of Connecticut.

Bulter-Por, N. (1987). *Underachievers in school: Issues and intervention.* New York: JohnWiley and Sons.

Colangelo, N. (1984). Counseling the gifted underachiever. Keynote address at the third Annual AEGUS (Association for the Education of Gifted Underachieving Students) Conference. St. Paul, Minnesota: College of St. Thomas.

Cray-Andrews, M., Baum, S.M. & Gubbins, E.J. (1987). Gifted students as creative producers. *The Gifted Child Today, 10*(1), 22–24.

Crittenden, M. R., Kaplan, M. H. & Heim, J. K. (1984). Developing effective study skills and self-confidence in academically able young adolescents. *Gifted Child Quarterly, 28*(1), 25–30.

Delcourt, M. (1993). Creative productivity among secondary school students: combining energy, interest and imagination. *Gifted Child Quarterly, 37*(1), 23–31.

Delisle, J. R. (1981). *The revolving door model of identification and programming for the academically gifted: The correlates of creative production.* Unpublished doctoral dissertation. University of Connecticut.

Emerick, L. J. (1992). Academic underachievement among the gifted: Students' perceptions of factors that reverse the pattern. *Gifted Child Quarterly, 36*(3), 140–146.

Gubbins, E. J. (1982). *Revolving Door Identification Model: Characteristics of talent pool students.* Unpublished doctoral dissertation. University of Connecticut.

Hastings, J. M. (1982). A program for gifted underachievers. *Roeper Review, 4*(4), 42.

Jick, T. D. (1979). Mixing qualitative and quantitative methods: Triangulation in action. *Administrative Science Quarterly, 24* (4), 602–611.

Karafellis, P. (1986). *The effects of the tri-art drama curriculum on the reading comprehension of students with varying levels of cognitive ability.* Unpublished doctoral dissertation. University of Connecticut.

Kaufman, F. (1991). The courage to succeed: A new look at underachievement. Keynote address at fourth Annual AEGUS (Association for the Education of Gifted Underachieving Students) Conference. Tuscaloosa, AL: University of Alabama.

An empirical study concerning the incidence, diagnosis, treatments, and follow-up of academically underachieving children. Khartoum, Sudan: University of Khartoum. (ERIC Document Reproduction Service No. ED 166 922)

Mitchell, E. S. (1986). Multiple triangulation: A methodology for nursing science. *Advances in Nursing Science, 8*(3), 18–26.

Moon, S. M. (1991). Case study research in gifted education. In N. Buchanan & J. Feldhusen (Eds.), *Conducting research and evaluation in gifted education.* (pp. 157–178). New York: Teachers College Press.

Owen, S.V. & Baum, S. M. (1991). SEAT: Self-efficacy for academic tasks. In Baum, S.M., Owen, S.V., & Dixon, J. *To be gifted and learning disabled: From identification to practical intervention strategies.* Mansfield Center, CT: Creative Learning Press.

Passow, A. H., & Goldberg, M. L. (1958). Study of underachieving gifted. *Educational Leadership, 16,* 121–125.

Reid, B. D. (1991). *Research needs in gifted education: A study of practitioners' perceptions.* Unpublished doctoral dissertation. University of Connecticut.

Reis, S. M. (1981). *An analysis of the productivity of gifted students participating in programs using the revolving door identification model.* Unpublished doctoral dissertation. University of Connecticut.

Reis, S. M. & Cellerino, M. B. (1983). Guiding gifted students through independent study. *Teaching Exceptional Children, 15*(3), 136–139.

Reis, S. M. & Hébert, T. P. (1985). Creating practicing professionals in gifted programs: Encouraging students to become young historians. *Roeper Review, 8*(2), 101–104.

Renzulli, J. S., & Baum, S. M. (1989). *Development of characteristics of creative productivity.* Storrs, CT: University of Connecticut. Unpublished manuscript.

Renzulli, J. S., & Reis, S. M. (1985). *The schoolwide enrichment model: A comprehensive plan for educational excellence.* Mansfield Center, CT: Creative Learning Press.

Renzulli, J. S. (1977a). *The enrichment triad model: A guide for developing defensible programs for the gifted.* Mansfield Center, Connecticut: Creative Learning Press.

Renzulli, J. S. (1977b). *The interest-a-lyzer.* Mansfield Center, Connecticut: Creative Learning Press.

Renzulli, J., Smith, L., White, A., Callahan, C. M., & Hartman, R. K. (1977). *Scales for rating the behavioral characteristics of superior students.* Mansfield Center, CT: Creative Learning Press.

Rimm, S. B. (1986). *Underachievement syndrome: Causes and cures.* Watertown, Wisconsin: Apple Publishing.

Scruggs, T. E. & Cohn, S. J. (1983). A university-based summer program for a highly able but poorly achieving Indiana child. *Gifted Child Quarterly, 27*(2), 90–93.

Smith, H. W. (1975). Triangulation: The necessity for multi-method approaches. In W.H. Smith (Ed.), *Strategies of social research: The methodological imagination.* (pp. 271–292) Englewood Cliffs, NJ: Prentice-Hall.

Strauss, A .L. (1987). *Qualitative analysis for social scientists.* New York: Cambridge University Press.

Whitmore, J. R. (1980). *Giftedness, conflict and underachievement.* Boston: Allyn & Bacon.

12

Mentors for Gifted Underachieving Males: Developing Potential and Realizing Promise

Thomas P. Hébert

The University of Georgia

F. Richard Olenchak

The University of Houston

The literature focusing on mentorships and underachieving gifted young men is almost nonexistent. To address this need, the researchers examined the mentorship experiences of three students who characterized various aspects of giftedness and underachievement in males. The findings of the study revealed a single core category with three attendant subcategories. The influence of a significant adult on a young person was the dominant

---

Editor's Note: From Hébert, T. P., & Olenchak, F. R. (2000). Mentors for gifted underachieving males: Developing potential and realizing promise. *Gifted Child Quarterly, 44*(3), 196-207. © 2000 National Association for Gifted Children. Reprinted with permission.

category. Several related subcategories reinforced the importance of the mentor: mentors' open-minded and nonjudgmental characteristics; consistent and personalized social/emotional support and advocacy; and strength and interest-based strategies for intervention to reverse underachievement. These results underscore the critical effectiveness of mentorships on underachievement, regardless of age, environment, and socioeconomic background. Implications of the findings are presented that highlight the successful features of the mentor-protégé relationship.

Mentorships have historically been viewed as one avenue to the acquisition of knowledge and perfection of skill among child prodigies. Spontaneous mentorships arise naturally when adult experts recognize strong potential and motivation in individuals with whom they share common interests. The experts then take the protégés under their tutelage, offering protection, nurturance, and guidance while the prodigies work to fulfill their potential. Seminal studies in the field of gifted education have noted the frequent presence of mentors in the lives of highly successful, eminent people (Torrance, 1984; Kaufman, Harrel, Milam, Woolverton, & Miller, 1986) and have captured the attention of educators searching for effective strategies to develop the talents of special populations of students.

Increasingly, evidence exists that gifted young men are at special risk for developing academic and social problems that include serious academic and behavioral problems, self-identity and self-esteem concerns, and even denial of talent (Alvino, 1991; Ford, 1996; Hébert, 1997; Olenchak, 1995; Seeley, 1993). Thanks to numerous research studies, professionals have uncovered some factors contributing to underachievement among gifted youth (Baum, Renzulli, & Hébert, 1995; Ford, 1993; Frasier, Passow, & Goldberg, 1958; Rimm, 1986; Whitmore, 1980); but, there remains limited and inconclusive research on effective strategies for reversing it.

Putting the Research to Use

If schools will strive to identify, and match appropriate men willing to serve as mentors for underachieving male students, enhancement of both academic and nonacademic performance, as well as social/emotional development is likely to result. The power of mentors to serve each of the young men in the three case studies reinforces the broader notion that males who model productivity and understanding themselves, are in good stead to precipitate positive changes in their underachieving protégés. It is essential that each mentorship be arranged with the strengths and interests of the young man as the overarching focus. Learning how to achieve can apparently come about best by working alongside an adult who shares at least some of the young man's own interests and is willing to overlook the child's underachievement history, viewing it as irrelevant to their mentor-protégé relationship. Moreover, as a significant segment of that relationship, the mentor must serve as advocate, spokesman, and confidante for the young man with whom he works.

Schools and other education-related agencies should not attempt to supplant the pivotal roles of parents in the lives of young men. Rather, educational leaders must recognize that to effect gifted-like behaviors from young men who present patterns of underachievement, adult males aside from family members frequently must be introduced to those students. Potential mentors must be open-minded about and committed to forging long-term, personal relationships with young men who have grown accustomed to underachieving, and they must be passionate about sharing their own interests and strengths with their protégés. Schools can serve as mentorship brokers by creating opportunities for such mentor-protégé relationships to develop and by extending the positive results derived from the mentorships into the schoolhouse.

Previous research has examined the effects of family counseling (Colangelo & Peterson, 1993; Silverman, 1993), educational interventions (Emerick, 1992; Lemley, 1994; Rimm & Olenchak, 1991; Scruggs & Cohn, 1983; Whitmore, 1980), and using behavior management techniques (Rimm, 1986). In addition, examinations have been conducted of underachievement interventions among students with learning, behavioral, and developmental differences (Baum, Olenchak, & Owen, 1998; Olenchak, 1995).

The literature contains relatively few studies, however, that have examined the role of a mentor relationship in reversing patterns of underachievement (Clasen, 1993). Although gifted students collectively are likely to attract mentors on their own, several subpopulations of gifted students, including underachievers, do not experience this advantage. Arnold and Subotnik (1995) asserted that the gifted youngster's talent and motivation alone are not enough to attract a prospective mentor. They indicated that the closer the protégé's gender, social class, ethnicity, experiential background, values, and attitudes match those of the mentor, the more likely the child will find the status and lifestyle of the profession attractive and the mentor will be interested in the young person. This scenario poses a problem for disadvantaged, minority, or underachieving gifted young people who often are less likely to reflect socioeconomic characteristics similar to those of potential mentors (White-Hood, 1993; Wright & Borland, 1992). As a result, they are often overlooked.

Aside from the dichotomous personal and socioeconomic characteristics of the mentor and protégé, several studies of formal mentorships cite demonstrated task commitment as one of the primary criteria for selection as a protégé (Edlind & Haensly, 1985; Goh & Goh, 1996; Reilly, 1992). The importance of this criterion is understandable, considering that most mentorship programs utilize professionals from the community as mentors. Such professionals are apt to lead busy lives and have difficulty finding time for their protégé. Coordinators of mentor programs recognize this sacrifice and often select those young people who have demonstrated a high degree of commitment to task to ensure that the mentor's time will not be wasted.

Despite the body of research examining mentor-protégé relationships, studies that have explicitly explored mentorships as interventions for underachievement among high-ability students are limited (Noller & Frey, 1994); those that have examined this issue among high-ability males are virtually nonexistent (Clasen & Clasen, 1997). Although mentorships have been examined broadly without regard to gender (Flaxman, Ascher, & Harrington, 1988; Reilly, 1992; Torrance, 1984), Levinson and colleagues' (1978) work specifically explored mentorships among males. Their impression of mentorship, based on interviews with 40 men, includes being a teacher, supporter, adviser, nurturer of skills and intelligence, guide, and model. Further, "the mentor has another function and this is developmentally the most crucial one: to support and facilitate the realization of the Dream" (p. 98), or the image that each young man has for his adulthood.

Flaxman, Ascher, and Harrington (1988) provided an even more apt perspective for mentorships involving young people: a supportive relationship between a youth or young adult and someone more senior in age and experience who offers support, guidance, and concrete assistance as the younger partner goes through a difficult period, enters a new area of experience, takes on an important task, or corrects an earlier problem. In general, during mentoring, protégés identify with, or form a strong interpersonal attachment to, their mentors; as a result, they become able to do for themselves what their mentors have done for them.

Torrance's (1980, 1984) seminal study of mentor relationships presents conclusive evidence that mentorships have a significant impact on the creative achievements of gifted individuals. Reporting that having a mentor was a statistically significant factor in adult creative achievement for both men and women, Torrance's 22-year longitudinal study strongly suggests that a critical component for facilitating achievement among economically disadvantaged youngsters is mentors (Torrance, Goff, & Satterfield, 1998).

In another seminal investigation, Kaufman et al. (1986) investigated the lives of 139 Presidential Scholars from 1964 to 1968 to determine the characteristics of spontaneous mentors and their influences on the lives of academically gifted young people. As a whole, the participants in this study valued the role model, support, and encouragement aspects of their mentorship far more than the professional interaction. Fifty-nine percent reported that they adopted some of the characteristics of their mentors, including their attitudes toward work, personal habits, or general outlook on life.

In another study, Shaughnessy and Neely (1991) also examined the attributes of effective mentors. Among the traits most frequently cited in their sample of academically gifted individuals were providing security, building confidence, and being enthusiastic and patient. Underscoring a relationship between traits and action, Ambrose, Allen and Huntley (1994) found that successful mentors of gifted young people guided them through difficult times in their personal lives and were able to enhance their development and the likelihood that they would reach their potential.

Associated with mentorships is the incorporation of experiences that not only can transpire within the context of school, but also can be extended beyond the academic day. Heath and McLaughlin (1993) indicated that involvement in organizations beyond school provided opportunities for gifted young people to build a sense of self-efficacy and success in different events. These experiences enabled youth to construct positive perceptions of self and raise aspirations for the future. Halpern (1992) indicated that involvement in after-school programs offered young people structure and predictability that might be missing in their lives and an opportunity to learn something about the distinction in behavior required in settings outside their school environment. Moreover, such extracurricular experiences can often serve as forums in which young people can begin to develop deeper relationships with adults that are less likely to be complicated by academic expectations. As a result, out-of-school activities present opportunities for close mentorships to develop in a fashion that allows for personal growth of gifted youth that can be virtually free of any negative school-related attitudes.

Heath and McLaughlin (1993) noted that involvement in activities focusing on producing tangible products or performances reinforced this positive sense of self through building a sense of accomplishment and success within young people. The activities gave youth concrete evidence that something could be gained by sticking with an effort and provided opportunities for success. These experiences also taught the youngsters that choices matter, that effort can make a difference, and that some adults believe that what they do with their talents is important.

The value of cocurricular activities, those in which students extend the regular school program into related areas of study beyond the basic curriculum, was also highlighted in a longitudinal study of 200 talented teenagers. In this study, Csikszentmihalyi, Rathunde, and Whalen (1997) reported that these experiences were the most likely school activities to engage youngsters fully in learning—the most consistent source of interest and flow (Csikszentmihalyi, 1990) for students. Such activities were important in alerting youngsters to the fact that important work was not always aversive and alienating. The researchers proposed that cocurricular activities combined feelings of spontaneous involvement with a focus on important goals and perceptions of high skill with correspondingly high challenges.

To enhance the understanding of the significance of mentorships in reversing the underachievement of gifted males, this article describes three case studies of high-ability young men and the mentors who had a critical impact on their lives. Following a discussion of the methodology, the case studies are presented, and implications across the studies are discussed.

METHODS

To understand the experience of the young men described in this study, the investigators chose a comparative case study research design for qualitatively examining the intensive, holistic relationships and activities associated with the subjects (Merriam, 1998). The goal of the study was to examine the lives of three gifted young men and to understand how a significant adult engaged each subject in a relationship that ultimately reversed underachievement. Case studies are often used when attempting to answer "how" and "why" questions, such as those posed in this study (Yin, 1989): How did the mentor-protégé relationship develop, and why was the relationship successful in helping to reverse underachievement? Case studies are designed to investigate the interrelationships among a series of complex human variables within their real-life contexts (Yin, 1989). As a tool for inquiry, case studies enable researchers to understand complicated social phenomena, while retaining the holistic and meaningful characteristics of everyday events (Yin, 1993). They are particularly useful when the researcher needs to understand some specific group of people, particular problem, or unique situation in great depth. When the researcher can identify cases within this group, problem, or situation, case study research can yield valuable information (Patton, 1990; Stake, 1995).

Although ethnographic works depict persons, places, and events as they exist amidst the instability of real life, effort was made by the researchers to satisfy what Denzin (1997) called the quantitative investigator's quest for "stable pictures of reality" (p. 45). One means for enhancing interpretations of single-subject ethnographic case studies is to increase the number and diversity of subjects to permit cross-study comparisons. However, despite these efforts at experimental research, such comparisons are more akin to matching photographs in a series of pictorial essays than they are like statistical comparisons (Denzin, 1997). When qualitative researchers examine a range of similar and contrasting cases, the inclusion of multiple illustrations enhances the external validity or generalizability of the researcher's findings (Merriam, 1998; Miles & Huberman, 1994). As a result, the researchers chose to apply single-subject ethnographic methods to a multiple case approach, thereby enhancing the potential for more global conclusions to be extracted from the data. The research described in this article involved three cases of gifted males who underachieved. The names of the people, places, and institutions described were changed to protect the identities of the participants.

Selection of the Participants

The young men featured in this study, ranging from elementary-age through later adolescence, either had been formally identified for participation in special programming for gifted students or were being considered for those programs. Each of the three participants in the study was selected through purposeful sampling procedures to provide insight about gifted males across several developmental periods: early elementary years, early middle school years, and early collegiate years. The objective of purposeful sampling is to select information-rich cases whose study will illuminate the research questions being investigated. "Information-rich cases are those from which one can learn a great deal about the issues of central importance to the purpose of the research, thus the term purposeful sampling" (Patton, 1990, p. 169). More specifically, criterion sampling was implemented, whereby all cases had to meet some predetermined criterion of importance. The criteria for selecting the three participants were as follows: (1) the subjects were male; (2) each had been recognized or referred during his public school years for gifted characteristics (Davis & Rimm, 1994); and (3) each one was currently underachieving academically as reflected by a preponderance of grades of C or lower. Subjects in this study were located through field work in academic settings. Information from academic portfolios was used to validate their inclusion in this research.

Data Collection

A combination of semi-structured interviews and document review was used to gather data for this qualitative study. Along with transcribed interviews with participants, the review of formal and informal documents, such as the students' records and samples of their written work, provided a clearer picture of the school life experiences being examined. Six or more in-depth interviews were conducted with each of the gifted males featured in this article. Data were collected that encompassed individual interviews with their teachers, school counselors, advisors, and other professionals significant in their educational placements. These semi-structured interviews consisted of open-ended questions designed to explore a few general topics in order, not only to gain information directly from the participants, but also to develop insight on how the young men interpreted aspects of their school experiences. Through the interviews of the subjects themselves, a picture emerged of what each young man believed was happening, enabling each to tell his own story. The following research questions guided the qualitative case studies:

1. How did the relationship between each subject and his mentor develop and endure?

2. What circumstances influenced patterns of underachievement among three intelligent young men?

Data Coding and Analysis

The transcribed interviews were coded and analyzed according to Strauss and Corbin's (1990) three-stage process. The first stage consists of open coding, in which all transcribed interviews were read and analyzed line by line to generate initial categories. A second stage of coding then identified consistent themes and relationships in each of the three sources: student interviews, interviews with all other participants, and document review. After these general categories emerged, each source was reviewed once more to locate additional evidence in the data. Strauss and Corbin described this process as axial coding since it involves analysis to be focused individually around the axis of each category. A third stage, selective coding, then compared the general themes across all sources of data, identifying even broader, more consistent themes.

Following a description of the participants, a discussion of the findings is provided, and implications are discussed.

RESULTS

Jackson

Twelve-year-old Jackson, a light-skinned African American fifth grader at a neighborhood elementary school in an industrialized suburb of a large Southern city, was referred to the researchers by the school principal, who expressed concern for him not only academically, but also socially. At first sullen and unwilling to talk unless directly asked a question, rapport quickly developed when one of the researchers leaped up and yelled, "Now, what do you suppose a honky like me has to offer you?" A smile cracked across Jackson's face, followed by giggles more characteristic of a child several years his junior. Henceforth, communication between the researchers and Jackson was open and forthright.

Eldest of five children in a family receiving welfare, Jackson had significant challenges simply to sustain his life each day. When he was barely age 10, Jackson's mother was sent to prison for burglary and repeated incidents of shoplifting; neither he nor his siblings knew their fathers. As a result, the children were legally placed with an 80-year-old grandmother who, as time went on, became increasingly afflicted with arthritis. Forced to assume many of the duties his grandmother had previously handled, Jackson quickly became more like a surrogate parent than an older brother to his siblings. Among the most important of these obligations was "hawking" them, or making sure that each of his brothers and sisters was staying out of trouble. In a neighborhood of older, single-family residences, some of which have been abandoned and boarded up, tending to small children was more than a cursory assignment. A child himself, Jackson's role appeared to be overwhelming, though he undertook it in stride and managed to find time to interact with other young males in the neighborhood. It was these relationships that most troubled the school principal.

Several weeks before meeting the research team, Jackson had been caught trespassing in an abandoned warehouse a few blocks from his grandmother's home. The warehouse, known for serving as a meeting site for several youth gangs, had also been the scene of a gang-related murder only a year before. Though it could not be confirmed, Jackson's popularity with his peers led the school principal to surmise that Jackson was being courted by at least one of the gangs. Moreover, having been retained in first grade for failure to achieve the competencies requisite for promotion, Jackson continued to experience academic problems in all areas. In fourth grade, his teacher referred him for screening for behavior disorders, but he did not qualify behaviorally, despite his tendency to be withdrawn with adults. Instead, the battery of tests revealed that Jackson actually possessed nonverbal ability ranking well into the superior range. Although at times Jackson refused to complete his school assignments, teachers felt it was because he often seemed overtired to the point of exhaustion. In fact, a developing history of truancy and tardiness was attributed by the principal to Jackson's significant responsibilities for his brothers, sisters, and grandmother. Visits to Jackson's home by social service agents revealed that, despite the grandmother's condition and age, the family was functioning fairly well, though "the oldest son [Jackson] has many more chores than children his age should have."

Intervention. With the support of the school, a weekly 45-minute support group session was developed for Jackson and five other young men with similar profiles: from economically impoverished backgrounds, a history of academic problems, and either already involved in gangs or considered susceptible to such involvement. Aimed at providing each participant with a forum for discussion of topics of interest to them, as well as instruction in an array of problem resolution strategies, each meeting of the group opened with each participant sharing brief descriptions of one or two positive and one or two negative events from the preceding week. Early on, the group members were administered a locally designed interest inventory. Jackson's interests clustered around the sciences, mathematics, and spatial activities like building, designing, and manipulating objects. Thereafter, every member of the group was paired with one or more mentors specializing in an appropriate area of interest, and efforts were made to ensure compatibility through a series of interest-related outings involving each group member and his mentor, as well as one of the researchers. For Jackson, a day-long weekend visit to a NASA museum, an afternoon at a university science laboratory, and a hands-on session in a commercial design business served both to solidify the relationship with his mentor, and to acquaint him with career opportunities.

Meanwhile, specific curricular adaptations were undertaken to alter Jackson's school program. Using funding for remedial education, the school district provided 50 of its teachers, who taught students who were particularly at risk of school failure (including Jackson's), with training in talent development techniques and problem-solving approaches. Specifically, teachers learned ways to compact time spent on basic skills where mastery could be documented with less drill and practice. They learned strategies gauged to emphasize student strengths while de-emphasizing weaknesses and ways to differentiate curriculum. In addition, the teachers were trained not only in the problem-solving and decision-making heuristics inherent in level I of the CoRT Thinking Skills Program (deBono, 1986), but they also were taught how to integrate them into day-to-day academic content. In the case of each of the six members of the special group, teachers agreed to be monitored in their implementation of the enrichment and problem-solving strategies. Monitoring included lesson plans teachers maintained, unannounced observations by the research team, and evaluation-linked scrutiny by the principal, who was also trained in the curriculum alteration procedures.

To arrange for and monitor efforts to personalize his curriculum, Jackson's teacher scheduled meetings with him every six weeks, held additional meetings as needed along with the mentor, and maintained a daily journal thoroughly capturing reflections about activities in which Jackson participated, his reactions, and the relationships with teachers, peers, and family. Each meeting produced a contract for material and skills he had to master in each major content field and interest-based activities in which Jackson could engage once he had demonstrated mastery. Of critical importance before the first contract, Jackson's mentor arranged a luncheon where Jackson was introduced to an African American attorney who explained the nature of contracts, what they mean, how they are handled, and the penalties for violation. Afterward, Jackson met again with his teacher to make sure that he understood the seriousness of the contracts in which he was going to become a partner.

Findings. After the first six weeks, Jackson discussed with both his teacher and the mentor his feelings about the potential for his personally tailored program:

> I just can't think y'all would do anything like this. I mean, you know, that I'm just a boy from the 'hood and I think it's hot. I get to do experiments and hot stuff, but it's like what that lawman called a contract that if I violate it I might as well go to jail. The difference is I don't have to sign, but if I don't, I don't get to work on experiments. . . . The contract lets me move out of the school's stuff fast if I want to.

During that first six-week period, his teacher held almost daily meetings with Jackson to sustain his interest and commitment to the contract he had signed. He not only successfully accomplished his required assignments, he found that he had sufficiently compacted his curriculum in math and in science to permit undertaking a study of space. Although his mentor was not a space specialist, he facilitated access to a teacher at a nearby high school who had once held a position as a NASA Space Camp instructor. His teacher's journal entry after the third meeting with the mentor and former NASA instructor captured the essence of a metamorphosis:

> I can't believe that this is happening so fast! Jackson walked into the classroom this morning and was actually toting a book that he was protecting! The book was one on space from NASA. He asked me if I would make a safe place for him to keep his space materials so that they didn't get lost because he really had no place at home. This is more interest than any teacher has ever seen from Jackson since he walked in the door in Head Start. I am stunned!

As days passed, Jackson never agreed to sign a contract unless he felt he could adhere to it. Over an academic year, he declined signing only once, during the third six-week period when Jackson pronounced the proposed contract was "too much work right now. Let's change it so that there's not so much." When he was reminded that the time he could earn for his space study would have to be reduced if he spent more time completing basic requirements, he expressed appreciation for the fact he was in charge of the pacing of his educational program: "I forget that I be in charge of my schoolin' now." Thereafter, a more diligent effort was undertaken to involve Jackson in even the earliest development of each contract. This allowed the young man to see exactly which basic skills and content material were required and which assignments were needed to demonstrate mastery.

Occasionally, Jackson's own comments, as well as those from his teacher's journal, indicated that, as might have been predicted, commitment fluctuated. Shortly before the end of the first semester, Jackson told his mentor:

> I'm about done on this. It's work, work, work, and like it's too much. I've been reading late, and my granny wants me to be asleep. So, I hide under the blanket, and she thinks I'm asleep. What a game! I am fired and don't think this is as fun . . . there's all that work just so I can have time for [my] space [project].

However, the mentor and teacher remained supportive throughout the year. The teacher's journal entry made the same day Jackson expressed his frustration indicated her own wavering commitment, yet willingness to persevere:

> Jackson is feeling the pressure of what it means to use one's abilities. He is tired and angry that school can't be totally his own way, that work is required in addition to the space interest. After talking about this with Bob [his mentor], I sat down with Jackson during lunch, and we talked about what we could do to make it better. We agreed that his space work could also be done during lunch and recess, but that he'd have to be in charge of himself in my classroom. Mrs. Lewis [the principal] told him

that if he made just one mistake when he was using this time, he'd lose it forever. Jackson then told her it had to be in the contract in order to be the law, so we renegotiated the contract and built this in. He is smart!!!

By the time school resumed after the winter vacation, Jackson and Bob had developed a plan for building his own telescope, only part of which was from a kit; the former NASA instructor would supervise mostly from afar but, on occasion, would meet one-to-one with Jackson. Using the time he had freed from the basic curriculum, as well as that contracted from lunches and recesses, Jackson made significant headway on his telescope and had even worked with an optics expert on grinding the lenses for it.

There was also evidence that other aspects of the intervention plan were having a meaningful impact on Jackson's life. One day on his way home after school, just before spring vacation and the unveiling of his completed telescope, Jackson was approached by some gang members. Threatening him, Jackson told them, that he was going to form his own gang, but it would be a different gang—one that was going to learn all about space so that every member could one day take shuttle trips to other planets. They laughed and teased him, but they left. Making specific reference to one of the problem resolution skills on which teachers were concentrating in his intervention, Jackson later related the encounter to his mentor:

You know, I was scared they'd draft me, but I used that CoRT from school. I used, you know, CAF [Consider All Factors] and OPV [Other Points of View], and I was thinking that they'd laugh at me if I sound like a space person . . . they think I am crazy. That's okay; gangs leave crazies alone.

By the end of the school year, Jackson had not only utilized his telescope to begin tracking various stars and planets, but with assistance from Bob and the teacher, he had founded a space club for other students in the school. With nearly a dozen members meeting at lunch each Wednesday, the group also had met three nights under the watchful eyes of the mentor, the high school teacher who had been a Space Camp instructor, and Jackson's own teacher. Her final journal entry for the year set the stage for later interventions:

Jackson is going off to Carver [middle school] next year. He has made such great headway that I can't let him fail. Bob, Mrs. Lewis, and I have already arranged for the counselor over there and the school's new enrichment teacher to work with Jackson and set up a new mentorship in the same way we have . . . they need to keep him going . . . The principal there has already built in Jackson's space club as one of the middle school mini-courses in the school's schedule, so I think it's going to be real follow-through. He is too bright to be squandered to the streets.

Nathan

Nathan's expressive dark eyes, stocky build, and trendy attire made him typical of his environment. He came from an intact family residing in the suburbs of a large East Coast city. The younger of two children, at age eight, Nathan lived in a small, but tidy brick bungalow with his elder sister, Carol, and both parents. His mother, a nurse, traveled among several medical facilities, while his father, a commercial seaman, was frequently away on shipping assignments to other nations.

From the start of his life, Nathan seemed destined to live in Carol's shadow. Carol was identified early for participation in the school district's gifted program, had maintained outstanding scholastic and behavioral performance all through school, and had been accelerated one grade level after completing third grade. As a result, at age 13, Carol was enrolled as a freshman at a nearby high school, was participating with distinction in a rigorous precollegiate curriculum, and had earned critical acclaim for her piano debut with a suburban symphony orchestra. In contrast, Nathan's mother said in reference to her son, "I always hold my breath when I am paged to the phone at work. I just know that Nate has done something else."

Upon meeting the researchers, Nathan refused to be seated, but was communicative. Nathan explained that, "Sitting down makes me look like I choose to be here, and I do *not*! This must be another third-degree inquiry or something." An examination of his school records revealed a hefty file of disciplinary infractions; virtually all of the disciplinary actions were related either to calling out, talking too much, or acting out behaviors. A review of referrals and testing showed that, on two occasions Nathan had been referred for special services for students with learning and behavior disorders. Results did not indicate qualification for special educational services either time, and ability and aptitude testing indicated an uncooperative client for whom test results were believed to be unrepresentative. At that, it was noted anecdotally that Nathan placed in the upper ranges of average ability, though his verbal skills were consistently superior. Moreover, Nathan's school records indicated that he always managed to salvage his academic work, as well as his behavioral problems just enough to avoid grade retention.

Intervention. Working with Sue, Nathan's third-grade teacher, at the beginning of the academic year, the researchers developed a plan to accentuate the student's obvious verbal strengths while de-emphasizing his tendency to talk out of turn and act out. Believing that at least part of Nathan's concern might have been related to his sister's seeming stardom, the teacher was most willing to work with the young man's parents to design a well-orchestrated program to develop Nathan's abilities. The plan, based on research about the importance of student interests in developing talent (Emerick, 1992), was aimed at identifying areas that appealed to Nathan and then imbedding those in his day-to-day curriculum. It was hoped that he might eventually develop enough enthusiasm to produce a high-quality project.

Using an interest inventory, Sue found that Nathan was intrigued about a number of topics that perhaps had been overlooked by both his school and family. When asked "What is the most interesting place you ever visited?" he quickly responded with sophisticated oratory:

> That's easy; I have a tie. First, I was astounded when we first went downtown to The Smithsonian. I was five, and I liked it all, but I was especially amazed by the displays at the Museum of American History. Since then, I have been back to the MAH—that's what I call it now because I feel like the Museum and I are best friends—lots of times. Second, I was just as interested in the Gettysburg Battlefield when we went there last year. Both places have caused me to collect books and tapes on American history, and I like to sit alone in my room reading and watching information about every part of our country. Did you know that Benjamin Banneker was the first man to build a clock in this country, and he took over the design of Washington after Mr. L'Enfant was fired? And he was Afro-American!

Convinced that Nathan was deeply committed to history, Sue elected to halt the interest assessment at that point. Enlisting the support of his parents and the principal, Sue held a meeting where Nathan was present to discuss openly opportunities available to him were he to refrain from disrupting class for others. A detailed discussion ensued, as summarized in the thorough journal Sue maintained about Nathan and his emerging program:

> We all agreed that Nathan's interest in history, especially American history with special interest in African American history, was one that had strong appeal. Nathan was adamant that, if school would allow him time to work on his interest instead of spending time only on the basics, he would be able to control himself Although both his morn and dad and I remain skeptical, we decided that I should adjust curriculum so that history could be built in more often. Nathan assured us he would "be good."

During the next few weeks after the initial meeting, Sue had to remind Nathan occasionally about the agreement. Each time, he quickly acceded to the prompting, but Sue wondered if the intervention was going to work:

> Whew! Another day at the salt mines! Nathan may drive me and himself mad! I had to remind him 17 times today to be quiet and to do whatever he was supposed to be doing. Once he was singing a song he had made up about the Civil War and slavery—it was almost a dirge it was so sad. His neighbors kept telling him to shut up, and finally I had to intervene by separating him to the carrel for a few minutes. I reminded him repeatedly of his agreement, and he reminded me that we needed to find more time for him to study his history.

Over the next several weeks, Sue, working with the research team as facilitators, contacted a professor of African American history at a nearby university, who referred Sue to one of her undergraduate students, Amman. Amman agreed to work with Nathan on a regular basis once each week at a mutually convenient time, and Nathan's parents resolved to arrange for Nathan and Amman to meet at least one additional time each week during nonschool hours. Henceforth, Sue and Amman worked together to integrate facets of African American history into virtually every portion of the curriculum. This allowed Nathan to identify his interests in African American history in many aspects of the classroom program. Further, with the assistance of the researchers, Sue worked with the school's gifted education teacher to arrange an interview to determine whether Nathan's interest could develop into a guided study. Nathan was quick to identify exactly the direction of his project:

> Hey, you mean I can make a movie of my own for kids my age? I want to write, design, and direct a video production about famous African Americans in the U.S.A. and how they have had a major impact on our history. After I write it, all I need to do is figure out how to get some of the other kids to star in it. Do you think we could advertise it and show it to grown-ups, too?

Findings. Although Nathan's overall behavior and academic success wavered, he largely sustained his commitment to both his project and controlling his behavior. The school principal met with Nathan for counseling infrequently, but most of his success was attributable to the curricular alterations and the work with Amman. Nathan described his improved situation as follows:

> It has been difficult for me to keep my end of the bargain. I have had to bite my tongue a lot in class because I need to tell everyone what I think and what I feel. But, my teacher has really made school interesting for me. It is like whatever Amman and I are doing on my movie ends up in my class, and then everybody ends up talking about the topics I am studying to put into my script. This has really helped me. Oh, I'm not perfect, but my sister, Carol, has congratulated me on my success. She even told me that she can't wait to see my movie!

While the school year concluded before Nathan's film could be completed, all of the adults involved in Nathan's plan, as well as the teacher with whom Nathan will work next school year, have met. They delineated a detailed plan for continuing to integrate African American history with the general curriculum, and they revised Nathan's proposal for completing his film. Barring any unforeseen obstacles, Nathan is planning the premiere of his film by the middle of his fourth-grade year. In assessing the intervention, Sue's journal concluded:

Anything was worth a shot! I am thrilled at the progress Nathan has made. Not only are his overall grades up to above average, he has qualified for the gifted program. He has not been sent to the office at all since Christmas, and the other kids all want to know what part they can play in his movie. From now on, he won't ever have to find the attention he deserves by calling out and disrupting.

Stephen

As Stephen sat in his college advisor's office, he explained his problem to Dr. Kirkland, a new professor in the College of Education assigned to him for academic counseling. With nervousness reflected in his voice, Stephen explained he had been involved in dormitory pranks with other freshman males, and the good times had gotten him into some trouble academically. Previously at his suburban high school, Stephen had achieved a strong, academic, athletic, and extracurricular record replete with excellent grades in advanced placement courses. Nicknamed "the Viking" throughout his high school years, Stephen's Scandinavian features indicated his Norwegian descent.

Stephen came to the university from an upper-middle-class community in the South whose industrial base was centered around the space industry and depended on major contracts from NASA. The technological orientation of the community was reflected in the school district's curriculum, and Stephen explained that his peer group had been high-powered academic achievers all through school, many of them pursuing intellectually challenging math and science courses at an early age. Stephen's mother, a single parent with 2 children, worked for the space industry as a computer software designer. Often referring to himself as "the man of the house," Stephen explained that his parents had divorced when he was two years old, and his father had not been a part of his life since. Stephen's older sister, three years his senior and with whom he was close, was in her final year of an undergraduate program in zoology at a neighboring institution in the South and was planning on applying to medical school following her graduation.

With embarrassment, he explained that his first semester grade point average was a pitiful 1.6 and that he was dissatisfied with his performance. He also indicated that he was no longer involved in sports and had not been lifting weights, something he had done religiously throughout high school. Overwhelmed by his rather lackluster beginning as a college student, he turned to his advisor for help.

During their initial meeting, Dr. Kirkland could see that Stephen was troubled by his academic underachievement as a college freshman. At that time, Dr. Kirkland sensed that Stephen's high school years, during which he had excelled athletically and academically, had been very important to him. Facing such a dismal beginning as a freshman appeared to be overwhelming to the young man, who suddenly saw himself as just "another small fish in a big pond." As

Dr. Kirkland and Stephen chatted about his academic and athletic success in high school, his advisor shared with Stephen one of his research projects. For his examination of successful coaches of scholar-athletes, Dr. Kirkland explained he needed help with a review of literature that he was writing and asked Stephen if he would be willing to assist with library searches to locate research articles on this topic. Stephen explained that he had benefited from a healthy coach-athlete relationship with his football coach in high school, and he was pleased to assist his new advisor with the research. Stephen agreed to spend some time in the university's sport studies library working for his new advisor. Following arrangements with the library's director, Stephen went to work for Dr. Kirkland.

Intervention. Dr. Kirkland explained to Stephen that he wanted to meet with him on a weekly basis to discuss the research articles he was able to obtain. He would look forward to their weekly sessions since whatever literature Stephen might uncover would be a great help to the research professor. Dr. Kirkland was also honest with Stephen as he explained he had other motives. He wanted to be able to stay in touch with his new advisee to check his academic efforts on a weekly basis and provide any support he could for the very capable student. Stephen agreed that this seemed like a good plan for him. The following week, they met for lunch at the student union, reviewed the journal articles Stephen had uncovered, and discussed his events of the week. Dr. Kirkland informed Stephen that he would be contacting his mother to explain the plan they had agreed on as a strategy for getting Stephen "back on track" academically. Stephen's mother was delighted to hear from Dr. Kirkland and approved of his plan to reverse Stephen's underachievement.

During their weekly meetings, Stephen and his advisor arrived at an important conclusion concerning why Stephen had failed academically during his first semester. Stephen reflected on how much busier he had been during high school with his heavy load of advanced placement courses and involvement in the high school band and several varsity sports. The busier he was, the better he was at managing his time. The unstructured time in the dormitory was apparently an aspect of collegiate life that Stephen was not able to handle.

As part of his academic advising, Dr. Kirkland agreed to Stephen's enrollment in an innovative electronic music class that was being offered at the university for the first time. Stephen had explained that the music course would serve as a creative outlet that he had been missing since his high school band experience. Although Dr. Kirkland hesitated about enrolling Stephen in a course that was not part of his undergraduate core requirements, he realized that such an experience might help Stephen feel better about his abilities.

The following August, Stephen gladly reported he was not living in the dormitory during his sophomore year; he and a friend were renting a small apartment on campus, which he felt would provide a quieter environment for serious study. Again, Stephen and his advisor mapped out a plan for keeping him on track academically. The two men agreed that Stephen would benefit from a part-time job on campus, and Dr. Kirkland suggested a lifeguard position at the university recreation center. Realizing that athletics had been such an important part of Stephen's high school experience, Dr. Kirkland was delighted to hear that Stephen was also planning on getting involved with the university's rugby team and encouraged him to try out. Although the research project from the previous year was completed, the two men agreed that staying in touch on a weekly basis would help keep Stephen focused academically.

Findings. The role as research assistant to Dr. Kirkland, coupled with the weekly meetings with his mentor, helped pave the way for continuing reversal of underachievement. The electronic music course also proved to be an appropriate complement; Stephen enjoyed the instructor tremendously, he discovered a new peer group that shared his passion for electronic rock music, and he achieved a grade of A in a challenging course. Dr. Kirkland celebrated Stephen's success in the course by attending a culminating concert in which the course participants performed original electronic music. Along with his success in the electronic music class, Stephen made tremendous progress during his second semester, raising his grade point average to a respectable level. Describing the successes he experienced during that second semester, Stephen said:

> I think the biggest thing for me was walking into his office my freshman year, knowing that I had screwed up my grades, and seeing that he was there listening to me. I felt that I needed a second chance, and I knew that I could work hard. I knew that I had to bring up my grades. He listened to me and told me that he believed in me and told me that I was going to be able to do it. That really gave me a push and the motivation to achieve. He emphasized several points—that I was a freshman in college, a large university, a new place for me, and I needed some time to get the partying out of my system. He told me I wasn't the first bright young man who had been distracted from studying during his first semester in college. I guess I was feeling so low that day, and somehow he focused on the positive. Dr. Kirkland also showed me that he was also concerned about other things about me outside of the academics. He wanted to know how my family was doing, what kind of extracurricular activities I was involved in, and what I liked to do for fun, what my life was all about. He didn't just focus on which courses I should select for the semester. He was interested in me as a whole person. I was very intimidated when I first came to the office. I guess there was a sense of shame on my part. All I had to share with him that day was that I had been put on academic probation. It was an embarrassing thing. His telling me that he believed in me made me feel that I couldn't let him down.

The combination of a new housing arrangement, a part-time job, and his involvement on the rugby team also appeared to make a difference. Since he worked as a lifeguard early in the morning his sophomore year, he found that his time spent at the swimming pool allowed him additional opportunity to study "on the job." The rugby team gave him the athletic outlet he needed along with a new circle of friends. Stephen also found time to get involved with a small group of musicians from his apartment complex who planned to form a rock band. Despite the fact that fall semester of his sophomore year was very busy for him, he was successful at managing his time more carefully because he had established a serious study schedule and continued to improve his grades.

Dr. Kirkland continued to meet weekly with Stephen and was pleased to hear about his success as he reversed his pattern of underachievement. He helped Stephen to see how much more confident he appeared to be, noting that he had begun to develop dating relationships with several young women. Stephen also indicated that his success in his education major was making a difference; further, he was enjoying his clinical experiences in local public school classrooms working with young children. The time spent working with elementary school youngsters was similar to the positive experience he had found working with children as a lifeguard at the water slide in his hometown. These confidence-building experiences assured him that his change of major had been right for him.

Due to changes in Stephen's family situation, it became necessary for him to change universities after the first semester of his junior year. Though he hated to leave his new friends and his new rock band that was successful in "landing gigs at frat houses," Stephen felt good about his accomplishments since the dismal spring semester of his freshman year. With a B average, he was grateful to Dr. Kirkland for his supportive mentorship and, even more importantly, his friendship. As he left campus, he visited his advisor's office one last time and promised to send Dr. Kirkland the first invitation to his commencement ceremony at the University of Utah. Not long thereafter, Dr. Kirkland shared a letter from Stephen with the researchers containing the following excerpt:

> There was always something more that made me feel we had a friendship rather than just a student-advisor relationship. We had a comfortable relationship. You believed in me from the beginning. You weren't just trying to cheer me up and make me feel better. You believed in me from the beginning, from day one. I picked up on that right away. I appreciated what you were doing for me. You were always checking in with me to see that things were okay. Not just in my classes, but other things outside of school, like my social life and whether I was meeting new people and making new friends. You were concerned about my development as a person. Just knowing that there was a person out there who cared about me is important to me. I'll be honest, every time I hear that someone has a doctorate, that's pretty intimidating to me. To have someone at that level listening to me and telling me that he believed in me and telling me he knew that I could do it really made me feel good.

DISCUSSION AND IMPLICATIONS

Based on the findings revealed in each case, a single core category emerged: the influence of a significant adult on a young person. There were, however, several related subcategories. First, the open-minded and nonjudgmental characteristics of the mentor were required to sustain an on-going relationship. Second, as a natural quality of a caring adult friend, each mentor provided his protégé with consistent and personalized social/emotional support and advocacy beyond that associated with simple instructor-student relationships. Finally, a plan of strength and interest-based strategies for intervention to reverse patterns of underachievement was implemented successfully in each case.

Corroborating Torrance's (1984) investigation, the mentor relationship experienced by the three young men described in this study revealed that each matured socially and emotionally, becoming a colleague of an accepting adult who cared about him as an individual. In each case, the significant adult was a man who helped the young person contemplate the barricades to his creative productivity and then to develop appropriate plans and strategies for leaping those hurdles.

It is interesting to note that each mentor experienced substantial growth himself. In the case of Jackson, the mentor was willing to learn about the trials and tribulations confronting urban youth in poor neighborhoods. Similarly, Nathan's mentor, Amman, was willing to expand his repertoire of skills from African American history to pedagogical techniques appropriate for a child. And the college professor was willing to set his typical academic obligations aside to monitor his protégé's progress. Paralleling Torrance's (1984) findings, each mentor in the present investigation developed an association with his protégé that "was a deeper and more caring one than coach and sponsor relationship" (p. 8).

Another important implication of this study also parallels the longitudinal work of Torrance (1984) in which his subjects reported that they "saw their mentors as teaching them 'how to play the game'" (p. 10). For Jackson, this instruction equated to persevering academically in order to free school time and also allow him the opportunity beyond school for his studies of space and astronomy. Amman taught Nathan how to use his interests in the struggles of African Americans throughout history as a means for becoming enthused about school and uncovering hidden talents in film production. Dr. Kirkland taught Stephen "how to play the game" by keeping busier to maintain his focus and encourage him to use his time more productively.

Unlike previous results, the present case studies reveal that school personnel were pivotal in helping to establish mentorships for the young subjects. Without purposeful intervention in designing these matches, the mentor relationships could not have developed. The cases reinforce the notion that parents are often so overwhelmed with their own circumstances that they are unable to provide such opportunities. Moreover, parents often lack the contacts for locating appropriate mentors in a community.

The importance of the mentor as advocate or as spokesman for each young man was prevalent in all three cases. Bob, Jackson's mentor, met frequently with school personnel to monitor his academic program and to ensure that he had adequate contact with the NASA instructor for developing his space project and founding his space club. Amman made sure that Nathan had sufficient opportunities for building connections from African American history to the regular content in his classroom. Dr. Kirkland spoke in Stephen's behalf when he was forced to miss numerous classes due to mononucleosis.

Focusing on personal strengths and interests was found to be effective in helping each young subject improve his motivation, self-regulation, and academic efforts. These results underscore Renzulli's (1994) recommendations for talent development. Across the three case studies, each young man discovered how his interest could be connected to his academic responsibilities. Whether it was Jackson's interest in space, Nathan's fascination with African American history, or Stephen's passion for electronic music, each young man began to see a link between his personal desires and traditional academic expectations. This realization produced improved school behavior and academic achievement in all three subjects.

Jackson and Nathan each experienced improved relationships with peers, while Stephen expanded the range and quality of peer interactions. Jackson realized that a positive peer group need not be a street gang, but could be a collection of students interested in a space club. Nathan suddenly became popular because his interest in producing a movie about African American history prompted his peers to seek his approval for their participation. Meanwhile, Stephen developed much stronger and richer friendships based not on dormitory pranks, but on mutual interests and values. These results highlight the findings of Baum, Renzulli, and Hébert (1995) where students made friends with peers who achieved academically and shared common interests.

Supporting the findings of several previous studies (Emerick, 1992; Hébert, 1997; Olenchak, 1995; Reilly, 1992; Torrance, 1984), the current investigation revealed that the mentor in each case genuinely cared for his protégé, believed in him, and appreciated and respected him as a unique individual with special talents and abilities beyond the academic tasks at hand. In every case study, the mentor could see beyond the underachieving behaviors to focus on the strengths of the protégé.

Ultimately, this study has indicated that mentor relationships can be effective in reversing the pattern of underachievement in gifted young men. Regardless of age, socioeconomic background, and environment, the mentorship approach was successful in discerning personal interests and in nurturing strengths in the young men. Educators and other professionals must purposefully seek to encourage relationships between caring adults and talented young men who are underachieving. To do otherwise is to obscure potential and promise.

REFERENCES

Alvino, J. (1991). An investigation into the needs of gifted boys. *Roeper Review, 13,* 174–180.

Ambrose, D., Allen, J., & Huntley, S. (1994). Mentorship of the highly creative. *Roeper Review, 17,* 12–134.

Arnold, K., & Subotnik, R. (1995). Mentoring the gifted: A differentiated model. *Educational Horizons, 73,* 118–123.

Baum, S. M., Olenchak, F. R., & Owen, S. V. (1998). Gifted students with attention deficits: Fact and/or fiction? Or, can we see the forest for the trees? *Gifted Child Quarterly, 42,* 96–104.

Baum, S. M., Renzulli, J. S., & Hébert, T. P. (1995). Reversing underachievement: Creative productivity as a systematic intervention. *Gifted Child Quarterly, 39,* 224–235.

Clasen, D. R. (1993). Resolving inequities: Discovery and development of talents in student populations traditionally underrepresented in gifted and talented programming. *Journal of the California Association for the Gifted, 23*(4), 25–29.

Clasen, D. R., & Clasen, R. E. (1997). Mentoring: A time-honored option for education of the gifted and talented. In N. Colangelo & G. A. Davis (Eds.), *Handbook of gifted education* (2nd ed., pp. 281–229). Boston: Allyn and Bacon.

Colangelo, N., & Peterson, J. S. (1993). Group counseling with gifted students. In L. K. Silverman (Ed.), *Counseling the gifted and talented* (pp. 111–129). Denver, CO: Love.

Csikszentmihalyi, M. (1990). *Flow: The psychology of optimal experience.* New York: Harper and Row.

Csikszentmihalyi, M., Rathunde, K., & Whalen, S. (1997). *Talented teenagers: The roots of success and failure.* New York: Cambridge University Press.

Davis, G. A., & Rimm, S. B. (1994). *Education of the gifted and talented.* Boston: Allyn and Bacon.

deBono, E. (1986). *CoRT Thinking Skills Program.* Oxford, England: Pergamon Press.

Denzin, N. K. (1997). *Interpretive ethnography: Ethnographic practices for the 21st century.* Thousand Oaks, CA: Sage.

Edlind, E., & Haensly, P. (1985). Gifts of mentorships. *Gifted Child Quarterly, 29,* 55–60.

Emerick, L. J. (1992). Academic underachievement among the gifted: Students' perceptions of factors that reverse the pattern. *Gifted Child Quarterly, 36,* 140–146.

Flaxman, E., Ascher, C., & Harrington, C. (1988). *Youth mentoring: Programs and practices.* New York: ERIC Clearinghouse on Urban Education.

Ford, D. Y. (1993). An investigation of the paradox of underachievement among gifted Black students. *Roeper Review, 16,* 78–84.

Ford, D. Y. (1996). *Reversing underachievement among gifted Black students.* New York: Teachers College Press.

Frasier, A., Passow, A. H., & Goldberg, M. L. (1958). Curriculum research: Study of underachieving gifted. *Educational Leadership, 16,* 121–125.

Goh, B. E., & Goh, D. (1996). Developing creative writing talent through a mentorship program. *Gifted Education International, 11,* 156–159.

Halpern, R. (1992). The role of after school programs in the lives of inner-city children: A study of the "urban youth network." *Child Welfare, 71,* 215–230.

Heath, S. B., & McLaughlin, M. W. (1993). *Identity and inner-city youth: Beyond ethnicity and gender.* New York: Teachers College Press, Columbia University.

Hébert, T. P. (1997). Jamison's story: Talent nurtured in troubled times. *Roeper Review, 19,* 142–148.

Kaufman, F., Harrel, G., Milam, C., Woolverton, N., & Miller, J. (1986). The nature, role, and influence of mentors in the lives of gifted adults. *Journal of Counseling and Development, 64*, 576–577.

Lemley, D. (1994). Motivating underachieving gifted secondary students. *Gifted Child Today, 17*(4), 40–41.

Levinson, D. J., Darrow, C. N., Klein, E. B., Levinson, M. H., & McKee, B. (1978). *The seasons of a man's life.* New York: Alfred A. Knopf.

Merriam, S. B. (1998). *Qualitative research and case study applications in education.* San Francisco: Jossey-Bass.

Miles, M. B., & Huberman, A. M. (1994). *Qualitative data analysis: An expanded sourcebook* (2nd ed.) Thousand Oaks, CA: Sage.

Noller, R. B., & Frey, R. (1994). *Mentoring: Annotated bibliography 1982–1992.* Sarasota, FL: Center for Creative Learning.

Olenchak, F. R. (1995). Effects of enrichment on gifted/learning disabled students. *Journal for the Education of the Gifted, 18*, 385–399.

Patton, M. Q. (1990). *Qualitative evaluation and research methods* (2nd ed.). London: Sage.

Reilly, J. M. (1992). *Mentorship: The essential guide for schools and businesses.* Dayton, OH: Ohio Psychology Press.

Renzulli, J. S. (1994). *Schools are places for talent development: A practical plan for school improvement.* Mansfield Center, CT: Creative Learning Press.

Rimm, S. B. (1986). *Underachievement syndrome: Causes and cures.* Watertown, WI: Apple.

Rimm, S. B., & Olenchak, F. R. (1991). How FPS helps underachieving gifted students. *Gifted Child Today, 14*(2), 19–22.

Scruggs, T. E., & Cohn, S. J. (1983). A university-based summer program for a highly able but poorly achieving Indian child. *Gifted Child Quarterly, 27*, 90–93.

Seeley, K. (1993). Gifted students at risk. In L. K. Silverman (Ed.), *Counseling the gifted and talented* (pp. 263–276). Denver, CO: Love.

Shaughnessy, M., & Neely, R. (1991). Mentoring gifted children and prodigies: Personological concerns. *Gifted Education International, 7*, 129–132.

Silverman, L. J. (1993). Counseling families. In L. K. Silverman (Ed.), *Counseling the gifted and talented* (pp. 151–178). Denver, CO: Love.

Stake, R. (1995). *The art of case study research.* Thousand Oaks, CA: Sage.

Strauss, A., & Corbin, J. (1990). *Basics of qualitative research: Grounded theory procedures and techniques.* Newbury Park, CA: Sage.

Torrance, E. P. (1980). Growing up creatively gifted: A 22-year longitudinal study. *Creative Child and Adult Quarterly, 5*(1), 148–158, 170.

Torrance, E. P. (1984). *Mentor relationships: How they aid creative achievement, endure, change, and die.* Buffalo, NY: Bearly Limited.

Torrance, E. P., Goff, K., & Satterfield, N. B. (1998). *Multicultural mentoring of the gifted and talented.* Waco, TX: Prufrock Press.

White-Hood, M. (1993). Taking up the mentor challenge. *Educational Leadership, 51*(3), 76–78.

Whitmore, J. R. (1980). *Giftedness, conflict, and underachievement.* Boston: Allyn and Bacon.

Wright, L., & Borland, J. H. (1992). A special friend: Adolescent mentors for young, economically disadvantaged, potentially gifted students. *Roeper Review, 14*, 124–129.

Yin, R. K. (1989). *Case study research: Design and methods.* London: Sage.

Yin, R. K. (1993). *Applications of case study research.* London: Sage.

13

The Underachievement of Gifted Students: What Do We Know and Where Do We Go?

Sally M. Reis

D. Betsy McCoach

The University of Connecticut

The process of defining underachievement, identifying underachieving gifted students, and explaining the reasons for this underachievement continues to stir controversy among practitioners, researchers, and clinicians. Despite this interest, the underachievement of gifted students remains an enigma. This article reviews and analyzes three decades of research on the underachievement of gifted students in an attempt to clarify the present state

Editor's Note: From Reis, S. M., & McCoach, D. B. (2000). The underachievement of gifted students: What do we know and where do we go? *Gifted Child Quarterly, 44*(3), 152-170. © 2000 National Association for Gifted Children. Reprinted with permission.

of research. The problems inherent in defining and identifying underachieving gifted students are given special attention. The authors also include suggestions for those interested in pursuing potentially promising new lines of research and inquiry in this area.

The underachievement of gifted students is a perplexing phenomenon. Too often, for no apparent reason, students who show great academic promise fail to perform at a level commensurate with their previously documented abilities, frustrating both parents and teachers (Whitmore, 1986). The process of defining underachievement, identifying underachieving gifted students, and explaining the reasons for this underachievement continues to stir controversy among practitioners, researchers, and clinicians. Legitimate problems exist in determining whether these students are at greater risk for social or emotional problems than other students, and most interventions to reverse underachievement have met with limited success. Practitioners who responded to a National Research Center on the Gifted and Talented needs assessment identified underachievement as a major research problem (Renzulli, Reid, & Gubbins, 1992). Despite this interest, the underachievement of gifted students remains an enigma.

DEFINING UNDERACHIEVEMENT IN GIFTED STUDENTS

Any discussion of issues relating to underachievement in gifted students must carefully define both the constructs of giftedness and underachievement. Defining underachievement in gifted students seems as if it should be an easy and straightforward task. Unfortunately, no universally agreed upon definition of underachievement currently exists. Several recent researchers' operational and conceptual definitions of gifted underachievement are summarized in Tables 1, 2, 3, and 4. The most common component of the various definitions of underachievement in gifted students involves identifying a discrepancy between ability and achievement (Baum, Renzulli, & Hébert, 1995a; Butler-Por, 1987; Dowdall & Colangelo, 1982; Emerick, 1992; Redding, 1990; Rimm, 1997a; Supplee, 1990; Whitmore, 1980; Wolfle, 1991).

Putting the Research to Use

How can educators help bright students who are underachieving in school? Underachievers are a very heterogeneous group. Like gifted students in general, they exhibit great variability and diversity in their behaviors, interests, and abilities. Because students underachieve for so many different reasons, no one intervention strategy can possibly reverse these behaviors in all underachieving gifted students. We need to individualize programs for underachieving gifted students at least as much as we individualize programs for achieving gifted students. The most successful programs to reverse underachievement behaviors will provide a menu of intervention options for different types of underachieving gifted students. These menus should include curricular modification and differentiation options such as curriculum compacting, counseling components, and self-regulation training activities.

Educators must also realize that home, peer, and cultural environments may impact students' levels of achievement. As educators, we may or may not be able to change the external factors that contribute to the underachievement of certain gifted students. However, students who have reversed their underachievement behaviors have noted that having a teacher who supported and believed in them helped them overcome their underachievement. Therefore, in the absence of developing formal programs for underachievers, providing underachievers with support, attention, and positive feedback could help these students reverse their underachievement.

Three general themes emerge from the many operational and conceptual definitions of gifted underachievement (Dowdall & Colangelo, 1982; Ford, 1996). The first theme, displayed in Table 1, portrays underachievement as a discrepancy between potential (or ability) and performance (or achievement). A second, smaller number of authors define underachievement as a discrepancy between predicted achievement and actual achievement. This genus of this definition, illustrated in Table 2, views underachievement as a regression equation involving human potential and performance (Frick et al., 1991). If a student performs more poorly on measures of achievement than one would expect based on measures of ability, then he or she is underachieving. The third theme, presented in Table 3, views underachievement as a failure to develop or utilize latent potential without reference to other external criteria. Researchers proposing definitions in this category make no attempt to explicitly define or measure

Table 1   Definitions of Gifted Underachievement That Include a Discrepancy
Between Potential and Performance

Author	Date	Key Concept
Baum, Renzulli, & Hébert	1995a	High potential as evidenced by intelligence, achievement tests, or tests of specific aptitude, teacher observation, grades; underachievement as evidenced by discrepancy between performance and potential.
Butler-Por	1987	Large discrepancy between school performance and potential.
Dowdall & Colangelo	1982	Discrepancy between potential and actual performance.
Emerick	1992	Evidence of giftedness included standardized achievement test scores, scores on tests of general aptitude, or other indicators of potential for well-above average academic performance . . . . Evidence of underachievement included average or below average academic performance as assessed by test scores, grades, and teacher observations.
Whitmore	1980	High aptitude scores but low grades and achievement test scores, or high achievement test scores but low grades due to poor daily work.

potential. In this conception of underachievement, underachievers may be viewed as individuals who fail to self-actualize.

Definitions of gifted underachievement as a discrepancy between potential and performance are by far the most common. However, if one accepts the general premise that underachievement involves a discrepancy between ability and achievement, a need exists to operationally define these key concepts.

A common method of defining ability involves the use of an IQ test, such as the WISC-III or the Stanford-Binet IV. However, the criteria needed to identify giftedness vary from state to state and from district to district. In some states, students must achieve an IQ score at or above a certain cut-off in order to acquire the gifted label. Many states mandate the use of multiple criteria to determine giftedness. Because different school systems use different criteria to label a student gifted, the populations of students who are identified as gifted vary; and, in some cases, they are not comparable. This phenomenon is sometimes called "geographic giftedness" (Borland, 1989).

Defining achievement is even more problematic. Two common measures of achievement are standardized achievement test scores (e.g., the California Achievement Tests, the Iowa Test of Basic Skills, the Stanford Achievement Tests, Metropolitan Achievement Tests, the Terra Nova, etc.) and classroom performance as evidenced by course grades. Standardized achievement tests offer one advantage over classroom grades: They provide documented, empirical evidence of reliability. However, because standardized achievement tests do not directly reflect the actual school experience, they may not be indicative of a student's classroom performance. Classroom grades, though unreliable and

Table 2   Definitions that Emphasize Specific IQ/Ability Test Score as a Criterion for Identification as a Gifted Underachiever

Author	Date	Key Concept
Colangelo et al.	1993	Giftedness as evidenced by scores at the 95th percentile or above on the ACT; underachievement as evidenced by GPA of 2.25 or below in high school coursework.
Gowan	1957	Giftedness as evidenced by an IQ of 130 or above. Diagnosis of underachievement occurs when a student falls in the middle third in scholastic achievement in grades, and severe underachievement occurs when a student falls in the lowest third in scholastic achievement.
Green, Fine, & Tollefson	1988	Giftedness as evidenced by scores in the top 2% of the Tollefson norm group on an intelligence test. Underachievement as evidenced by one of the following criteria: (a) earning a C or below in at least one major academic subject; (b) having at least a one-year difference between expected and actual performance on a standardized achievement test; or (c) failing to complete work or submitting incomplete work at least 25% of the time as indicated by teacher records.
Krouse & Krouse	1981	Underachievers—those individuals who consistently, over a number of years, perform at higher levels on instruments of academic aptitude or intelligence than they do in regular classroom situations.
Supplee	1990	High academic ability as assessed through an IQ score or through achievement test scores at the eighth or ninth stanine. Low achievement as evidenced by achievement test scores that were at least two stanines lower than the IQ score, or by teacher ratings, or by school grades showing a marked discrepancy from expected achievement based on IQ or achievement tests.

teacher dependent, provide one of the most commonly used methods to assess and evaluate students. Almost all colleges and universities use high school grades in their admissions procedures. Students who are required to repeat grade levels or courses are rarely singled out as a result of low standardized achievement test scores. Rather, they are retained as a result of their classroom performance.

Distinguishing exactly what constitutes a discrepancy between ability and achievement also poses challenges. If a student scores in the 99th percentile on an IQ test, that does not mean that he or she should also score in the 99th percentile on standardized measures of achievement. No reason exists to believe that all gifted students should achieve well academically (Janos & Robinson, 1985) or that ability and achievement should be perfectly correlated (Thorndike, 1963). Pirozzo (1982) asserted that, generally, about half of the

Table 3   Definitions of Gifted Underachievement That Stress Predicted
Achievement vs. Actual Achievement

Author	Date	Key Concept
Gallagher	1991	"If the actual achievement scores fall some distance lower than what was predicted the student can be labeled underachiever" (p. 223).
Lupart & Pyryt	1996	1. Determine the correlation between IQ and achievement. 2. Estimate the expected IQ in relation to achievement for each student using the standard error of estimate. 3. Individuals with a discrepancy beyond one standard error of estimate were targeted as possible underachievers.
Redding	1990	"Underachievement—the discrepancy between actual GPA and predicted GPA, based upon a regression procedure used to predict GPA based upon full-scale WISC-R IQ scores" (p. 7).
Thorndike	1963	Underachievement refers to the fact that a group of pupils all of the same age, the same IQ, the same type of home background, will still vary in the scores they receive in school.

Table 4   Definitions of Gifted Underachievement That Stress
Development of Potential

Author	Date	Key Concept
Richert	1991	"1. Achievement among gifted students—developing four aspects of giftedness: Ability, Creativity, Productivity Performance, Motivation-Emotions-Values. 2. Underachievement among gifted students—underachievement in any of the four areas necessary for the manifestations of giftedness" (p. 142).
Rimm	1997a	"If students are not working to their ability in school, they are underachieving" (p. 18).

gifted children who score in the top 5% of intellectual ability on individualized
IQ tests do not demonstrate comparable school achievement. Thorndike's four
reasons that explain why the correlation between measured intelligence and
measured achievement is less than perfect provide insight into current issues
regarding underachievement.

Errors of Measurement

No test is 100% reliable. Differences in scores will arise as a result of
sampling errors, student mood and health on the testing days, and other extra-
neous variances. Confidence intervals are usually reported with the standardized
test scores. For example, an observed score of 130 on WISC-III is in the 98th

percentile. The 90% confidence interval for a score of 130 is 124–134. In other words, if a student were to take the same IQ test again, there is a 90% probability that his or her score would fall between 124 and 134. A score of 124 would place the student in the 95th percentile, while a score of 134 would place the student in the 99th percentile. In other words, one can stipulate with 95% confidence that this student's IQ places him or her in the top 5% of the population on this measure. Conversely, there is a 10% chance that this student's "real" IQ score is lower than 124 or higher than 134. Because of these errors of measurement, psychologists can never determine with 100% certainty a student's "true" score on the original measure.

Using the estimation of the first true score to predict a student's expected score on another related measure compounds these measurement uncertainties. For example, statistical regression to the mean further complicates the comparison of two aptitude or achievement measurements. When a person scores at one extreme of the testing continuum on one testing occasion, he or she is more likely to score closer to the mean on the next testing occasion. Therefore, operational definitions of underachievement as a discrepancy will overidentify underachievement in students with higher ability levels and underidentify students with lower ability levels (Frick et al., 1991). Thorndike (1963) cautioned educators and psychologists not to waste their time and effort attempting to provide explanations arising solely from measurement errors, discussed below.

Heterogeneity of the Criterion

"Criterion heterogeneity is the extent to which a criterion score of either aptitude or achievement changes its nature and meaning from one person to another" (Raph, Goldberg, & Passow, 1966, pp. 11–12). If the criterion is academic achievement defined in terms of course grades, it is impossible to compare grades across subject areas or even across students because of the variability in content and presentation. It is erroneous to equate an A in third grade math with an A in advanced placement calculus. In fact, even comparing grades in the same course becomes impossible because of the differences in different teachers' curricular emphases, grading policies, and testing procedures.

The use of standardized achievement test scores also results in a certain amount of heterogeneity in the criterion variable. Part of this variability is explained by the error of measurement of the criterion. Just as IQ scores are not completely reliable, standardized achievement test scores are also subject to errors of measurement due to content sampling, time sampling, and other issues. Furthermore, the correspondence between school districts' adopted curricula and the content of the standardized tests used to assess student achievement is usually imperfect.

Two methods can help reduce heterogeneity of the criterion variable (Raph et al., 1966). The first method involves using a large random sample of subjects in order to dilute the effects of criterion heterogeneity. The second approach is to use a sample of subjects that is "homogeneous with respect to the variables thought to be significant determinants of criterion scores" (Raph et al., p. 12). Neither approach seems logical or practical for school-based research.

Limited Scope in the Predictors

As Thorndike (1963) explained,

> all behavior is complexly determined. No one predictor will ever include all the determinants of a behavioral outcome. We have tended to become preoccupied with scholastic aptitude measures because they do correlate substantially with later achievement, and consequently do permit some improvement in the accuracy of predictions. But neither our psychological insights nor our statistical evidence give us reason to believe that a scholastic aptitude test measures all of the significant determiners of scholastic achievement. (p. 5)

The estimated correlation between IQ scores and estimated GPA is approximately .5 (Neisser et al., 1996). This moderate correlation between the intelligence test scores and school grades means that IQ scores explain only 25% of the variance between school grades and IQ scores, leaving 75% of the variance in achievement test scores unaccounted for by IQ scores. More recent studies (e.g., Anderson & Keith, 1997) report correlations as high as .67 between measures of ability and achievement. However, even if the correlation between ability tests and grades is as high as .70, this still only explains 49% of the variance between the two measures, leaving slightly more than half of the variance in grades unexplained by ability. Obviously, factors other than ability, such as motivation, personality characteristics, family environment, school environment, and peer pressure, influence achievement. Conceivably, the combination of these factors may account for more variance in achievement than ability alone.

Impact of Varied Experiences on the Individual

Environmental influences and events have a major impact on students' achievement. Consider an extreme example: No one would be surprised if a student who had been ill for a long period of time scored significantly lower on a standardized achievement test or a final exam than a healthy classmate of similar ability. However, other intervening environmental influences and experiences that may not be obvious to school personnel or parents also affect achievement. For example, a student who is clinically depressed or has other emotional or drug-related problems may experience a sudden decline in school grades. Being aware of these factors could change teacher and parent perceptions of the student as an underachiever. Moreover, a student's family, school, or community environment or peer influences may also influence his or her level of achievement.

THE UTILITY OF DEFINING UNDERACHIEVEMENT

If a certain amount of variation between aptitude measures and achievement measures is normal, how does one distinguish between normal variability in scores and a discrepancy that indicates a cause for concern? As previously mentioned, most definitions of underachievement involve a discrepancy between ability and academic achievement/performance. Some of the definitions included in Tables 1–4 (e.g., Mather & Udall, 1985; Redding, 1990) are specific operational definitions. Other definitions (Butler-Por, 1987; Ford, 1996; Rimm, 1997a) are broader and more inclusive. Defining underachievement operationally provides researchers and readers with a clearer picture of the composition of the sample being studied and enables the comparison of results of different studies. However, although operational definitions provide clarity, they sacrifice flexibility and inclusiveness in a quest for precision. Operational definitions categorize a continuous variable (academic performance), thereby creating arbitrary divisions between achievement and underachievement at a certain cut-off point. Ford advocated using a more holistic approach to defining and identifying gifted underachievers: "Broad, inclusive definitions of underachievement support the notion that underachievement is a multidimensional construct that cannot be assessed with unidimensional instruments" (Ford, 1996, p. 54).

Defining underachievement based strictly upon scholastic success or failure may also be limiting. If a student spends much of his or her free time reading about world religions or volunteering at the local hospital, but fails to complete mundane homework assignments, does that represent underachievement or a personal decision reflecting a wise use of time? This student may have consciously decided not to expend the time or effort to do seemingly meaningless homework and willfully chose to engage in more self-actualizing activities. Schweitzgebel (1965) alluded to this phenomenon when he observed that "underachievers, in contrast to slower learners, may in fact learn rapidly and well, but what they learn may not coincide with the content of our examinations" (p. 486).

The manifestation of underachievement may reflect a mismatch between the student and the curriculum. Recently, Reis (1998) suggested that gifted students who are not challenged in school may actually demonstrate integrity and courage when they choose not to do required work that is below their intellectual level. Labeling this phenomenon "dropping out with dignity," she concluded that some students may underachieve as a direct result of an inappropriate and unmotivating curriculum. Recent research (Reis, Hébert, Diaz, Maxfield, & Ratley, 1995), provides further evidence that boredom may contribute to underachievement. The results of the four-year longitudinal study with gifted high school students who either achieved or underachieved in high school suggested that boredom with the regular curriculum in elementary and middle school often contributes to underachievement in high school. When teachers expect students to complete work involving content and concepts mastered several years earlier, high-ability students become difficult to motivate.

Students who are difficult to motivate are often categorized as underachievers. Whitmore (1986) suggested that "the problem of gifted students who lack motivation to participate in school or to strive to excel academically is, in most cases, a product of a mismatch between the child's motivational characteristics and the opportunities provided in the classroom" (p. 67).

Finally, several fundamental philosophical issues surround the entire concept of underachievement. Who should make the decision as to what is considered achievement and, by extension, what is worth achieving? Labeling a student an underachiever requires making a value judgment about the worthiness of certain accomplishments. A teacher may believe that reading *Huckleberry Finn* is more worthwhile than mastering a new video game, but a child may not. This behavior illustrates a values conflict between adult and child (Whitmore, 1986). At what age should an individual gain control over his or her own destiny and make decisions regarding his or her priorities and goals? Finally, should adults place higher expectations on gifted students, or does this represent an elitist and utilitarian view of humanity? Certain responses to these questions may lead to the conclusion that underachievement does not exist or is not a problem that adults should remedy. The remainder of this article assumes that underachievement exists and merits attention and research; however, the authors recognize that even this most fundamental concept evokes value judgments and debates.

Definitions of gifted underachievement are inconsistent and sometimes incompatible. Vocabulary facilitates communication; without a common vocabulary, professionals cannot assume that they are discussing the same construct. Clarifying the myriad definitions of underachievement that exist in our field will enable professionals and scholars to communicate and investigate this phenomenon more effectively.

IDENTIFYING UNDERACHIEVERS

Since the identification of gifted underachievers depends on defining both underachievement and giftedness, discussing criteria for identification is no less complicated. One fact seems certain: The identification procedure should flow directly and logically from the definition of gifted underachievement. However, identifying underachieving gifted students by locating discrepancies between ability and achievement as measured by standardized achievement tests may lead to the underidentification of this population. In addition, bright students who receive poor grades may demonstrate mastery in standardized achievement testing situations (Colangelo, Kerr, Christensen, & Maxey, 1993; Lupart & Pyryt, 1996). Therefore, any system of defining, identifying, and eventually reversing underachievement should include students whose classroom performance falls significantly below their standardized test performance.

Identifying an underachiever using one of the broader, more inclusive definitions is also problematic. Rimm (1997a) believes that "if students are not working to their ability, they are underachieving" (p. 18). This definition could include most gifted students, as many receive top grades in school without expending sustained effort. One could even argue that Rimm's definition includes almost all students. However conceptually sound this notion may be, a definition that does not differentiate between a straight-A student and a student who is in jeopardy of failing may have little practical utility for the practitioner. In other words, using an overly narrow definition may increase Type II error, leading to a failure to identify a truly underachieving gifted student. Conversely, using a very broad definition may promote Type I error, causing overidentification of underachieving students.

Criteria for identifying gifted underachievers should include a method for determining observable discrepancies between ability and achievement. In addition, many professionals add a temporal dimension to the identification procedure (Mandel & Marcus, 1995). Often, students may not be classified as underachievers unless they have exhibited low performance for at least a year. Students may experience short-term lags in achievement that may not be indicative of a long-term underachievement problem. However, whenever a student's performance drops substantially over a short time period, it should merit the attention of a teacher or a counselor.

Some professionals may try to gauge an age/performance discrepancy when identifying underachievers (Mandel & Marcus, 1995). In other words, they may not identify a student as an underachiever unless performance in at least one major subject area is at least one year below grade level. Although this may be a suitable method for identifying underachievers from the general school population, such an age/performance discrepancy may only identify the most severely underachieving gifted students. One would expect a gifted student's performance to be above grade level in some subject areas, especially those areas in which that student has been identified as gifted. When a gifted student is performing only at grade level in those content areas, there may be a justifiable cause for concern. Using such an identification method to identify gifted underachievers may lead to problems of underidentification.

Rimm, Cornale, Manos, and Behrend (1989) suggested using longitudinal test data in order to screen for possible underachievement. Such a method may provide more insight into the nature of the child's achievement since children are repeatedly compared to the same norm group. IQ test scores, achievement percentile scores, or grades that have declined for three years in a row are strong indicators of an underachievement problem. However, using such a formula to screen for gifted underachievement may underestimate the number of students who are falling into patterns of underachievement. Often, standardized tests have low ceilings, and when gifted students score at the ceiling of a testing instrument, it is impossible to know how much higher the student's performance might have been if the ceiling had been raised. Therefore, even though a gifted student's performance may decline over time, he or she could still appear to be at the top of the norm group. In other words, "tests may not register the decline since the first test did not discriminate accurately" (Rimm et al., 1989, p. 62).

We propose an imperfect, yet workable operational definition for defining and identifying underachievers in general, as well as gifted underachievers. Underachievers are students who exhibit a severe discrepancy between expected achievement (as measured by standardized achievement test scores or cognitive or intellectual ability assessments) and actual achievement (as measured by class grades and teacher evaluations). To be classified as an underachiever, the discrepancy between expected and actual achievement must not be the direct result of a diagnosed learning disability and must persist over an extended period of time. Gifted underachievers are underachievers who exhibit superior scores on measures of expected achievement (i.e., standardized achievement test scores or cognitive or intellectual ability assessments). Ideally, the researcher would standardize both the predictor and the criterion variables and would identify as underachievers those students whose actual achievement is at least one standard deviation below their expected achievement level. In reality, the standardization of classroom grades may be neither feasible nor meaningful.

CHARACTERISTICS OF GIFTED UNDERACHIEVERS

Attempting to define overarching psychological constructs to describe gifted underachievers is virtually impossible. Underachievers are a diverse population, and lists or description of their traits that may be hypothesized and/or researched—"common personality traits" abound. The range of characteristics ascribed to gifted underachievers by numerous authors are summarized in Table 5. Synthesizing the hypothesized characteristics of gifted underachievers becomes a nearly impossible task, and legitimate questions exist regarding the utility of such a list. For each personality trait common to gifted underachievers, there are many other underachieving gifted students who do not exhibit that trait. In addition, students who are not underachievers may exhibit one or several of these characteristics. Often, the lists of common personality traits contradict one another. Even the research on common characteristics in underachieving gifted students is often inconsistent. For example, low self-concept is one of the most common characteristics ascribed to underachieving gifted students (Belcastro, 1985; Bricklin & Bricklin, 1967; Bruns, 1992; Clark, 1988; Diaz, 1998; Fine & Pitts, 1980; Fink, 1965; Ford, 1996; Kanoy, Johnson, & Kanoy, 1980; Schunk, 1998; Supplee, 1990; Van Boxtel & Mönks, 1992; Whitmore, 1980). Even so, several studies have found that underachievers do not exhibit lower self-concepts than their achieving counterparts (e.g. Holland, 1998). After reviewing the research in the field of gifted underachievement, Emerick (1992) observed that "the picture of the underachiever which emerges is complex and often contradictory and inconclusive" (p. 140). Interestingly, some recent research suggests that underachieving gifted students share more common characteristics with underachievers in general than they do with achieving gifted students (Dowdall & Colangelo, 1982; McCall, Evahn, & Kratzer, 1992).

Several authors (Heacox, 1991; Mandel & Marcus, 1988, 1995; Rimm, 1995; Schneider, 1998) have created profiles for different types of underachievers. Three of these paradigms are compared and contrasted in Table 6. Although considerable overlap exists among the three authors' conceptions of under-achievement typologies, each author has described at least one underachiever type that is not mentioned by either of the other authors. In fact, only three types—the "anxious underachiever," the "rebellious underachiever," and the "complacent/coasting underachiever"—have approximate parallels in all three authors' schema. Although these profiles may provide educators with conve-nient categories for various underachievers whom they encounter, they also illustrate the difficulty in trying to create a coherent profile of a "typical" under-achiever. Furthermore, Rimm (1995) developed her underachiever profiles to reflect the variety of students she had treated in her clinical practice. However, underachievers who receive formal, clinical counseling do not necessarily represent the entire population of underachievers. Finally, the differences among the three authors' typical categories of underachievers further illustrate the fact that none of the lists are definitive or immutable.

FAMILY DYNAMICS

Research on the family characteristics of underachieving gifted students suggests that certain types of home environments may be related to the development of students' underachievement patterns (Baker, Bridger, & Evans, 1998; Brown, Mounts, Lamborn, & Steinberg, 1993; Rimm & Lowe, 1988; Zilli, 1971). Families with underachieving children tend to exhibit less positive affect (Mandel & Marcus, 1988). Whereas parental emphasis on achievement tends to inspire higher academic achievement (Brown et al., 1993), parents of underachievers may exhibit disinterested attitudes towards education (Jeon & Feldhusen, 1993).

Rimm (1995) emphasized the importance of parenting styles and parental influence on the development of children's achievement and underachieve-ment behaviors and found that inconsistent parenting techniques appeared to occur more frequently in the homes of underachieving children (Rimm & Lowe, 1988). She found that parents frequently oppose each other when disciplining their children. "In 95% of the families, one parent played the role of the parent that challenges and disciplines, and the other took the role of the protector. There was an increasing opposition between parents as the challenger became more authoritarian and the rescuer became increasingly protective" (p. 355). Rimm and Lowe concluded that particular styles of parenting appear to be less important than maintaining consistency within a parenting approach.

Parents of high-achieving students seem to utilize an authoritative parent-ing style more often than parents of low-achieving students (Taylor, 1994). Parents of underachievers often tend to be overly lenient or overly strict (Pendarvis, Howley, & Howley, 1990; Weiner, 1992). By contrast, families of underachieving students may tend to be more restrictive and punishment-oriented (Clark, 1983). In addition, bestowing adult status on a child at too young an age may contribute to the development of underachievement (Fine & Pitts, 1980; Rimm & Lowe, 1988). High-achieving parents often provide positive role-modeling of achievement-oriented behaviors (Rimm & Lowe, 1988; Zilli, 1971). In contrast, although the parents of underachieving gifted children may verbally espouse the values of achievement, they may have lives characterized by frustration and lack of fulfillment (Rimm & Lowe, 1988). In addition, families of high-achieving students seem to encourage self-motivation, environmental engagement, and autonomy more than families of low-achieving students (Taylor, 1994). Underachieving students may not want to identify with their parents (Clark, 1983; Weiner, 1992). Fine and Pitts speculated that more family conflicts occur in underachievers' homes, and recent research (Reis, Hébert, Diaz, Maxfield, & Ratley, 1995) has supported this view. In their recent study of gifted urban underachievers, the family dysfunction that characterized the lives of the gifted underachievers contrasted with the happier home lives of the gifted achievers (Reis et al., 1995). It is impossible to establish a causal relationship from case study reports of family conflict and underachievement. Do students underachieve because they come from families in conflict? Does the underachievement of the child create problems in the family unit? Or, is there a dynamic interaction between the underachiever and the family?

In another study comparing the families of underachievers to those of achievers, "families with underachieving gifted students were not classified as dysfunctional any more frequently than families with achieving gifted students" (Green, Fine, & Tollefson, 1988, p. 271). However, dysfunctional families with achieving gifted students reported greater satisfaction with their family lives than did dysfunctional families of underachieving students. Perhaps the family discord is a result of, rather than a cause of, the child's underachievement.

THE INFLUENCE OF PEERS

Peer issues may also contribute to the achievement and underachievement of adolescents. Peer relationships impact adolescent behavior (Brown, 1982; Clasen & Brown, 1985). Reis, Hébert, Diaz, Maxfield, and Ratley (1995) found that high-achieving peers had a positive influence on gifted students who began to underachieve in high school. Positive peer interaction contributed to some students' reversal of underachievement. Likewise, negative peer attitudes can often account for underachievement (Clasen & Clasen, 1995; Weiner, 1992). Underachieving students frequently report peer influence as the strongest force impeding their achievement (Clasen & Clasen, 1995). "Sixty-six percent of the students named peer pressure or attitude of the other kids, including friends, as the primary force against getting good grades" (pp. 68–69).

Table 5   Common Characteristics of Gifted Underachievers

Characteristics of Gifted Underachievers	Citation
Personality characteristics	
1. Low self-esteem, low self-concept, low self-efficacy.	Belcastro, 1985; Bricklin & Bricklin, 1967; Bruns, 1992; Clark, 1988; Diaz, 1998; Dowdall & Colangelo, 1982; Fine & Pitts, 1980; Fink, 1965; Ford, 1996; Kanoy, Johnson, & Kanoy, 1980; Schunk, 1998; Supplee, 1990; Van Boxtel & Mönks, 1992; Whitmore, 1980
2. Alienated or withdrawn; distrustful, or pessimistic.	Delisle, 1982; Fink, 1965; Ford, 1996; Mandel & Marcus, 1988,1995; Van Boxtel & Mönks, 1992; Whitmore, 1980
3. Anxious, impulsive, inattentive, hyperactive, or distractible; may exhibit ADD or ADHD symptoms.	Bruns, 1992; Clark, 1988; Diaz, 1998; Frick et al., 1991; Mandel & Marcus, 1988; Redding, 1990; Rimm, 1995; Whitmore, 1980
4. Aggressive, hostile, resentful, or touchy.	Butler-Por, 1987; Diaz, 1998; Mandel & Marcus, 1988; Whitmore, 1980
5. Depressed.	Mandel & Marcus, 1988; Rimm, 1995
6. Passive-aggressive trait disturbance.	Bricklin & Bricklin, 1967; Bruns, 1992; Dowdall & Colangelo, 1982; Fine & Pitts, 1980; Khatena, 1982; Pendarvis, Howley, & Howley, 1990; Weiner, 1992
7. More socially than academically oriented. May be extroverted. May be easygoing, considerate, and/or unassuming.	Mandel & Marcus, 1988; Rimm, 1995; Van Boxtel & Mönks, 1992; Whitmore, 1986
8. Dependent, less resilient than high achievers.	Bruns, 1992; Rimm, 1995, 1997b
9. Socially immature.	Clark, 1988; Dowdall & Colangelo, 1982; Fink, 1965; Weiner, 1992; Whitmore, 1980; Wolfle, 1991
Internal Mediators	
10. Fear of failure; gifted underachievers may avoid competition or challenging situations to protect their self-image or their ability.	Bricklin & Bricklin, 1967; Butler-Por, 1987; Diaz, 1998; Gallagher, 1991; Laffoon, Jenkins-Friedman, & Tollefson, 1989; McNabb, 1997; Rimm, 1995,1997a; Richert, 1991; Weiner, 1992
11. Fear of success.	Bricklin & Bricklin, 1967; Butler-Por, 1987; Ford, 1996; Weiner, 1992; Whitmore, 1986

(Continued))

Table 5 (Continued)

Characteristics of Gifted Underachievers	Citation
12. Attribute successes or failures to outside forces; exhibit an external locus of control, attribute successes to luck and failures to lack of ability; externalize conflict and problems.	Butler-Por, 1987; Clark, 1988; Ford, 1996; Gallagher, 1991; Kanoy et al., 1980; Weiner, 1992; Whitmore, 1980
13. Negative attitude toward school.	Bruns, 1992; Clark, 1988; Colangelo, Kerr, Christensen, & Maxey, 1993; Diaz, 1998; Ford, 1996; Frankel, 1965; Lupart & Pyryt, 1996; McCall et al., 1992; Rimm, 1995
14. Antisocial or rebellious.	Bricklin & Bricklin, 1967; Clark, 1988; Dowdall & Colangelo, 1982; Emerick, 1992; Mandel & Marcus, 1988; Richert, 1991; Rimm, 1995; Whitmore, 1980
15. Self-critical or perfectionistic; feeling guilty about not living up to the expectations of others.	Bricklin & Bricklin, 1967; Bruns, 1992; Diaz, 1998; Weiner, 1992
Differential Thinking Skills/ Styles	
16. Perform less well on tasks that require detail-oriented or convergent thinking skills than their achieving counterparts.	Redding, 1990
17. Score lower on sequential tasks such as repeating digits, repeating sentences, coding, computation, and spelling.	Silverman, 1993
18. Lack insight and critical ability.	Fink, 1965
Maladaptive Strategies	
19. Lack goal-directed behavior; fail to set realistic goals for themselves.	Clark, 1988; Emerick, 1992; Van Boxtel & Mönks, 1992; Weiner, 1992

(Continued))

Table 5   (Continued)

Characteristics of Gifted Underachievers	Citation
20. Poor coping skills; develop coping mechanisms that successfully reduce short-term stress, but inhibit long-term success.	Gallagher, 1991
21. Possess poor self-regulation strategies; low tolerance for frustration; lack perseverance; lack self-control.	Baum, Renzulli, & Hébert, 1994,1995a; Bricklin & Bricklin, 1967; Bruns, 1992; Diaz, 1998
22. Use Defense mechanisms.	Bricklin & Bricklin, 1967; Mandel & Marcus, 1988; Rimm, 1995; Van Boxtel & Mönks, 1992
Positive Attributes	
23. Intense outside interests, commitment to self-selected work.	Baum, Renzulli, & Hébert, 1994, 1995a; Reis, 1998; Weiner, 1992
24. Creative.	Ford, 1996
25. Demonstrate honesty and integrity in rejecting unchallenging coursework.	Reis, 1998

An examination of the NELS: 88 data revealed that students with friends who cared about learning demonstrated better educational outcomes than those with less educationally interested or involved friends (Chen, 1997). A more recent study of peer influence on students' adjustment to school (Berndt, 1999) measured students' grades and behavior in the fall and spring of one academic year. Berndt found that students seemed to resemble more closely their friends at the end of the school year than they did at the beginning of the school year. Students' grades decreased between fall and spring if their friends had lower grades in the fall. This finding does not imply causality, since "students often select friends whose characteristics are already similar to theirs" (Berndt, p. 18). However, these findings support the notion that there is a correlation between a student's achievement and the achievement of his or her closest peer group.

Table 6   Underachiever Descriptions

Heacox (1991)	Rimm (1995)	Mandel & Marcus (1995)	Shared Characteristics
I. Underachiever types that resemble at least one other author's description of underachiever types.			
The Rebel	"Rebellious Rebecca" Dominant Nonconformer	The Defiant Underachiever	May be disruptive, delinquent; may be hostile, touchy, temperamental.
The Conformist	"Social Sally, Jock Jack, and Dramatic Dick" Dominant Conformers		May succumb to peer pressure; doesn't want to be labeled a "nerd."
The Stressed Learner	"Perfectionistic Pearl" Dependent Conformer	The Anxious Underachiever	Anxious, perfectionistic, worry about failure.
	"Depressed Donna" Dependent Nonconformer	The Sad/Depressed Underachiever	Sad, depressed, low self-esteem.
The Victim	"Poor Polly" Dependent Conformer		Reluctant to accept responsibility, dependent on adults
	"Creative Chris" Dominant Nonconformer	Identity Search Underachiever	Does not want to conform.
The Distracted Learner	"Torn Tommy" Dominant Conformer/ Nonconformer		May be experiencing stress/anxiety for personal reasons that are unknown to school personnel.
	"Manipulative Mary" Dominant Nonconformer	The Wheeler-Dealer Underachiever	Manipulative; places emphasis on social circle, but the friendships are unstable; may be insecure or have a low self-concept.
The Complacent Learner	"Passive Paul" Dependent Conformer	The Coasting Underachiever	Procrastinates; easily distracted from doing work; seems unconcerned about work.

(Continued)

Table 6   (Continued)

Heacox (1991)	Rimm (1995)	Mandel & Marcus (1995)	Shared Characteristics
II. Underachiever types that do not resemble either of the other authors' descriptions of underachiever types.			
The Single Sided Achiever			Achieves in one area, underachieves in other areas.
	"Hyper Harry" Dominant Nonconformer		May be disorganized, impulsive, inconsistent.
The Bored Student			May need more challenging activities; may be afraid of failure.
The Struggling Student			May be a bright student who never learned proper study skills. He/she may perceive lack of success as loss of intelligence.

From Heacox, 1991; Mandel and Marcus, 1988,1995; and Rimm, 1995.

CULTURALLY DIVERSE UNDERACHIEVERS

The construct of underachievement in gifted students differs across cultures. Unfortunately, little research has focused specifically on culturally diverse underachievers (Ford, 1996; Reis, Hébert, Diaz, Maxfield, & Ratley, 1995). Culturally diverse students face unique barriers to their achievement for several reasons. Minority students are often underrepresented in programs for the gifted and talented (Ford, 1996; Tomlinson, Callahan, & Lelli, 1997). Culturally diverse students continue to face unintentional bias at school and in society at large (Ford, 1996). The definition of achievement in a particular subculture may be very different from that of the dominant culture.

Several issues pose potential problems for understanding the under-achievement of African American students. First, psychometric definitions tend to ignore important behavioral causes and correlates of underachievement (Ford, 1996). Second, the psychometric or standardized tests that are used to screen for gifted underachievement may not be valid or reliable indices of the abilities of students from diverse cultural backgrounds. Research suggests that using IQ scores as the sole criterion for inclusion in gifted programs can create a bias against African American students (Baldwin, 1987; Ford, 1996; Frasier & Passow, 1994). Current identification practices that underidentify gifted African American students hinder the identification of gifted underachievers of African American descent. If tests provide invalid inferences about a student's ability or achievement, they must, by extension, be invalid indices of underachievement (Ford, 1996). Finally, African American students often exhibit an attitude-achievement paradox; they report positive attitudes toward education, yet they manifest poor academic achievement. This attitude-achievement paradox makes understanding and reversing their underachievement difficult to those unfamiliar with the phenomenon (Mickelson, 1990).

A longitudinal study of 35 culturally diverse, gifted urban high school students compared successful students to a similar group of high-ability students who did not achieve (Reis et al., 1995). The researchers found no relationship between poverty and achievement, between parental divorce and achievement, or between family size and achievement. High-achieving students acknowledged the importance of being grouped together in honors and advanced classes for academically talented students. Successful students received support and encouragement from each other and from supportive adults, including teachers, guidance counselors, coaches, and mentors. Students who achieved in school participated in multiple extracurricular activities, both after school and during the summer. Most high-achieving females in this study chose not to date so they could concentrate their energies on their studies. In contrast, students who underachieved had developed neither a strong belief in self nor the resilience to overcome negative experiences with their families, their schools, and their communities. In addition, Diaz (1998) found that the absence of early appropriate academic experiences impeded Puerto Rican students' opportunities to develop their abilities when they reached high school. Although her model of underachievement stresses the interaction of family, personal, community, and school factors on the behavioral manifestations of underachievement in Puerto Rican youth, it could prove helpful in understanding the nonachievement behaviors in a wider range of ethnically diverse students.

Latino students may also confront unique barriers to their academic achievement. Some researchers have suggested that minority language background may adversely affect Hispanic students' academic achievement (Fernandez, Hirano-Nakanishi, & Paulsen, 1989). However, the relationship between language proficiency and school is complex. English language proficiency in school tends to improve across generations of immigrants, but test scores, grades, and other forms of educational achievement do not, especially among Latinos (Rumberger & Larson, 1998). Rumberger and Larson found that

> Mexican American students who came from Spanish-speaking backgrounds and who became proficient in English (FEP) were generally more successful in school than were those from Spanish-speaking backgrounds who were not proficient (LEP students) in English or than

Latino students from English speaking backgrounds. The findings suggest that achieving proficiency in English is a necessary, but not sufficient condition for Latino students to succeed in American schools. (p. 86)

Finally, educators must consider the different value systems within the Hispanic American community in order to understand the achievement of Hispanic American youth (Reis et al., 1995).

Due to the difficulty in defining underachievement, it appears that the concept of underachievement may be regarded as a subjective, rather than an objective, classification. In a culture that generally prizes both childhood and adult achievement, we label as underachievers those students who do not perform as well as we might expect them to perform. This raises several important issues. Let us define underachievement as a discrepancy between expected achievement and actual achievement. If we hold low expectations for students who then achieve at low levels, they are not underachievers. In other words, if we predict that students will not succeed, and then they fail, they have not performed below our initial expectations. The problem in this case lies in our initial predictions, not in the students' levels of achievement. When we hold low expectations for students, we may be unable to recognize, and therefore reverse, these students' underachievement behaviors.

The issues surrounding the identification of culturally diverse gifted students have received greater attention in recent years, and several points seem clear. First, we must recognize the talents in culturally diverse youth. Only after we recognize potential can we assess whether performance is below potential. Students whose gifts and subsequent underachievement go unrecognized are sometimes called "hidden underachievers" (Ford, 1996) who underachieve because educational systems do not recognize their potential. Cultural relativism also becomes a factor when identifying underachievement in diverse groups. What is prized in one culture may not be valued in another, and it is difficult to impose one belief system on a culture that may define achievement and underachievement differently. Do we help or hurt a child when we ask him or her to assimilate into the majority culture? How many researchers have explored how success can be achieved in the mainstream in the United States without assimilation?

Equality of educational opportunity also affects underachievement. Unfortunately, what is viewed as achievement in a poor school may be viewed as underachievement by a more competitive school or by society at large. Students who are not given adequate opportunities to develop their talents often become "involuntary underachievers." Recent research suggests that quality of schooling (Anderson & Keith, 1997; Baker, Bridger, & Evans, 1998) and completion of academic coursework research (Anderson & Keith) appear to be significant predictors of achievement for at-risk high school students. In fact, "it appears each additional academic course that an at-risk student completes can be expected to result in an increase of one eighth of a standard deviation in academic achievement test scores" (Anderson & Keith p. 264).

Researchers and educators may need to adjust their views of both giftedness and underachievement when attempting to identify and address the phenomenon within a culturally diverse student population. In addition, a discussion of the cultural connotations of the construct of underachievement deserves further attention.

UNDERACHIEVEMENT AND SPECIAL POPULATIONS OF GIFTED STUDENTS

Recently, researchers have begun to probe the relationships among underachievement, attention deficit disorders, and learning disabilities (Hinshaw, 1992a, 1992b). Students who seem unmotivated may have attention deficits (Busch & Nuttall, 1995) or hidden learning disabilities. Recent research indicates that many twice-exceptional students underachieve in school. However, "the current conceptualization and the literature on the underachieving gifted and on special populations (such as gifted/LD, gifted/ADD or ADHD, gifted students with physical disabilities or behavioral or emotional problems) appear to treat the two groupings as separate and unrelated" (Lupart & Pyryt, 1996, pp. 39–40). High-ability students can have learning problems (Barton & Starnes, 1988; Baum, Owen, & Dixon, 1991; Bireley, 1995) or attention deficits (Baum, Olenchak, & Owen, 1998) of various types that affect or cause underachievement. Distinguishing between a chronic underachiever and a gifted student who has processing deficits, learning disabilities, or attention deficits is crucial because the interventions that are appropriate for these subgroups may be radically different.

INTERVENTIONS

The causes and correlates of gifted underachievement have received considerable attention in recent research literature (Dowdall & Colangelo, 1982; Van Boxtel & Mönks, 1992; Whitmore, 1986). However, research on effective intervention models for this population remains scarce. Although conducting case studies and qualitative research on underachieving gifted students has become quite popular, few researchers have attempted to utilize true quasi-experimental designs to study the efficacy of various interventions. Most of the interventions reported in the literature (i.e., Supplee, 1990; Whitmore, 1980) were designed to effect immediate results with a group of acutely underachieving gifted students. Ethically, it may be difficult to have a true comparison group in such studies because the researcher must withhold treatment that he or she believes is valuable for underachieving gifted students.

The documented effectiveness of most interventions designed to reverse underachievement in gifted students has been inconsistent and inconclusive (Emerick, 1988). Furthermore, the majority of interventions have attained limited long-term success (Dowdall & Colangelo, 1982; Emerick, 1992). Interventions aimed at reversing gifted underachievement fall into two general categories: counseling and instructional interventions (Butler-Por, 1993; Dowdall & Colangelo, 1982).

Counseling interventions concentrate on changing the personal or family dynamics that contribute to a student's underachievement. Counseling interventions may include individual, group, or family counseling (Jeon, 1990). Many early attempts to improve underachievers' academic achievement through counseling treatments were unsuccessful (Baymur & Patterson, 1965; Broedel, Ohlsen, Proff, & Southard, 1965). In most counseling situations, the counselor's goal is not to force the underachiever to become a more successful student, but rather to help the student decide whether success is a desirable goal and, if so, to help reverse counter-productive habits and cognitions.

Weiner (1992) outlined four different interventions for four distinct groups of low achieving students: (1) strengthening deficient reward systems, (2) alleviating cognitive and emotional handicaps, (3) filling educational gaps, and (4) modifying passive-aggressive propensities. Counselors and therapists can help underachievers strengthen deficient reward systems, modify passive-aggressive propensities, and alleviate emotional deficits; educators can help students fill educational gaps and alleviate or compensate for cognitive handicaps. Unmotivated underachievers may see no compelling reasons for becoming better students. When working with this type of underachiever, a counselor should find ways of implementing reward systems that will encourage the student's scholastic efforts and reinforce academic successes. The parents of unmotivated underachievers may also benefit from therapeutic strategies that encourage them to speak positively about education, show an interest in their child's schoolwork, and praise their child's accomplishments.

Although passive-aggressive underachievement may be more likely to indicate psychological disturbance than underachievement attributable to motivational, educational, and cognitive components, this type of underachievement seems fairly responsive to psychotherapy (Weiner, 1992). Counseling interventions for passive-aggressive underachievers are most effective when the student seeks counseling or at least participates willingly in the counseling process. Because the passive-aggressive behavior of such children is usually directed against their families, family counseling interventions may also help reverse passive-aggressive underachievement. One strategy for counseling passive-aggressive underachievers "involves helping adolescents to recognize their abilities and interests, clarify their personal value systems and preferred goals, and pursue their studies to serve their own purposes rather than to meet or frustrate the needs of others" (Weiner, p. 290). Although clinicians report success with counseling interventions, research on therapeutic approaches has documented limited success in reversing students' underachievement patterns (Baymur & Patterson, 1965; Butler-Por, 1993; Jeon, 1990).

The most well-known educational interventions for gifted students have established either part-time or full-time special classrooms for gifted underachievers (e.g., Butler-Por, 1987; Fehrenbach, 1993; Supplee, 1990; Whitmore, 1980). In these classrooms, educators strive to create a favorable environment for student achievement by altering the traditional classroom organization. Usually, a smaller student/teacher ratio exists, teachers create less-conventional types of teaching and learning activities, teachers give students some choice and freedom in exercising control over their atmosphere, and students are encouraged to utilize different learning strategies.

Whitmore (1980) designed and implemented a full-time elementary program for gifted underachievers. Supplee (1990) instituted a part-time program for gifted elementary underachievers. Both programs stressed the importance of addressing affective education, as well as the necessity of creating student-centered classroom environments. Both Whitmore and Supplee designed their programs to effect immediate change in student behaviors, as well as to research the construct of underachievement. Both programs provided anecdotal and some qualitative evidence of at least partial success. However, neither study used a control or comparison group; therefore, the results of their studies may not be generalizable to the entire population of underachievers. Neither study utilized a truly longitudinal design, and neither researcher was able to fully track the progress of the students once they left the elementary school. Although some underachieving students appear to progress during academic interventions, the long-term effects of such programs are less clear. What happens when the student reenters the regular class and is once again faced with unstimulating schoolwork? How can the underachievement of older students be reversed? These and many other questions remain unanswered.

Emerick (1992) investigated the reasons that some students are able to reverse their academic underachievement without the assistance of formal interventions. Her qualitative research study examined the patterns of underachievement and subsequent achievement of 10 young adults. Several common factors appeared to play a part in the students' reversal of underachievement. Participants in Emerick's study perceived that out-of-school interests and activities, parents, development of goals associated with grades, teachers, and changes in "selves" had a positive impact on achievement. Other research also suggests that students who are more involved in extracurricular activities (Colangelo et al., 1993; Reis et al., 1995) are less likely to be underachievers. The participants in Emerick's study believed that a specific teacher had the greatest impact in reversing their underachievement behavior. In addition, participants were most likely to develop achievement-oriented behaviors when they were stimulated in class and given the opportunity to pursue topics of interest to them. These findings suggest that "reversing the underachievement pattern may mean taking a long, hard look at the underachiever's curriculum and classroom situation. The responses and actions of the students in this study suggest that when appropriate educational opportunities are present, gifted underachievers can respond positively (Emerick, p. 145).

Emerick's study indicated that one type of effective intervention may be based on students' strengths and interests (Renzulli, 1977; Renzulli & Reis, 1985,

1997). In a recent study, researchers used self-selected Type III enrichment projects as a systematic intervention for underachieving gifted students. This approach (Renzulli, 1977) specifically targets student strengths and interests in order to help reverse academic underachievement (Baum, Renzulli, & Hébert, 1995b). In a qualitative study of this intervention technique, five major features of the Type III enrichment process contributed to the success of the intervention. These factors were the relationship with the teacher, the use of self-regulation strategies, the opportunity to investigate topics related to their underachievement, the opportunity to work on an area of interest in a preferred learning style, and the time to interact with an appropriate peer group. Almost all of the students who completed Type III investigations showed some positive gains in either behavior or achievement during the course of the school year. Eleven of the 17 participants showed improved achievement; 13 of the 17 students appeared to exert more effort within their classes; and 4 of the 17 students showed marked improvement in their classroom behavior. The results of this research suggest that flexible, student-centered enrichment approaches may help reverse underachievement in gifted students.

Certain treatments aimed at combating underachievement combine counseling and school-centered interventions. For example, Rimm's trifocal model is a three-pronged approach that involves parents and school personnel in an effort to reverse student underachievement (Rimm, 1995; Rimm, et al., 1989). Because the factors that influence the development and manifestation of underachievement vary, no one type of intervention will be effective for the full range of underachieving gifted students. Rather, a continuum of strategies and services may be necessary if we are to systematically address this problem. Model-based interventions provide an internal consistency between diagnostic and prescriptive elements. Therefore, future researchers in this field should posit coherent, complete models of gifted underachievement and design interventions in accordance with their proposed models.

AREAS FOR FUTURE RESEARCH

We do not know how many talented students underachieve, but we know that this issue is foremost in the minds of practitioners (Renzulli, Reid, & Gubbins, 1992). Future research must attempt to unravel the complex causes of academic underachievement and provide interventions that help reverse underachievement behavior. Several lines of research remain inadequately explored.

We need to move beyond correlational studies of common characteristics of underachieving students and begin to explore linkages and flow of causality among these different characteristics and student achievement. For example, according to several authors (e.g., Belcastro, 1985; Bricklin & Bricklin, 1967; Bruns, 1992; Diaz, 1998; Dowdall & Colangelo, 1982; Fine & Pitts, 1980; Fink, 1965; Ford, 1996; Kanoy, Johnson, & Kanoy, 1980; Schunk, 1998; Supplee, 1990; Van Boxtel & Mönks, 1992; Whitmore, 1980), positive self-concept appears to correlate with student achievement, raising an interesting but unanswered question: Does low self-concept cause underachievement or does under-achievement result in a deterioration of self-concept, or does a third exogenous variable influence both self-concept and scholastic achievement? If low self-concept causes underachievement, interventions that raise self-concept should enhance student achievement. Therefore, one might expect counseling approaches to effectively address the problem of underachievement. However, counseling treatments have met with limited success. This direction of causation between self-concept and underachievement has not been adequately addressed. Both longitudinal studies of achievers and underachievers and the development of structural equations models of achievement and under-achievement may help clarify the direction of causality between these two variables. Similar research on the flow of causality between student achievement and self-efficacy, self-regulation, student attitudes, peer attitudes, and other factors believed to influence underachievement will help researchers develop more effective intervention strategies to combat underachievement in gifted students.

Another area for research involves studying whether and how gifted under-achievers differ significantly from nongifted underachievers. McCall, Evahn, and Kratzer (1992) observed that most of the comparison group research within the area of gifted underachievement equates gifted underachievers to their mental ability cohorts. Many of these studies have found qualitative differences between gifted achievers and gifted underachievers. However, an interesting, though less studied, line of research involves comparing gifted underachievers to other students who are at the same achievement level as measured by GPA, achievement test scores, and so forth, regardless of their measured mental ability. Do gifted underachievers resemble lower achieving students? Do gifted underachievers have more in common with gifted students who do achieve or low-achieving students who are not gifted? Dowdall and Colangelo (1982) observed that gifted underachievers seem to share more characteristics with underachievers than they do with gifted achievers. Future research could explore the generality of the underachievement phenomenon and investigate whether interventions that are successful with gifted students might also apply to the wider spectrum of underachieving students. Whether gifted students actually require interventions that are qualitatively different from nongifted underachievers has yet to be determined.

Finally, researchers and practitioners must translate knowledge and insights about causes and correlates of underachievement into models and strategies that educators can use to develop more effective prevention and intervention programs. First, researchers should begin to explore the relationship between classroom practices and academic underachievement. If unchallenging scholastic environments produce underachieving gifted students, then providing intellectual challenge and stimulation at all grade levels should decrease underachievement. Do schools that differentiate instruction for high-ability students have fewer incidences of underachievement? Does providing part- or full-time gifted programming the occurrence of academic underachievement among the gifted? Is providing intellectual challenge especially critical during a particular age range? Bright, underachieving students might benefit from curriculum differentiation techniques (Renzulli & Smith, 1978; Reis, Burns, & Renzulli, 1992), such as curriculum compacting or Type III enrichment opportunities. These classroom strategies can provide attractive and interesting curricular replacement options and enrichment to advanced students. The literature also presents a variety of other classroom designs, such as self-contained classrooms, and home and school partnerships. Unfortunately, little research has addressed the effectiveness of these options. Most of the self-contained classroom studies lacked suitable control groups. Future research on the effectiveness of separate classes for gifted underachievers should attempt to utilize a quasi-experimental design.

Family, school, and individual factors all seem to contribute to the emergence of underachievement behaviors (Baker, Bridger, & Evans, 1998). Because causes and correlates of underachievement differ, no one intervention reverses underachievement patterns in the full spectrum of gifted underachievers. Further research in this area must focus on developing multiple approaches to both preventing and reversing underachievement. Such approaches would differentiate among different types of underachievement, incorporating both proactive and preventative counseling and innovative instructional interventions. Deficits in self-control or self-regulation may engender underachievement (Borkowski & Thorpe, 1994; Krouse & Krouse, 1981). In addition, researchers should incorporate the knowledge gained from social cognitive theory to combat underachievement (Dai, Moon, & Feldhusen, 1998; Schunk, 1998; Zimmerman, 1989). Interventions that enhance self-efficacy or develop self-regulation may complement other intervention strategies and increase the effectiveness of other interventions. Different types of underachievers may require different proportions of counseling, self-regulation training, and instructional or curricular modifications. Unfortunately, the need for multiple approaches to treatment will complicate the research designs necessary to test the efficacy of underachievement interventions. Therefore, such studies will require the attention of researchers who can utilize sophisticated design techniques.

CONCLUSIONS

The concept of underachievement, though often discussed, is still vaguely defined in the professional literature. The absence of any clear, precise definition of gifted underachievement restricts research-based comparisons and hinders the quest for suitable interventions. Although using a precise operational definition of gifted underachievement clarifies the exact nature of the population being studied, it may also prevent the identification of certain types of potential gifted underachievers. Broad, inclusive definitions of gifted underachievement allow more flexibility in the identification of gifted underachievers. However, such definitions may not adequately distinguish between gifted students who achieve and those who underachieve. The psychological characteristics ascribed to gifted underachievers vary and sometimes contradict each other. The plethora of definitions and identification methods contribute to the difficulty in studying the characteristics of this population. In general, inadequate research has examined the interventions aimed at reversing underachievement. Further research is needed in this area in order to unravel the mystery of why gifted students underachieve and how we can help them succeed.

The research literature mentions only a small number of interventions. Further research and inquiry into this area should address the need for clearly defined, well-researched, and effective interventions for gifted underachievers. These interventions should probably involve counseling and some form of curriculum modification or differentiation. Future research should focus on evaluating the efficacy of both instructional and counseling treatments. As the next millennium approaches, researchers must move beyond describing this educational dilemma and instead strive to find solutions.

REFERENCES

Anderson, E. S., & Keith, T. Z. (1997). A longitudinal test of a model of academic success for at-risk high school students. *The Journal of Educational Research, 90*, 259–268.

Baker, J. A., Bridger, R., & Evans, K. (1998). Models of underachievement among gifted preadolescents: The role of personal, family, and school factors. *Gifted Child Quarterly, 42*, 5–14.

Baldwin, A. Y. (1987). I'm Black but look at me, I am also gifted. *Gifted Child Quarterly, 31*, 180–185.

Barton, J. M., & Starnes, W. T. (1988). Identifying distinguishing characteristics of gifted and talented learning disabled students. *Roeper Review, 12*, 23–29.

Baum, S. M., Owen, S. V., & Dixon, J. (1991). *To be gifted and learning disabled: From identification to practical intervention strategies.* Mansfield, CT: Creative Learning Press.

Baum, S. M., Olenchak, F. R., & Owen, S. V. (1998). Gifted students with attention deficits: Fact and/or fiction? Or, can we see the forest for the trees? *Gifted Child Quarterly, 42*, 96–104.

Baum, S. M., Renzulli, J. S., & Hébert, T. P. (1995a). *The prism metaphor: A new paradigm for reversing underachievement* (CRS95310). Storrs, CT: University of Connecticut, The National Research Center on the Gifted and Talented.

Baum, S. M., Renzulli, J. S., & Hébert, T. P. (1995b). Reversing underachievement: Creative productivity as a systematic intervention. *Gifted Child Quarterly, 39*, 224–235.

Baymur, F., & Patterson, C. H. (1965). Three methods of assisting underachieving high school students. In M. Kornrich (Ed.), *Underachievement* (pp. 501–513). Springfield, IL: Charles C. Thomas.

Belcastro, F. P. (1985). Use of behavior modification strategies: A review of the research. *Roeper Review, 7*, 184–189.

Berndt, T. J. (1999). Friends' influence on students' adjustment to school. *Educational Psychologist, 34*, 15–28.

Bireley. M. (1995). *Crossover children: A sourcebook for helping students who are gifted and learning disabled*. Reston, VA: The Council for Exceptional Children.

Borkowski, J. G., & Thorpe, P. K. (1994). Self-regulation and motivation: A life-span perspective on underachievement. In D. H. Schunk & B.J. Zimmerman (Eds.), *Self-regulation of learning and practice* (pp. 45–74). Hillsdale, NJ: Lawrence Erlbaum.

Borland, J. H. (1989). *Planning and implementing programs for the gifted*. New York: Teachers College Press.

Bricklin B., & Bricklin, P. M. (1967). *Bright child—poor grades: The psychology of underachievement*. New York: Delacorte.

Broedel, J., Ohlsen, M., Proff, F., & Southard, C. (1965). The effects of group counseling on gifted underachieving adolescents. In M. Kornrich (Ed.), *Underachievement* (pp. 514–528). Springfield, IL: Charles C. Thomas.

Brown, B. B. (1982). The extent and effects of peer pressure among high school students: A retrospective analysis. *Journal of Youth and Adolescence, 11*, 121–133.

Brown, B. B., Mounts, N., Lamborn, S. D., & Steinberg, L. (1993). Parenting practices and peer group affiliation in adolescence. *Child Development, 64*, 467–482.

Bruns, J. H. (1992). *They can but they don't*. New York: Viking Penguin.

Busch, B., & Nuttall, R. L. (1995). Students who seem to be unmotivated may have attention deficits. *Diagnostique, 21*(1), 43–59.

Butler-Por, N. (1987). *Underachievers in school: Issues and intervention*. Chichester, England: John Wiley and Sons.

Butler-Por, N. (1993). Underachieving gifted students. In K. A. Heller, F.J. Mönks, & A. H. Passow (Eds.), *International handbook of research and development of giftedness and talent* (pp. 649–668). Oxford: Pergamon.

Chen, X. (1997, June). *Students' peer groups in high school: The pattern and relationship to educational outcomes*. (NCES 97055). Washington, DC: U.S. Department of Education.

Clark, B. (1983). *Growing up gifted* (2nd ed.). Columbus, OH: Merrill.

Clark, B. (1988). *Growing up gifted* (3rd ed.). Columbus, OH: Merrill.

Clasen, D. R., & Brown, B. (1985). The multidimensionality of peer pressure in adolescence. *Journal of Youth and Adolescence, 14*, 451–467.

Clasen, D. R., & Clasen, R. E. (1995). Underachievement of highly able students and the peer society. *Gifted and Talented International, 10*(2), 67–75.

Colangelo, N., Kerr, B., Christensen, P., & Maxey, J. (1993). A comparison of gifted underachievers and gifted high achievers. *Gifted Child Quarterly, 37*, 155–160.

Dai, D. Y., Moon, S. M., & Feldhusen, J. F. (1998). Achievement motivation and gifted students: A social cognitive perspective. *Educational Psychologist, 33*, 45–63.

Delisle, J. (1982). Learning to underachieve. *Roeper Review, 4*, 16–18.

Diaz, E. I. (1998). Perceived factors influencing the academic underachievement of talented students of Puerto Rican descent. *Gifted Child Quarterly, 42*, 105–122.

Dowdall, C. B., & Colangelo, N. (1982). Underachieving gifted students: Review and implications. *Gifted Child Quarterly, 26*, 179–184.

Emerick, L. J. (1988). *Academic underachievement among the gifted: Students' perceptions of factors that reverse the pattern*. Unpublished doctoral dissertation, University of Connecticut, Storrs.

Emerick, L. J. (1992). Academic underachievement among the gifted: Students' perceptions of factors that reverse the pattern. *Gifted Child Quarterly, 36*, 140–146.

Fehrenbach, C. R. (1993). Underachieving students: Intervention programs that work. *Roeper Review, 16*, 88–90.

Fernandez, R. M., Hirano-Nakanishi, M., & Paulsen, R. (1989). Dropping out among Hispanic youth. *Social Science Research, 18,* 21–52.

Fine, M. J., & Pitts, R. (1980). Intervention with underachieving gifted children: Rationale and strategies. *Gifted Child Quarterly, 24,* 51–55.

Fink, M. B. (1965). Objectification of data used in underachievement self-concept study. In M. Kornrich (Ed.), *Underachievement* (pp. 79–86). Springfield, IL: Charles C. Thomas.

Ford, D. Y. (1992). Determinants of underachievement as perceived by gifted, above average, and average Black students. *Roeper Review, 14,* 130–136.

Ford, D. Y. (1996). *Reversing underachievement among gifted Black students.* New York: Teachers College Press.

Frankel, E. (1965). A comparative study of achieving and underachieving boys of high intellectual ability. In M. Kornrich (Ed.), *Underachievement* (pp. 87–101). Springfield, IL: Charles C. Thomas.

Frasier, M. M., & Passow, A. H. (1994). *Toward a new paradigm for identifying talent potential* (Research Monograph 94112). Storrs, CT: University of Connecticut, The National Research Center on the Gifted and Talented.

Frick, P. J., Kamphaus, R. W., Lahey, B. B., Loeber, R., Christ, M. A. G., Hart, E. L., & Tannenbaum, L. E. (1991). Academic underachievement and behavior disorders. *Journal of Consulting and Clinical Psychology, 59,* 189–194.

Gallagher, J. J. (1991). Personal patterns of underachievement. *Journal for the Education of the Gifted, 14,* 221–233.

Gowan, J. C. (1957). Dynamics of the underachievement of gifted students. *Exceptional Children, 24,* 98–101.

Green, K., Fine, M.J., & Tollefson, N. (1988). Family systems characteristics and underachieving gifted males. *Gifted Child Quarterly, 32,* 267–272.

Heacox, D. (1991). *Up from underachievement.* Minneapolis, MN: Free Spirit.

Hinshaw, S. P. (1992a). Academic underachievement, attention deficits, and aggression: Comorbidity and implications for intervention. *Journal of Consulting and Clinical Psychology, 60,* 893–903.

Hinshaw, S. P. (1992b). Externalizing behavior problems and academic underachievement in childhood and adolescence: Causal relationships and underlying mechanisms. *Psychological Bulletin, 111*(1), 127–155.

Holland, V. (1998). Underachieving boys: Problems and solutions. *Support for Learning, 13,* 174–178.

Janos, P. M., & Robinson, N. (1985). Psychosocial development in intellectually gifted children. In F. Horowitz & M. O'Brien (Eds.), *The gifted and talented: Developmental perspectives* (pp. 149–195). Washington, DC: American Psychological Association.

Jeon, K. (1990, August). *Counseling and guidance for gifted underachievers.* Paper presented at the First Southeast Asian Regional Conference on Giftedness. Manila, Philippines. (ERIC Document Delivery Service ED328051)

Jeon, K. W., & Feldhusen, J. F. (1993). Teachers' and parents' perceptions of social-psychological factors of underachievement of the gifted in Korea and the United States. *Gifted Education International, 9,* 115–119.

Kanoy, R. C., Johnson, B. W., & Kanoy, K. W. (1980). Locus of control and self-concept in achieving and underachieving bright elementary students. *Psychology in the Schools, 17,* 395–399.

Khatena, J. (1982). *Educational psychology of the gifted.* New York: John Wiley and Sons.

Krouse, J. H., & Krouse, H. J. (1981). Toward a multimodal theory of underachievement. *Educational Psychologist, 16,* 151–164.

Laffoon, K. S., Jenkins-Friedman, R., & Tollefson, N. (1989). Causal attributions of underachieving gifted, achieving gifted, and nongifted students. *Journal for the Education of the Gifted, 13*, 4–21.

Lupart, J. L., & Pyryt, M. C. (1996). "Hidden gifted" students: Underachiever prevalence and profile. *Journal for the Education of the Gifted, 20*, 36–53.

Mandel, H. P., & Marcus, S. I. (1988). *The psychology of underachievement.* New York: John Wiley and Sons.

Mandel, H. P., & Marcus, S. I. (1995). *Could do better.* New York: John Wiley and Sons.

Mather, N., & Udall, A. J. (1985). The identification of gifted underachievers using the Woodcock-Johnson psychoeducational battery. *Roeper Review, 8*, 54–56.

McCall, R. B., Evahn, C., & Kratzer, L. (1992). *High school underachievers: What do they achieve as adults?* Newbury Park, CA: Sage.

McNabb, T. (1997). From potential to performance: Motivational issues for gifted students. In N. Colangelo & G. A. Davis (Eds.), *Handbook of gifted education* (2nd ed., pp. 408–415). Boston: Allyn and Bacon.

Mickelson, R. A. (1990). The attitude achievement paradox among Black adolescents. *Sociology of Education, 63*, 44–61.

Neisser, U., Boodoo, G., Bouchard, T. J., Boykin, A.W., Brody, N., Ceci, S. J., Halpern, D. F., Loehlin, J.C., Perloff, R., Sternberg, R. J., & Urbina, S. (1996). Intelligence: Knowns and unknowns. *American Psychologist, 51*, 77–101.

Pendarvis, E. D., Howley, A. A., & Howley C. B. (1990). *The abilities of gifted children.* Englewood Cliffs, NJ: Prentice Hall.

Pirozzo, R. (1982). Gifted underachievers. *Roeper Review, 4*, 18–21.

Raph, J. B., Goldberg, M. L., & Passow, A. H. (1966). *Bright underachievers.* New York: Teachers College Press.

Redding, R. E. (1990). Learning preferences and skill patterns among underachieving gifted adolescents. *Gifted Child Quarterly, 34*, 72–75.

Reis, S. M. (1998). Underachievement for some—dropping out with dignity for others. *Communicator, 29*(1), 1, 19–24.

Reis, S. M., Burns, D. E., & Renzulli, J. S. (1992). *Curriculum compacting: A guide for teachers.* Mansfield, CT: Creative Learning Press.

Reis, S. M., Hébert, T. P., Diaz, E. P., Maxfield, L. R., & Ratley, M. E. (1995). *Case studies of talented students who achieve and underachieve in an urban high school* (Research Monograph 95120). Storrs, CT: University of Connecticut, National Research Center for the Gifted and Talented.

Reis, S. M., Neu, T. W., & McGuire, J. M. (1995). *Talents in two places: Case studies of high ability students with learning disabilities who have achieved.* (Research Monograph 95114). Storrs, CT: University of Connecticut, National Research Center for the Gifted and Talented.

Renzulli, J. S. (1977). *The Enrichment Triad Model: A guide for developing defensible programs for the gifted and talented.* Mansfield Center, CT: Creative Learning Press.

Renzulli, J. S., Reid, B. D., & Gubbins, E.J. (1992). *Setting an agenda: Research priorities for the gifted and talented through the year 2000.* Storrs, CT: University of Connecticut, The National Research Center on the Gifted and Talented.

Renzulli, J. S., & Reis, S. R. (1985). *The Schoolwide Enrichment Model: A comprehensive plan for educational excellence.* Mansfield Center, CT: Creative Learning Press.

Renzulli, J. S., & Reis, S. R. (1997). *The Schoolwide Enrichment Model: A how-to guide for educational excellence.* Mansfield Center, CT: Creative Learning Press.

Renzulli, J. S., & Smith, L. H. (1978). *The Learning Styles Inventory: A measure of student preference for instructional techniques.* Mansfield Center, CT: Creative Learning Press.

Richert, E. S. (1991). Patterns of underachievement among gifted students. In J. H. Borland (Series Ed.) & M. Bireley & J. Genshaft (Vol. Eds.), *Understanding the gifted adolescent,* (pp. 139–162). New York: Teachers College Press.

Rimm, S. (1995). *Why bright kids get poor grades and what you can do about it.* New York: Crown Trade Paperbacks.

Rimm, S. (1997a). An underachievement epidemic. *Educational Leadership, 54*(7), 18–22.

Rimm, S. (1997b). Underachievement syndrome: A national epidemic. In N. Colangelo & G. A. Davis (Eds.), *Handbook of Gifted Education* (2nd ed., pp. 416–435). Boston: Allyn and Bacon.

Rimm, S., Cornale, M., Manos, R., & Behrend, J. (1989). *Guidebook for implementing the tri-focal underachievement program for schools.* Watertown, WI: Apple.

Rimm, S., & Lowe, B. (1988). Family environments of underachieving gifted students. *Gifted Child Quarterly, 32,* 353–358.

Rumberger, R. W., & Larson, K. A. (1998). Toward explaining differences in educational achievement among Mexican American language minority students. *Sociology of Education, 71,* 68–93.

Schneider, S. (1998, Fall). Overcoming underachievement. (Rev. ed.). *Bulletin of the Pennsylvania Association of Gifted Education,* 1–7.

Schunk, D. H. (1998, November). *Motivation and self-regulation among gifted learners.* Paper presented at the annual meeting of the National Association of Gifted Children, Louisville, KY.

Schweitzgebel, R. (1965). Underachievement: A common fallacy. In M. Kornrich (Ed.), *Underachievement* (pp. 484–487). Springfield, IL: Charles C. Thomas.

Silverman, L. K. (1993). Counseling families. In L. K. Silverman (Ed.), *Counseling the gifted and talented.* Denver, CO: Love.

Supplee, P. L. (1990). *Reaching the gifted underachiever.* New York: Teachers College Press.

Taylor, R. D. (1994). Risk and resilience: Contextual influences on the development of African American adolescents. In M. C. Wang & E. W. Gordon (Eds.), *Educational resilience in inner city America,* (pp. 119–137). Hillsdale, NJ: Lawrence Erlbaum.

Thorndike, R. L. (1963). *The concepts of over and underachievement.* New York: Teachers College Press.

Tomlinson, C. A., Callahan, C. M., & Lelli, K. M. (1997). Challenging expectations: Case studies of culturally diverse young children. *Gifted Child Quarterly, 41,* 5–17.

Van Boxtel, H. W., & Mönks, F. J. (1992). General, social, and academic self-concepts of gifted adolescents. *Journal of Youth and Adolescence, 21,* 169–186.

Weiner, I. B. (1992). *Psychological disturbance in adolescence* (2nd ed.). New York: John Wiley and Sons.

Whitmore, J. R. (1980). *Giftedness, conflict, and underachievement.* Boston: Allyn and Bacon.

Whitmore, J. R. (1986). Understanding a lack of motivation to excel. *Gifted Child Quarterly, 30,* 66–69.

Wolfle, J. A. (1991). Underachieving gifted males: Are we missing the boat? *Roeper Review, 13,* 181–184.

Zilli, M. G. (1971). Reasons why the gifted adolescent underachieves and some of the implications of guidance and counseling to this problem. *Gifted Child Quarterly, 15,* 279–292.

Zimmerman, B. J. (1989). A social cognitive view of self-regulated academic learning. *Journal of Educational Psychology, 81,* 329–339.

14

A Functional Model for Counseling Parents of Gifted Students

David F. Dettmann

Nicholas Colangelo

The purpose of this article is to present a model of parent-school involvement in furthering the educational development of gifted students. The major premise is that the involvement of parents in the education of their gifted child can be a significant positive force. In order for parents to effectively participate in this educational venture the cooperation and support of school personnel are needed. While many of the ideas presented in this paper are applicable to various school personnel such as teachers and administrators, our focus is specifically on the role of the school counselor in working with parents of gifted. School counselors have traditionally worked with parents; however, they have not usually played a major role in working specifically with parents of gifted (Colangelo & Zaffran, 1979). The model delineated here serves not only as a

Editor's Note: From Dettmann, D. F., & Colangelo, N. (1980). A functional model for counseling parents of gifted students. *Gifted Child Quarterly*, 24(4), 158-161. © 1980 National Association for Gifted Children. Reprinted with permission.

framework for parents to actively engage in the education of their children, but also gives specific direction for counselors in becoming actively involved in the education of gifted.

In a report to Congress, Marland (1972) noted that the most neglected minority in American education was that group of youngsters identified as gifted. Thus parents of gifted children face the probable situation that their child will be in an educational environment not appropriate to his or her needs. Parents aware of this possibility might become apprehensive about the kind of education their gifted child will receive.

Ross (1964) stated that when parents are told their child has been identified as gifted, they react similarly to parents who are told their child has a learning disability. What parents react to is not so much that their child is gifted, but that their child is different; thus raising concerns about the social adjustment and happiness of their child. Concomitantly, most parents have the experience of "normal" upbringing and anticipate raising "normal" children (Ross, 1964), thereby feeling uncertain and even threatened when they are confronted with raising an exceptional child.

Additionally, the field of gifted and talented is fraught with myths and stereotypes (Colangelo, 1979; Solano, Note 1) and parents are subject to various misconceptions about giftedness. Parents may hold stereotypic views which can interfere with understanding their own gifted child.

Historically, parents of exceptional children, (e.g., mentally retarded) have had little choice about their child's placement in a special program (Ross, 1964). However, parents of gifted students face a different situation. These parents are often faced with the decision of whether or not to allow their child to participate in a special gifted program. In virtually every gifted program in the country parents make the decision of letting a son or daughter participate. What is especially difficult in making such a decision is that there is considerable disagreement over the kinds of special programs which truly help gifted youngsters (Baer, 1980; Goldberg, 1965; Marland, 1972; Renzulli, 1977, 1980; Stanley, 1976a, 1976b; Weiler, 1978), and whether they might actually cause harm in terms of peer relations (Clark, 1979). In the face of this confusion, parents are asked to make decisions.

We believe that parents should have the opportunity to make decisions in planning for the education of their children. However, we cannot expect parents to be comfortable or make sound decisions if they are not well informed. Dunlap (1958) stressed that parents often sense that their child is bright but cannot accurately discern actual abilities of the child. In this situation it is difficult for parents to assess what would be the most beneficial program for their child.

Educators in the field of gifted essentially agree on the important benefits of parents and family in the education and social development of gifted children (O'Neill, 1978). Morrow and Wilson (1961) reported that healthy relations and parent-child interactions are important to the positive adjustment of gifted youngsters. Sanborn (1979) states, "It probably goes without saying that parents play powerful roles in the development of their children. For better or for worse, the capacities and proclivities of the child reflect the impact of the parents" (p. 396).

SUMMARY REVIEW OF LITERATURE ON PARENTS OF GIFTED

One of the important functions of educators, particularly counselors, is to work with parents. Since parents of gifted children have some needs peculiar to their children's high ability, counselors must be knowledgeable about these specific needs. In an exhaustive review of literature on the specific needs of parents of the gifted (Colangelo & Dettmann, Note 2) four main issues emerged that are of interest to educators, particularly counselors, in the area of gifted.

1. First, parents are confused about their role in identifying the gifted child. Some parents (and schools) feel that this is entirely the school's responsibility, while other parents want to be active in the identification process. Yet, many parents indicated that as much as they would like to be involved, they don't know what to look for in their children. Thus, parents lack knowledge about identifying characteristics of the gifted child, as well as clear direction about their role in the process.

2. A second general issue reflected the deep concern and anxiety parents have with their gifted child's achievement. The empirical literature in this area has failed to provide clear and consistent direction for parents. For example, parental pressure has been reported as associated with both achievement (Nichols, 1964) and underachievement (Raph, Goldberg, & Passow, 1966). The literature more readily available to parents of gifted consists largely of the recent proliferation of popular "how-to" books (e.g., Delp & Martinson, 1977; Ginsberg & Harrison, 1977). The typical formula for parents includes expanding reading and extracurricular activities for the child, as well as the very general admonition to be involved with the child at home. The problem with these kinds of resources is that they do not provide substantial information for parents nor do they address the complexities and subtleties of the family interactions involved with a gifted child.

3. A multitude of issues in the literature revolved around parental problems and concerns with family relationships and gifted children. Frequently cited areas of concern were discipline and preventing or reducing sibling rivalry. Like the achievement issues, there was no systematic attention to the solution of these problems. Also, parents often reported that they had personal difficulties resulting from having a gifted child in the family. Commonly voiced problems included marital relationship changes, lack of communication with each other about expectations and standards for the gifted child, and a host of fears about potential or perceived maladjustment of the child. The underlying concern in most fears seemed to be that parents of gifted feel inadequately prepared to provide for their gifted child.

4. Finally, the issue of parents' relationships with the school was frequently referred to in the literature. From our readings it was readily apparent that parents do want to participate and assist in the education of their gifted children, however, they are confused as to their roles in this area and what to expect from schools. Parents sometimes place all the responsibility with the schools, yet are dissatisfied with the results. At the other extreme, parents may be more aggressive in taking responsibility for determining and demanding that their child's educational needs be met, with the frequent result of fractured school-home relations.

From these key points it should be evident to counselors that parents of gifted students confront a variety of issues. It is important that counselors become aware of these issues if they are to provide assistance.

COUNSELING APPROACHES

In order for counselors to understand more fully the options and approaches they can take with parents of gifted, we have devised a model for assisting counselors. The model presented depicts our view of three basic counseling approaches. While we realize that the three approaches are not mutually exclusive, the primary focus for each approach is different. Also, each approach has advantages and disadvantages that need to be considered.

The *Parent-Centered Approach* relies almost exclusively on the motivation and resources of the parents. The advantages here are that parents are viewed as central in the intellectual and affective development of their children. This approach provides for an extensive role for parents, a role that has (in practice) diminished as schooling has become more institutionalized and separate from parent participation. This approach is critically limited by the resources, knowledge, and active interests of parents. Many parents simply cannot provide for the various needs of gifted and the opportunities for the development of talents in their children could be limited by such factors as socioeconomic status and amount of education.

The *School-Centered Approach* has more potential in terms of providing ongoing programs. Schools can institute long-term programs which can provide for a larger number of gifted students. (In the parent-centered approach, parents would typically only provide for their own child.) Also, schools can readily call upon trained experts (e.g., psychologists, consultants) to help them incorporate programs. While this approach has obvious advantages, there are also limitations that need to be noted. In the school-centered approach the needs of gifted are subject to the priorities of the school, and some schools do not have the resources or commitment to provide adequate services. Counselors and teachers for the most part would unilaterally make educational decisions, thus keeping the role of the parents at a minimum level. One consequence of this posture is that counselors cannot make use of insights based on information from parents. This is unfortunate since Sanborn (1979) noted that counselors

Figure I   Three approaches counselors can take in working with parents of gifted

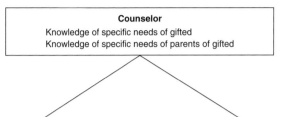

Counselor
Knowledge of specific needs of gifted
Knowledge of specific needs of parents of gifted

Parent-Centered Approach

Assumptions

- Parents are responsible for intellectual & affective development of child
- Home environment is most important to development of gifted
- Parents should seek outside experts or provide for enrichment activities if they feel child needs them

Role of Counselor

- Essentially provide information and advice as to what parents can do
- Encourage parents to actively seek suitable experiences for child

Role of Parents

- Very active in providing for their child
- Role is as active as financial sources and parent interest will allow

School-Centered Approach

Assumptions

- School are responsible for intellectual & affective development of child
- School environment is most important to development of gifted
- School should establish appropriate gifted programs

Role of Counselor

- Expert in providing for needs of gifted
- Help parents see that needs of gifted can be best met through experts and school programs

Role of Parents

- Passive participants
- Not seen as a teacher for their children
- Role of parents essentially confined to parent/ school organizations, etc.

Partnership Approach

Assumptions

- Counselors have expertise that can be beneficial to parents of gifted
- Parents of gifted have knowledge and expertise that the counselor & school need to understand child
- Parents are partners with educators in meeting educational and affective needs of gifted
- Parents, with help of counselor, can be actively involved in the learning process of their child

Roles of Counselor & Parents

- Team worker with parents
- Provide information to parents and elicit information about child
- Parents and counselor make joint decisions on best direction to meet educational needs of gifted

can be more effective with gifted when they receive extensive information from parents.

In considering long-term benefits, it is our contention that the most effective and promising approach is the *Partnership Approach*. Because it synthesizes the influences and resources of home and school, it requires active participation from both parents and counselors. Such joint responsibility is consistent with research studies that emphasize the importance of home and school in meeting the counseling needs of gifted. We also believe the partnership approach to be more rewarding to parents and counselors as well as to the child. Parents have an opportunity to actively participate in meeting the educational needs of their child. The counselor would have support and access to extensive information that would not otherwise be available based on typical school observations. Both parents and counselors would be combining their resources and at the same time maintaining joint decision-making responsibility in educational planning. The gifted child would benefit from this partnership since he/she is not facing discord between home and school. For this child home and school life are integrated, making learning a continuous process.

IMPLICATIONS

Working with parents is being recognized by counselors and other school personnel as an important factor in the educational development of gifted youngsters. However, there is presently no coherent and systematic approach to working with parents. Essentially, parent participation in gifted programs has evolved haphazardly. The uniqueness of the model presented in this article is that it offers counselors (and other educators) a means of developing a coherent program with parents. Based on this model counselors can understand and describe which approach of the three mentioned they are presently using, as well as plan for which approach they want to incorporate. Using the model, counselors and other educators can formulate program objectives and evaluation procedures. Counselors thus have a framework for defining their role with parents of gifted.

REFERENCE NOTES

1. Solano, C. H. *Teacher and pupil stereotypes of gifted boys and girls.* Unpublished manuscript, The Johns Hopkins University, 1977.

2. Colangelo, N. & Dettmann, D. F. Parents of gifted children. In R. Greene & R. Weisburg (Eds.), *Exceptional children.* Interstate Publishers: in press.

REFERENCES

Baer, N. A. Programs for the gifted: A present or a paradox? *Phi Delta Kappan*, 1980, *61*, 621–623.

Clark, B. *Growing up gifted: Developing the potential of children at home and at school.* Columbus, OH: Charles E. Merrill, 1979.

Colangelo, N. Myths and stereotypes of gifted children: Awareness for the classroom teacher. In N. Colangelo, C. H. Foxley, & D. Dustin (Eds.), *Multicultural non-sexist education: A human relations approach.* Dubuque, IA: Kendall/Hunt, 1979.

Colangelo, N., & Zaffran, R. T. (Eds.). *New voices in counseling the gifted.* Dubuque, IA: Kendall/Hunt, 1979.

Delp, J. L., & Martinson, R. A. *A handbook for parents of gifted and talented.* Ventura, CA: Ventura County Superintendent of Schools Office, 1977.

Dunlap, J. M. The education of children with high mental ability. In W. M. Cruickshank & G. O. Johnson (Eds.). *Education of exceptional children and youth.* Englewood Cliffs, NJ: Prentice-Hall, 1958.

Ginsberg, G., & Harrison, C. H. *How to help your gifted child: A handbook for parents and teachers.* NYC: Monarch Press, 1977.

Goldberg, M. L. *Research on the talented.* Columbia University: Bureau of Publications, 1965.

Marland, S. P. *Education of the gifted and talented.* Report to the Congress of the United States by the US Commissioner of Education. Washington, DC: US Government Printing Office, 1972.

Morrow, W. R., & Wilson, R. C. Family relations of bright high achieving and under-achieving high school boys. *Child Development*, 1961, *32*, 501–510.

Nichols, R. C. Parental attitudes of mothers of intelligent adolescents and creativity of their children. *Child Development*, 1964, *35*, 1041–1049.

O'Neill, K. K. Parent involvement: A key to the education of gifted children. *Gifted Child Quarterly*, 1978, 22, 235–242.

Raph, J. B., Goldberg, M. L., & Passow, A. H. *Bright underachievers.* NYC: Teachers College Press, 1966.

Renzulli, J. S. *The enrichment triad model: A guide for developing defensible programs for the gifted and talented.* Wethersfield, CT: Creative Learning Press, 1977.

Renzulli, J. S. What we don't know about programming for the gifted and talented. *Phi Delta Kappan*, 1980, *61*, 601–602.

Ross, A. O. *The exceptional child in the family.* NYC: Grune & Stratton, 1964.

Sanborn, M. P. Working with parents. In N. Colangelo & R. T. Zaffrann (Eds.), *New voices in counseling the gifted.* Dubuque, IA: Kendall/Hunt, 1979.

Stanley, J. C. Identifying and nurturing the intellectually gifted. *Phi Delta Kappan*, 1976a, *58*, 234–237.

Stanley, J. C. The case for extreme educational acceleration of intellectually brilliant youths. *Gifted Child Quarterly*, 1976b, *20*, 66–75.

Weiler, D. The alpha children: California's brave new world for the gifted. *Phi Delta Kappan*, 1978, *60*, 185–187.

15

Counseling Gifted Adolescents: A Curriculum Model for Students, Parents, and Professionals

Thomas M. Buescher

Northwestern University

Providing appropriate counseling for gifted and talented students requires deliberate effort to increase knowledge about self-development, awareness of social realities, and understanding about the interaction of conflict and intimacy in adolescence. This article presents an overview of a two-tiered curriculum model used to proactively counsel and support the growth of young gifted adolescents. Key developmental issues form the core of the curriculum, while integrated learning strategies are applied to two audiences: gifted adolescents themselves, and their parents, teachers, and counselors. Features of the model, a sample unit design, and suggestions for implementing the curriculum conclude the article.

Editor's Note: From Buescher, T. M. (1987). Counseling gifted adolescents: A curriculum model for students, parents, and professionals. *Gifted Child Quarterly*, *31*(2), 90-94. © 1987 National Association for Gifted Children. Reprinted with permission.

INTRODUCTION

Supporting and nurturing young people from a proactive or preventative stance is not unique to the counseling curriculum model described here. Counseling psychologists, social workers, and educational psychologists have emphasized the need to approach mental health issues primarily from an information and prevention perspective. But typically such strategies are focused on problems like substance abuse, depression, peer aggression, or sexual acting out as responses to normal problems of adjustment.

Recently, those who work with gifted and talented young people have begun to explore seriously and develop more proactive approaches in the area of individual and group counseling (Colangelo & Zaffran, 1979; Delisle, 1984a; Foster, 1985, Silverman, in press; Buescher and Higham, 1984). These have focused on particular behaviors and coping mechanisms employed by gifted students as they seek to accommodate or compensate for high levels of ability.

Effectively guiding and counseling gifted adolescents through the use of a specialized curriculum presupposes several important first principles enunciated by clinical and educational specialists. Three seem most pertinent for the moment. First, effective guidance and counseling occurs at a proactive, preventative stage rather than a reactive, intervening stage. Second, gifted adolescents can be immobilized by the conflictual "push" of others' expectations (parents, teachers, and peers) and the "pull" of their own extraordinary standards. And third, an individual adolescent's multiple talents (multipotentialities) and "over-exciteabilities" provide keen insight into the dynamics of adjustment being employed or ignored (Piechowski & Colangelo, 1982). Delisle has emphasized the need to start the counseling process at a less provocative, more supportive point in a young person's life (1984a). Crisis intervention, while desirable and necessary in some key moments, should never become the treatment of choice. Adolescents in particular are too efficient at hiding critical symptoms until difficult outcomes are inevitable.

The counseling curriculum described here has as its primary focus the elaborate discovery, conceptualization, and integration of essential developmental issues. Intensive problem solving and adjustment "under fire" are best accomplished in individual and family counseling situations.

IMPORTANT ASPECTS OF COMING TO KNOW

Knowledge, particularly about oneself, is not gained by accident. Incidental learning may account for some initial steps of novel learning, but it is more often than not only a shadow of the real knowledge that is eventually retained. If adolescents are to gain productive insight into their own growth and development, identity, and career potentials, an effective strategy for assuring their "coming to know" must be employed.

The core of the counseling curriculum is a three-step learning model developed by Smith, Goodman, and Meredith (1982) and refined by a number of curriculum designers interested in applying information processing theory to specialized areas of education (see Note). This model for *coming to know* assumes that new information is built on two foundations: (1) past, examined experience, and (2) present, constructed generalizations (concepts). An individual who is "coming to know" must work through three stages, *perceiving, ideating, and presenting*, before fully *knowing* a particular concept. Unfortunately, the first stage of the model, *perceiving*, is the step most often emphasized in the learning process. Educators and students alike are hounded by inservice activities and coursework that over stress the perception of new information. As subsequent research and evaluation has shown, perceiving is only the first part of coming to know; much more must follow before a concept is gained or a behavior affected and changed (Buescher, 1982).

The second stage of the process, *ideating*, is difficult to explain but easy to recognize. When new ideas or perceptions strike one's psyche, there is typically a good deal of clatter and noise. Old ideas and concepts are resistant to change. Piaget and others have described this phenomenon, remarking how an individual's conceptual framework is sometimes resistant to further accommodations—particularly when important values are linked to the status quo. Yet, disequilibrium, whether in the physical or conceptual sense, is a necessary partner in learning important new concepts. So it is in this curriculum's model for coming to know: perceptions give rise to dissonance, and it is this disturbance or ideating that drives the learner to a better resolution.

That is why the third and final stage, *presenting*, is so critical an element. By formally "presenting" the resolution of how new knowledge has meshed with or pushed aside the old, an individual achieves ownership of the product created, a new concept or generalization. Smith et al. (1982) argue that it is the new generalization—the artifact of perception, experience, and formalized thought—that sets the stage for further levels of perceiving, ideating, and presenting, and ultimately effects behavior change.

In the context of the counseling curriculum described below, the three stages of coming to know form an essential framework for the acquisition and use of new concepts about being or understanding adolescence among gifted and talented students. Giving adolescents information as a proactive strategy in counseling is insufficient; ideating and presenting must be equally facilitated before the process is complete.

KEY ISSUES FOCUS THE CURRICULUM

Four major topics focus the counseling curriculum: Adolescent growth and development; Identity and adjustment; Changes in relationships; and Career paths. These four broad topics provide an umbrella for a variety of investigations undertaken by individual learners, small groups, or classes. (See Figure 1).

Depending upon the nature of the audience (adolescents, or their parents, counselors, or teachers) and the length of time provided, emphasis can be given to one or more of the key issues. Since all four areas are integrally linked by experiences at home and school, it is easy to combine two or more into thematic investigations that cut across areas of study. Young adolescents, for example, might carefully explore how changes in body size, structure, and hormonal balance affect their image among peers, the stress they experience, and the feelings they have toward families and friends. By using all four issues to build the curriculum, natural interactions within the adolescent process and passage can be exploited to enhance learning.

Important resources for a counselor or teacher guiding the process might include: an overview of the adolescent process (Offer, Ostrov, & Howard, 1981; Elkind, 1984; Buescher, 1985); systematic examination of the landscape of adolescent life (Csikszentimihalyi & Larson, 1984); young people's own experiences and responses to being gifted (Galbraith, 1983; Delisle, 1984b); clinical information about problems encountered by adolescents (McCoy, 1982; Buescher & Higham, 1984); and descriptions of changes that occur in relationships between adolescents and their families and friends (Montemayor, 1984; Youniss & Smollar, 1985).

THE CURRICULUM MODEL IN ACTION

As described earlier (Buescher, 1984), the counseling curriculum is built upon a language and experience base. The major influence for that decision was James Britton's (1971) seminal work on the role of language for thinking and action among children.

In an elaborate exploration of the powerful mediating role of written language among older students, Britton and Burgess (1978) studied the structure, content, and style of young people's writing between the ages of eleven and eighteen. Their investigation verified the existence of a developmental progression within a writer's perspective: first as "expressive", then as "transactional", and finally as "poetic."

Prior to adolescence, young writers used written language primarily to *express* private feelings, personal responses, and formative experiences. By early adolescence, however, a second perspective had been assumed: using language to carefully communicate with a known (or at least presumed) *reader*. Young adolescents were visibly aware that a person would read what they had written, and as a result, sought to present ideas, personalities, and experiences in a concrete, tangible fashion. By later adolescence, the young writer was most interested in helping the reader develop new concepts or generalizations from what had been written. Fifteen and sixteen year olds become enamored of more poetic or metaphoric writing styles, urging readers to bring more of themselves into the reading in order to fully comprehend and exploit the writer's text.

Figure I Counseling Process Model

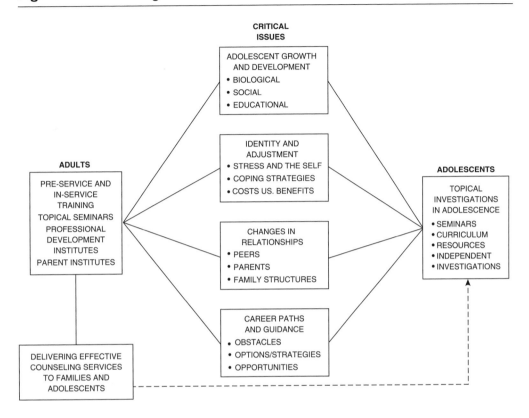

By using Britton's conceptualization of the path of writing process in adolescence, it is possible to create a curricular structure in which gifted adolescents can explore key facets of their lives through classic and popular literature, expository and creative writing, focused lectures and discussions, independent research, and the informal sharing of life experiences.

How is that accomplished? Figure 2 details the general structure of one of the curriculum's units that investigates an interconnected area of adolescent development: biological maturation and psychosocial adjustment.

The purpose of this unit was to have gifted adolescents discover and articulate for themselves several generalizations about the action of increased hormonal imbalance on emotional irritability around family and friends. The unit was initiated by engaging the group in two parallel activities: reading three preselected novels from the popular press that were related to the topic (every student selected two of the three), and constructing a preliminary "concept map" of the group's knowledge about the issue under investigation. Concept maps or webs provide essential clues to the counselor or teacher directing the curriculum about: known facts and concepts, real life experiences of the group members, hazy areas of information, and obvious myths and misconceptions.

Figure 2   Structure for a Unit to Investigate Aspects of Adolescence

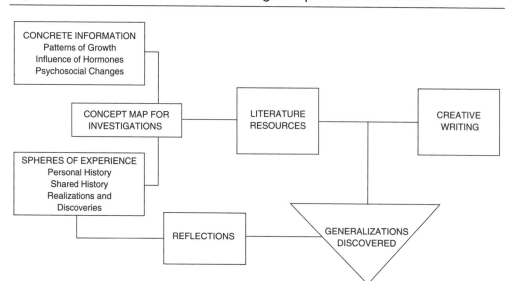

By selectively building new information onto this early concept map, either by direct teaching related to the area under study, or teasing pertinent items out of the literature being analyzed, the teacher and students achieve the first stage of the model, *perceiving*. The perceptions are enlivened by the addition of personal vignettes and experiences drawn from group members.

Having established a comfortable base of new information, the process moves forward to the second stage, *ideating*. Group discussion and parallel creative writing activities probe in what ways the students are working new facts and perceptions into their previous conceptual framework. For example, students might focus their efforts on developing pieces of dialogue between two adolescents. If the situation framing the dialogue is carefully constructed and primed by the teacher, important clues about the writers' underlying feelings, insights, or understanding of unpredictable fluctuations in behavior might be linked to factors analyzed and discussed earlier in the group. Another effective ideating stimulus is the introduction of a new, more complex short story or novel that lends itself to the critical factors under study.

The most rewarding aspect of the curriculum model, however, is the use of discovered generalizations in a formal process of *presenting*. In the sample unit outlined in Figure 2, a particular project activity termed "reflections" has been utilized to accomplish this stage. Given the language-based context of the unit, this *reflection* was expected to be an original piece of creative writing of unspecified length that was complete—in other words, a poem, short story, or dramatic sketch. No content is specified, but the reflections contain a depth of insight that is significant. Typically these pieces of writing "reflect" the most critical aspects of the concepts posed for study, an impressive feat since at no time were these generalizations actually taught! The final presentation product thus confirms and describes the concepts toward which the teacher or counselor was aiming the unit's activities.

SUGGESTIONS FOR IMPLEMENTATION

The counseling curriculum can be a flexible component within any middle school or high school program for gifted and talented students. Ideally, the program should be staffed and implemented by a team of professionals, including program area counselors, teachers, and coordinators. Content expertise in the area of adolescent growth and development can be provided by counseling staff personnel, social workers or psychologists, or outside consultants. With sufficient resources and preparation, qualified staff members can easily direct the learning activities included in the curriculum.

The curriculum can be implemented in several ways. The best use is to plan a definite period of time either within an existing course in personal growth and adjustment (usually taught at the high school level) or literature and writing. In that way, the curriculum can be wedded to other areas of interest and expertise. An equally effective approach is to use the curriculum as the content focus for a monthly series of special topical seminars with gifted and talented adolescents. The design allows students to undertake independent reading, meet as a group for specific discussions, and create particular "presentations" for sharing across grades and ages each month.

The efficacy of the model for training teachers, counselors, and parents of gifted adolescents should not be underestimated. Difficult issues, complex interactions, and the role of others' expectations can be economically addressed by the model's design. The curriculum has grown and improved as a result of its use with secondary school counselors and teachers engaged in inservice training with the Center for Talent Development during the last two years. On site implementation has occurred in a variety of middle school programs for gifted students.

As Benjamin Bloom has noted in his recent retrospective examination of the development of talent (1985), adolescents require sustained support to reach optimal levels of growth and success in areas of exceptional talent. The proactive approach of the counseling curriculum not only encourages accurate insight into one's own development and adjustment, but it emphasizes the important role empathic adults must serve during the adolescent passage.

NOTE

1. Curriculum design projects utilizing and evaluating the learning model include teacher inservice education programs, graduate training programs in curriculum and instruction, elementary and middle school language arts and social studies programs, and specific training activities in preschool special education. Primary investigators

include E. Brooks Smith, Carol Stenroos, David Wallace, and Thomas Buescher. All projects were conducted at Wayne State University, 1976–1982.

REFERENCES

Bloom, Benjamin (Ed.). (1985). *Developing talent in young people.* New York: Ballantine Books.

Britton, J. (1971). *Language and experience.* Miami: University of Miami Press.

Britton, J. and Burgess, T. (1978). *Developmental study of children's writing: 11 to 18.* London: Routledge-Kegan Paul.

Buescher, T. M. (1982). Immersion learning project: Comparative models for inservice training; A final report. Detroit: Wayne State University.

Buescher, T. M. (1984, April). Investigating adolescence through literature and writing with gifted middle school students. Paper presented at the Annual Convention Council for Exceptional Children, Washington, DC.

Buescher, T. M. (1985). A framework for understanding the social and emotional development of gifted and talented adolescents. *Roeper Review, 8*(1), 10–15.

Buescher, T. M. and Higham, S. J. (1984). Young gifted adolescents: Coping with the stresses and strains of being different. Paper presented at 61st Annual Meeting, American Orthopsychiatric Association, Toronto.

Colangelo, N. and Zaffran, R. (1979). Counseling with gifted and talented students. In *New voices in counseling the gifted.* Dubuque, IA: Kendall-Hunt.

Csikszentmihalyi, M. and Larson, R. (1984). *Being adolescent.* New York: Basic Books.

Delisle, J. (1984b). *Gifted children speak out.* New York: Walker and Company.

Delisle, J. (1984a). Vocational problems. In J. Freeman (Ed.), *The psychology of gifted children.* London: John.

Elkind, D. (1984). *All grown up and no place to go.* Reading, MA: Addison-Wesley.

Foster, W. (1985). Helping a child toward individual excellence. In J. Feldhusen (Ed.), *Toward excellence in gifted education.* Denver, CO: Love Publishing Company.

Galbraith, J. (1983). *The gifted kids survival guide for ages 11 to 18.* Minneapolis, MN: Free Spirit Press.

McCoy, K. (1982). *Coping with teenage depression: A parents' guide.* New York: New American Library, Mosby.

Montmayor, R. (1984). Changes in parent and peer relationships between childhood and adolescence: a research agenda for gifted adolescents. *Journal for the Education of the Gifted, 8*(1), 9–23.

Offer, D., Ostrov, E., and Howard, K. (1981). *The adolescent: A psychological self-portrait.* New York: Basic Books.

Piechowski, M. and Colangelo, N. (1982). Developmental potential of the gifted. *Gifted Child Quarterly, 8*(2), 80–88.

Silverman, L. (in press). Issues affecting the counseling of older gifted students. In T. M. Buescher (Ed.), *Counseling gifted and talented adolescents: A resource guide.* Evanston, IL: Midwest Talent Search Project, Northwestern University.

Smith, E. B., Goodman, K., and Meredith, R. (1982). *Language, thinking and reading in the elementary school.* New York: Holt, Rinehart and Winston.

Youniss, J. and Smollar, J. (1985). *Adolescent relations with parents and friends.* Chicago: University of Chicago Press.

16

Specialized Counseling Services for Gifted Youth and Their Families: A Needs Assessment

Sidney M. Moon, Kevin R. Kelly, and John F. Feldhusen

Purdue University

Although many authors have recommended counseling for the gifted (Colangelo, 1991; Kerr, 1986; Silverman, 1993b), little research has been done to find out what types of counseling services parents, teachers, and counseling professionals believe to be most beneficial to the development of gifted and talented individuals (Myers & Pace, 1986; Passow, 1991; Shore, Cornell, Robinson, & Ward, 1991). In this study 335 parents, school personnel, and related counseling professionals were surveyed to determine

Editor's Note: From Moon, S. M., Kelly, K. R., & Feldhusen, J. F. (1997). Specialized counseling services for gifted youth and their families: A needs assessment. *Gifted Child Quarterly, 41*(1), 16-25. © 1997 National Association for Gifted Children. Reprinted with permission.

their perceptions of the specialized counseling needs of gifted children and adolescents as part of a needs assessment for a proposed university-based counseling center. Results indicated that all groups of respondents believed that gifted and talented youth have important social, emotional, family, and talent and career development needs that can best be met by differentiated counseling services; and that such services are not readily available to gifted youth. Implications of the study for the development of counseling services and the training of counseling professionals are discussed.

COUNSELING SERVICES

A number of scholars have suggested that gifted students have unique counseling and guidance needs (Colangelo, 1991; Dettman & Colangelo, 1980; Hollingworth, 1926; Frederickson, 1986; McMann & Oliver, 1988; Milgram, 1991; Silverman, 1991, 1993b; Webb, Meckstroth, & Tolan, 1982). However, little research has been conducted to determine how different groups perceive those needs or the exact nature of the needs (Myers & Pace, 1986; Passow, 1991; Shore, Cornell, Robinson, & Ward, 1991). The purpose of this study was to determine the types of counseling services parents, teachers, counselors, and related professionals perceived is important for a university-based counseling center to offer to gifted youth and their families. Items for the needs assessment were generated after an extensive review of the literature related to the specialized assessment and counseling needs of gifted and talented youth.

REVIEW OF THE LITERATURE

Psychoeducational and Talent Assessment

The identification of talent, especially intellectual and academic talent, often involves some type of psychoeducational assessment. The instruments most frequently used in schools to identify intellectual and academic talent are group achievement tests. However, grade-level standardized achievement tests do not provide information on cognitive processing abilities, address only a narrow range of potential intellectual abilities (Gardner, 1983; Maker, 1996), are subject to ceiling effects (Feldhusen & Baska, 1989; Feldhusen & Jarwan, 1993; Silverman, 1989), and tend to be culturally and linguistically biased (Maker, 1996).

Putting the Research to Use

Our study suggests that parents and professionals perceive that talented youth and their families have unique social, emotional, and guidance needs that require differentiated counseling services. Historically, the field of gifted education has devoted a great deal of attention to meeting the learning needs of talented youth through differentiated curriculum and very little attention to meeting the social, emotional, and career development needs of talented youth through differentiated counseling services. If differentiated counseling services are to become routinely available to talented youth and their families, much work will need to be done. Universities will need to provide counselors-in-training with coursework on gifted and talented youth and experiences in working with talented youth and their families. Models of differentiated counseling will need to be developed and evaluated. Research will need to be conducted to determine what counseling strategies are most effective with what types of issues and whether traditional counseling models need to be altered when working with gifted or talented persons. The results of this study can be used by parents and professionals to advocate for increased attention to the development of differentiated counseling services for talented youth and their families.

Individual intelligence tests provide more accurate information on intellectual processing, but are more time consuming and expensive to administer and so are rarely available to gifted children through the schools. Individual intelligence testing has been recommended for the identification of intellectually gifted children, especially the highly gifted (Silverman, 1989), candidates for grade acceleration (Proctor, Feldhusen, & Black, 1988), underachievers (Rimm, 1995), and twice-exceptional children (Barton & Starnes, 1989). Boodoo, Bradley, Frontera, Pitts, and Wright (1989) conducted two statewide surveys and found that learning disabled gifted children were not being identified or served in most school districts. Individual intelligence tests that contain subscales related to different cognitive domains (such as verbal, spatial, and logical-sequential) are particularly helpful in assessing and serving gifted children with learning disabilities and/or attention deficit disorders. Such students tend to have significant amounts of scatter in subtest scores and subtest patterns specific to their ability-deficit profile (Barton & Starnes, 1989; Fox, 1983; Schiff, Kaufman, & Kaufman, 1981; Suter & Wolf, 1987).

In addition, assessment services are not widely available in schools for children talented in domains other than the intellectual-academic such as creativity, the visual and performing arts, the vocational arts, and the intra and interpersonal domains (Feldhusen, 1995; Gardner, 1983). This is due, in part, to the fact that these talent areas are difficult to assess psychometrically. For example, the assessment of creativity (Tannenbaum, 1983) and the identification of visual art talent (Clark & Zimmerman, 1984) have been hampered by a lack of reliable and valid assessment instruments. To identify talent in the visual and performing arts, Clark and Zimmerman (1984) recommended using a variety of methods including standardized art and creativity tests, portfolios of work completed, drawing tasks, structured nominations, behavioral checklists, biographical inventories, student interviews, and observations of artistic performance. However, such multiple-criteria assessment services for the visual and performing arts are usually not provided to talented youth in school settings. Similarly, few schools provide comprehensive assessment of specific talents in other nonacademic domains such as leadership, dance, or the vocational subjects (Feldhusen, 1995). This study addressed the perceived need for talent assessment services.

Psychosocial Adjustment

In general, researchers have found that mildly and moderately intellectually gifted youth exhibit better than average psychosocial adjustment (Janos & Robinson, 1985; Robinson & Noble, 1991). Most intellectually gifted youth also appear to have no major deficits in self-esteem, especially academic self-esteem (Hoge & Renzulli, 1991, 1993). However, clinical sources suggest that talented children are subject to unique stressors and are vulnerable to difficulties with social/emotional adjustment (Genshaft, Greenbaum, & Borovsky, 1995; Hoge & Renzulli, 1991; Hollinger, 1995; Silverman, 1993a, 1994; Webb, Meckstroth, & Tolan, 1982). Gifted children have characteristics such as intensity, sensitivity, overexcitabilities, high energy levels, low tolerance for frustration, pressure to meet internal and external expectations, and perfectionism that can make them vulnerable to social/emotional problems and bring them into conflict with their environment, especially when family or school conditions are not optimal (Ford, 1989; Hafenstein, 1995; Kitano, 1990; Lewis, Kitano, & Lynch, 1992; Lovecky, 1992; Mendaglio, 1993; Roberts & Lovett, 1984; Sowa, McIntire, May, & Bland, 1994; Waldroo, 1990).

Adolescence appears to be a time of particular vulnerability for gifted and talented youth (Robinson & Noble, 1991). Gifted adolescents experience conflicts between achievement and affiliation needs (Gross, 1989; Clasen & Clasen, 1995) and develop specific coping strategies to deal with anticipated peer rejection which may involve denying their talents (Cross, Coleman, & Terhaar-Yonkers, 1991; Clasen & Clasen, 1995). The subpopulations of gifted students most likely to use the denial strategy are the highly gifted, gifted females, and the verbally talented (Dauber & Benbow, 1990; Silverman, 1995; Swiatek, 1995).

Although most academically and intellectually talented students are high achievers, some underachieve in school (Colangelo, Kerr, Christensen, & Maxey, 1993; Dowdall & Colangelo, 1982; Peterson & Colangelo, 1996; Rimm, 1995). Many underachieving gifted children have psychosocial adjustment problems (Dowdall & Colangelo, 1982). Researchers have hypothesized a number of possible causes for underachievement among gifted children including poverty, boredom, inappropriate school environments, personal adjustment problems, peer influences, social self-defense, and family problems (Compton, 1982; Dowdall & Colangelo, 1982; Kolb & Jussim, 1993; Pirozzo, 1982; Rimm, 1995b, 1995c; Rimm & Lowe, 1988).

Many scholars have recommended that systematic efforts be made to address the unique social/emotional needs of gifted and talented children through differentiated psycho-educational and counseling interventions (Colangelo, 1991; Kerr, 1991; Milgram, 1991; Silverman, 1993a; Shore, Cornell, Robinson, & Ward, 1991; VanTassel-Baska, 1990; Webb & DeVries, 1993). Similarly, numerous counseling services have been recommended for intellectually and academically talented students who are underachieving in school including differentiated educational guidance (Peterson & Colangelo, 1996), family counseling (Zuccone & Amerikaner, 1986), and collaborative school-family planning (Fine & Pitts, 1980; Rimm, 1995). The present study was conducted to determine the extent to which parents, school personnel, and community counselors perceived a need for the development of specialized counseling services designed to help both achieving and underachieving gifted youth with psychosocial adjustment issues related to their giftedness.

Family Development

Giftedness appears to function as a stressor in many families, creating unique parenting challenges (Keirouz, 1990; Moon, Jurich, & Feldhusen, in press; Rimm, 1995). Concerns of parents of gifted children include family roles and relationships; parental self-concepts; family adaptations; peer relationships; underachievement; identification and labeling; and school programming (Colangelo, 1988, 1991; Hackney, 1981; Keirouz, 1990; McMann & Oliver, 1988; Silverman & Kearney, 1989; Wierczerkowski & Prado, 1991). Family values, relationships, and styles of parenting can influence the ways that giftedness develops as well as the social/emotional adjustment of gifted children (Bloom, 1985; Moon, Jurich, & Feldhusen, in press; Gelbrich & Hare, 1989; Olszewski, Kulieke, & Buescher, 1987). Parents of gifted children appear to benefit from specialized guidance and support groups (Meckstroth, 1991; Webb & DeVries, 1993), and several sources have recommended that differentiated counseling services be provided to families of gifted youth (Colangelo, 1991; Dettman & Colangelo, 1980; Silverman, 1993a; Moon, Nelson, & Piercy, 1993; Porter & Meyers, 1995). One of the goals of this study was to determine whether counselors, educators, and parents perceived families of gifted and talented children as needing differentiated counseling services.

Counselor Attitudes and Preparation

There appears to be a shortage of counseling personnel trained to work with gifted students and their families (Ford & Harris, 1995; Shore, Cornell,

Robinson, & Ward, 1991). Ford and Harris (1995) found that university counselors had little awareness of the special needs of gifted students. Deiulio (1984) cited the Marland report to support a claim that counselors and psychologists are more indifferent and/or hostile toward gifted students than any other group of professionals and Robinson (1986) found that such negative attitudes persisted over time. Attitudes of counselors toward gifted students appear to be more favorable in schools with gifted programs (Wiener, 1968), suggesting that awareness of the needs of talented students can improve attitudes and, presumably, the quality of services provided. Increased preservice and inservice training programs on working with gifted youth have been recommended for counselors (Ford & Harris, 1995). Perceptions of the need for specialized training for school teachers and principals, school counselors and psychologists, and community counselors were assessed in this study.

Educational and Career Development

Gifted adolescents also have a distinct pattern of career development. High academic talent has been reliably associated with career maturity (Kelly, 1992; Kelly & Colangelo, 1990). Gifted students begin to consider occupational options as early as elementary school and have more extensive knowledge of careers than their peers not identified as gifted (Kelly & Cobb, 1991). Because of their high level of accomplishment, gifted students also routinely aspire to occupations that require an extensive course of educational and professional training (Kelly, 1994). Because of their precocious career maturity and knowledge of careers and high level of aspiration, gifted students have unique counseling needs. For example, they are able to benefit from systematic career exploration and planning in early adolescence. They also need to be introduced to career information that is not routinely available in most high school guidance counseling curricula and to be helped to plan high school and college curricula that will enable the pursuit of graduate and professional training. Unfortunately, available evidence indicates that many gifted adults are dissatisfied with the quality of career counseling and educational planning they received as adolescents (Kerr & Colangelo, 1988; Montgomery & Benbow, 1992; Post-Kramer & Perrone, 1983). One of the goals of this study was to determine if parents and educators perceived gifted students as having differentiated career counseling needs.

PURPOSE OF THE STUDY

Although the need for psychosocial, educational, and career counseling for gifted students has been recognized, little research has been done to determine the types of counseling services that would be most beneficial to such students. The purpose of this study was to assess the types of counseling services parents, teachers, counselors, and related professionals perceived important for gifted youth and their families so that differentiated services could be developed to meet the perceived needs. A secondary purpose was to compare the perspectives of parents and professionals.

METHOD

Research Design

The study was a needs assessment in the traditions of action research (Borg, Gall, & Gall, 1993; King & Lonquist, 1995) and evaluation research (Madaus, Scriven, & Stufflebeam, 1983) conducted to guide local decision making and to add to the knowledge base about perceived counseling needs of talented youth. Borland (1989) argued that effective programming for gifted students "is more likely to emerge from a systematic, diagnostic-prescriptive approach to program planning" (p. 73) that takes into account the needs of stakeholders and includes an empirical needs assessment.

The needs assessment reported here was conducted to aid the systematic development of a multi-service counseling center for gifted youth and their families. A survey was designed and distributed to a regional sample of parents, school personnel, community counselors, and professors. The survey gathered information on the perceptions of the respondents regarding the counseling services that gifted children and their families needed that were different from the typical counseling services offered in schools and communities.

Participants

The survey was mailed to (a) *parents* of children enrolled in Saturday and summer programs at a midwestern university, (b) *coordinators of gifted education* with instructions to copy and distribute the survey as widely as possible to teachers, principals, school counselors, and parents within their school district, (c) *community counselors* identified from the yellow pages of the phone book with instructions to copy the survey and distribute it to their colleagues, and (d) *professors* in counseling-related fields. The manner of distribution was motivated by pragmatic considerations that made it impossible to keep an exact count of the number of surveys distributed. A total of 335 individuals responded to the survey. This total was comprised of four groups: *parents* ($n = 64$), *school personnel* (teachers, gifted program coordinators, school administrators, school principals) ($n = 238$), *counseling professionals* working in the community ($n = 15$), and *professors* in counseling-related fields ($n = 18$).

Data Collection

Three parallel forms of the survey were developed and used in the research: A Parent Form, a School Form, and a Counselor Form (for community counselors and professors in counseling-related disciplines). Items for the survey were generated by the authors after a thorough search of the literature on the counseling needs of gifted and talented youth and grouped into categories. An early draft of the survey was piloted with five adults. They were asked to complete the survey and write comments wherever they perceived errors, omissions, or lack of clarity. Their responses were used to generate a new version of the survey which was field tested on a small sample, found to be satisfactory, and used as the final survey instrument.

The different forms shared the same core items. The wording of each form was matched to the perspective of the respondent. Six core need areas were assessed: general needs (6 items), testing and assessment services (10 items), guidance services (5 items), training and educational services (4 items), counseling concerns (12 items), and consultation (4 items). Respondents used a five-point scale to respond to each item (definitely omit = 1; definitely include = 5). Thus higher scores reflected greater perceived need for the service described in each item. At the end of each core area, space was left for participants to write open-ended comments. Most participants wrote comments in at least some sections, and many wrote extensive comments.

Data Analysis

Both quantitative and qualitative methods of data analysis were employed. Two types of quantitative analyses were conducted, descriptive and inferential. For the descriptive analyses, responses to individual Likert scale items for the entire sample ($n = 335$) were examined. Means and standard deviations were calculated and relative highs and lows on these items were identified. For the inferential analyses, a composite score was calculated for each of the six core areas (testing and assessment, guidance services, etc.). Then scores in each of these areas were compared with ANOVAs for the four groups responding to the survey (parents, school personnel, community counselors, professors). Whenever there was a significant difference in the composite variable, individual ANOVAs were conducted for each scale item. A simple comparison between parents and school personnel was also conducted.

In addition, a qualitative, content analysis of the open-ended questions was conducted. Both school personnel and parents added many comments about counseling services for the gifted. These comments were categorized and analyzed using the techniques of analytic induction and enumeration (Goetz & LeCompte, 1984).

RESULTS

Quantitative Analysis

Means and standard deviations for general needs assessment items and the items for each service area are listed in Table 1. Means for the composites for all of the service areas were > 4.0, indicating that respondents perceived that differentiated services were needed in all six of the core need areas. In the general needs section, respondents were asked about the counseling needs of gifted youth in three different age ranges (children 3–11, adolescents, and young adults). The age group with the greatest perceived need for counseling services was adolescents ($M = 4.28$), followed closely by young adults ($M = 4.04$) and children ($M = 3.97$). Families of gifted children were also perceived as needing services ($M = 4.17$).

Testing and assessment services. The highest perceived needs in this area were career interest assessment ($M = 4.39$); individual intelligence testing ($M = 4.31$); and talent assessment in the creative and performing arts, sciences, and humanities ($M = 4.30$). The least urgent perceived needs were group achievement testing ($M = 3.14$) and group intelligence testing ($M = 3.30$). Respondent comments suggested that group testing was perceived as having lesser importance because group achievement and intelligence test results were readily available through the statewide testing program administered by the schools. The composite score for this area was $M = 4.00$.

Guidance services. Perceived need was high for all services in this area. The highest areas of need were guidance for parents of the gifted ($M = 4.47$) and educational planning ($M = 4.44$). The composite score for guidance services was $M = 4.34$.

Training and education services. The greatest perceived needs in this area were for training programs for teachers/principals ($M = 4.49$), training programs for school counselors and psychologists ($M = 4.46$), and educational programs for parents ($M = 4.35$). The least concern was expressed for training programs for community counselors ($M = 4.06$). However, this mean was still > 4.00, indicating that respondents perceived a need for specialized training for community counselors as well as school personnel and parents. The composite score for training and educational services was high ($M = 4.34$).

Counseling concerns. Great need was expressed for counseling in four areas: peer relationships ($M = 4.54$), emotional adjustment ($M = 4.53$), social adjustment ($M = 4.52$), and stress management ($M = 4.51$). Also deemed important were underachievement ($M = 4.38$), school and/or work relationships ($M = 4.27$), parenting and family relationships ($M = 4.26$ and 4.21, respectively), and depression ($M = 4.22$). The least need for specialized counseling services was perceived for death of a family member ($M = 3.70$), divorce and remarriage ($M = 3.92$), and alcohol/drug use ($M = 3.96$). Respondent comments suggested that the latter three areas were perceived as impacting all young people in similar ways and, therefore, not requiring differentiated counseling services for the gifted and talented.

Consultation. Respondents were asked whether they would consult with a university-based counseling center for emotional, behavioral, academic, and/or social problems. There was little variance in the responses. Means for all items

Table I   Descriptive Data for Individual Survey Items

	M	SD
General Needs Assessment		
1. Many gifted and talented adolescents would benefit from professional guidance and counseling services	4.28	0.77
2. Families of gifted children would benefit from professional guidance in raising their gifted children	4.17	0.80
3. Many gifted and talented young adults would benefit from professional guidance and counseling services	4.04	0.87
4. Many gifted and talented children (ages 3–11) would benefit from professional counseling and guidance services	3.97	0.86
Composite score	**4.12**	**0.84**
Testing and Assessment Services		
1. Career interest assessment	4.39	0.84
2. Individual intelligence testing	4.31	1.07
3. Talent assessment	4.30	0.87
4. Individual achievement testing	4.11	1.19
5. Learning disabilities testing	4.04	1.20
6. Personality testing	3.81	1.06
7. Group intelligence testing	3.31	1.26
8. Group achievement testing	3.15	1.27
Composite score	**4.00**	**0.96**
Guidance Services		
1. Guidance for parents of gifted	4.47	0.83
2. Educational planning	4.44	0.84
3. Talent development planning	4.33	0.80
4. Career planning	4.31	0.84
5. Career mentoring	4.14	0.91
Composite score	**4.34**	**0.84**
Training and Education Services		
1. Training programs for teachers and principals	4.49	0.76
2. Training programs for school counselors and psychologists	4.46	0.80
3. Educational programs for parents on parenting the gifted	4.35	0.81
4. Training programs for community counselors, family therapists, etc.	4.06	0.80
Composite score	**4.34**	**0.80**
Counseling Concerns		
1. Peer relationships	4.54	0.75
2. Emotional adjustment	4.53	0.77
3. Social adjustment	4.52	0.77
4. Stress management	4.51	0.78
5. Underachievement	4.38	0.83
6. School and/or work relationships	4.27	0.82

(Continued)

Table 1   (Continued)

	M	SD
7. Parenting	4.26	0.91
8. Depression	4.22	0.93
9. Family relationships	4.21	0.89
10. Alcohol/drug use	3.97	1.03
11. Divorce/remarriage/stepparenting	3.92	1.03
12. Death of a family member	3.70	1.10
Composite score	**4.25**	**0.92**
Consultation		
I would consult with a university-based counseling and		
guidance center for the gifted if:		
1. My child had emotional problems	4.05	0.90
2. My child had behavioral problems	4.09	0.94
3. My child had academic problems	4.05	0.90
4. My child had social problems	4.00	0.92
Composite score	**4.05**	**0.91**

were about 4.00 (see Table 1), suggesting that respondents felt they would receive moderately strong benefits from consultation with professionals trained in providing differentiated counseling services for the gifted and talented in all of the four problem categories.

Group differences on composite variables. Perceptions of need did not differ very much among the four different groups of respondents (parents, school personnel, community counselors, university professors), suggesting that in general all four groups of stakeholders held fairly similar views of the services needed. However, it should be noted that the groups were unequal in size and the size of the community counselor and professor groups quite small, so the power of the analyses to detect differences was not great.

There was a significant group effect for the testing and assessment composite; F (3, 316) = 3.10, $p < .03$. Post-hoc testing did not reveal any significant differences between groups even though the differences between the parent and community counselor composite means were 1.5 pooled standard deviations apart (parent $M = 3.54$; school personnel $M = 3.08$; community counselor $M = 2.08$; professor $M = 2.82$). There also was a significant group effect for the training and education services composite; F (3, 326) = 4.00, $p < .008$. There were significant group differences for items 1 (education programs for parents on parenting the gifted); F (3, 328) = 5.47, $p < .001$; and item 2 (training programs for teachers and principals); F (3, 327) = 4.14, $p < .007$. Regarding item 1, community counselors saw a greater need for training programs for parents ($M = 4.87$) than parents themselves reported ($M = 4.10$). For item 2, community counselors perceived a greater need for training programs for teachers and principals ($M = 5.00$) than school personnel judged themselves to need ($M = 4.43$).

Qualitative Analysis

Several respondents wrote comments that expressed a strong overall need for increased counseling services for the gifted. Overall support was expressed in many different ways. One parent said: "As a parent I think it would be a comfort to know I have someplace to turn for guidance in the above areas, if I felt I needed help."

Several respondents ($n = 14$) wrote some variation of "all" at the end of one or more of the core sections of the survey. "There is a definite need for assistance in all of these areas" said one school respondent. A parent agreed, "Every item in this section needs to be addressed. We have been confronted by each one."

The three categories of specific services mentioned most often by the respondents in their comments were (a) parent/family counseling and education ($n = 44$), (b) training for professionals ($n = 42$), and (c) educational planning and career development ($n = 38$). Each of these areas is discussed below.

Parent and family counseling services. Both parents ($n = 4$) and school personnel ($n = 6$) commented that parent and family guidance services are "much needed." Respondents felt parents needed education in order to understand the needs of their gifted child. For example, a school respondent wrote, "I think it is hard for parents of gifted children to understand how their child thinks" and a parent wrote, "All the parents we know of gifted kids are desperate for guidance, particularly about emotional issues. The older they get, the more we have anguish about academic habits, etc." Support for parents of gifted children was also perceived as an important need. "Parents need a support system involving other parents of gifted and talented students. This could include a combination of training and group counseling, but just time to interact would be helpful." Some school respondents ($n = 3$) felt that parental support and education would be important to the success of social/emotional counseling services. One school respondent suggested that counseling should also be made available to nongifted children of gifted parents.

Training. A number of parents and school personnel ($n = 10$) wrote that most educators need more training in understanding the social, emotional, and guidance needs of gifted children. School personnel had questions and suggestions about possible training formats and audiences for such services. Those perceived to need training included classroom teachers, secondary teachers, school counselors, and administrators. One school respondent wrote, "Obviously there is a great need for counselors in public schools to obtain training in gifted work. Teachers would benefit through observation of classroom strategies and counseling sessions. Administrators definitely need to avail themselves of as much information on the gifted as their school systems will allow." Concerns listed by school respondents as possible hindrances to training efforts included accessibility ($n = 3$) and time ($n = 2$).

Educational planning and career development. Several respondents wrote comments indicating that they perceived a need for specialized career assessment and guidance for gifted students, especially high school students ($n = 11$). Parents wrote comments like this, "These children definitely need help in focusing their career goals and aspirations," and "What I would like is for [gifted children] to be exposed to career choices and to become aware of their talents and how to productively use their talents for their enjoyment, productivity, and self-satisfaction." Parents expressed no additional concerns about career guidance services. School personnel expressed isolated concerns such as the inappropriateness of existing career assessment instruments for use with gifted populations ($n = 1$).

Special populations. In addition to the three areas of services mentioned most often, a small minority of both school personnel and parents commented on the needs of special populations such as underachieving ($n = 10$) and learning disabled ($n = 10$) gifted students. Comments about these special populations focused on the need for testing for students and support for parents and the importance of making gifted students who were at risk a priority emphasis. For example, one school respondent said, "A major need for me is a spot to get help in diagnosis for children that test high on intelligence but have problems in classroom work."

A parent of a learning-disabled gifted child expressed the need for support this way:

"Indeed, there are many gifted children who are not understood by their parents or community. As a parent of an LD student with an IQ of 130 or more and two above-average students I came to realize that as parents we have a greater need than we are educated to . . . Sharing from others' family experience(s) is very helpful when you feel so alone in trying to do your best for your child, and your family and friends feel you have a retarded child to deal with."

DISCUSSION

The purpose of this study was to determine the perceived need for university-based counseling services for gifted children and their families by parents, school personnel, and related professionals. Respondents indicated strong perceptions of need for almost all of the services included in the survey. Most prominent was the expression of need for specialized services in testing and assessment, career guidance and educational planning, family counseling, and training and education for parents and teachers of the gifted. Although the generalizability of the findings is limited by the regional focus of the survey, the convenience sampling procedures, and the small number of respondents in some of the groups, the study suggested that parents, school personnel, and related professionals are aware of the specialized counseling needs of the gifted, but tend to lack training on how to meet those needs. The survey respondents were united in their belief that differentiated counseling services should be more readily available to gifted and talented children and their families.

Many of the services perceived to be most valuable were either highly specialized or unavailable in the community at an affordable cost. For instance, a need was indicated for individual intelligence testing but not for group achievement testing. Talent assessment in the creative and performing arts, sciences, and humanities was also a perceived need. It is difficult for many able children to gain access to such specialized, expensive talent assessment services.

Many teachers and parents know that their students and children are very intelligent. However, far fewer seem to know the profile of their children's intellectual abilities. Diagnostic testing would be of particular value for parents and teachers of students who are highly able but have co-occurring learning or behavioral disabilities, especially when those disabilities are above the threshold required for identification through special education services or not included in state definitions of special education (as is often true of attention deficit hyperactivity disorder). Many parents and teachers do not know how to meet the challenges of such a child (Moon & Dillon, 1995; Nielsen, Hammond, Higgins, & Williams, 1994). Even for students who do not have disabilities, there seems considerable ambiguity on the part of parents about the level of ability of the child. Effective educational planning can be carried out best with accurate assessment of the individual child's intellectual strengths and weaknesses (Betts, 1985; Feldhusen, Hoover, & Sayler, 1990; Feldhusen & Moon, 1995). This study indicates that too few families and schools have access to this type of information.

There was a clear expression of need for career interest assessment and planning of postsecondary education. Although many schools and colleges provide guidance counseling, most do not provide information about the highly specialized occupations and training programs to which many gifted students aspire (Kerr, 1986; Schroer & Dorn, 1986). Neither do most school counselors, because of time limitations and heavy job demands, routinely work with parents and students to map out an educational plan to enable the talented child to maximize her or his development. There is a definite need for differentiated career planning for gifted students in conjunction with educational planning. For the gifted child, this should include planning for baccalaureate education and graduate or professional training.

An unequivocal need was expressed for family counseling with families with gifted children. Again, it should be appreciated that this is a specialized service. Family counseling is rather widely available. However, relatively few family counselors know how gifted children influence family dynamics.

Identification affects the child, the parents, and the child's siblings (Colangelo, 1991). Changes in the child's educational program and attempts by the parents to provide appropriate academic experiences for the gifted child affect all family members (Hackney, 1981; Keirouz, 1990; Moon, Jurich, & Feldhusen, in press; Rimm, 1995; Silverman, 1993b). These systemic effects have been well documented in the gifted education literature but are not well known outside the discipline. Widespread availability of family counseling would be welcomed by both parents and teachers.

Training and education services for school personnel and parents were also perceived as a high priority. This finding suggests that schools need to provide inservice training for teachers, administrators, counselors, and school psychologists on the unique counseling needs of the gifted and that colleges and universities should incorporate coursework on the gifted and talented into their undergraduate and graduate training programs for these groups of professionals. Parent education can be provided in a variety of settings and formats. Schools, mental health agencies, and universities can all sponsor parent support groups for parents of the gifted. Parents can also be encouraged to attend Supporting the Social and Emotional Needs of the Gifted (SENG) conferences or to join the National Association for Gifted and Talented Children or the Council for Exceptional Children's special interest group on the Talented and Gifted (TAG).

Overall, the needs assessment was informative. The results suggested that awareness of the specialized counseling needs of the gifted is generally quite high, but that services and trained personnel are not readily available. The results are being used by the authors to develop an interdisciplinary counseling center with three integrated services for gifted and talented youth: psychoeducational assessment; family counseling for social/emotional concerns and underachievement; and educational and career planning. The results also provide focus for others interested in providing counseling services for the gifted whether in school, community, or university settings. Such services should not duplicate existing services and resources. They should be differentiated for the special needs of the gifted and talented. The survey also indicated the need for interdisciplinary cooperation in order to provide the needed services. The differentiated counseling services needed by the gifted and talented cannot be provided by a single professional group. Schools or specialized centers that want to meet the counseling needs of the gifted must actively seek the cooperation of educators, counselors, social workers, family therapists, and psychologists.

REFERENCES

Barton, J. M., & Starnes, W. T. (1989). Identifying distinguishing characteristics of gifted and talented/learning disabled students. *Roeper Review, 12*(1), 23–28.

Betts, G. T. (1985). *The autonomous learner model for the gifted and talented.* Fort Collins, CO: Alps.

Bloom, B. S. (Ed.) (1985). *Developing talent in young people.* New York: Ballentine Books.

Boodoo, G. M., Bradley, C. L., Frontera, R. L., Pitts, J. R., & Wright, L. B. (1989). A survey of procedures used for identifying gifted learning disabled children. *Gifted Child Quarterly, 33,* 110–114.

Borg, W. R., Gall, J. P., & Gall, M. D. (1993). *Applying educational research: A practical guide.* New York: Longman.

Borland, J. H. (1989). *Planning and implementing programs for the gifted.* New York: Teachers College Press.

Clark, G. A., & Zimmerman, E. D. (1984). *Educating artistically talented students.* Syracuse, NY: Syracuse University Press.

Clasen, D. R., & Clasen, R. E. (1995). Underachievement of highly able students and the peer society. *Gifted and Talented International, 10,* 67–76.

Colangelo, N. (1988). Families of gifted children: The next ten years. *Roeper Review, 11,* 16–54.

Colangelo, N. (1991). Counseling gifted students. In N. Colangelo & G. A. Davis (Eds.), *Handbook of gifted education* (pp. 273–284). Boston, MA: Allyn & Bacon.

Colangelo, N., Kerr; B., Christensen, P., & Maxey, J. (1993). A comparison of gifted underachievers and gifted high achievers. *Gifted Child Quarterly, 37,* 155–160.

Compton, M. F. (1982). The gifted underachiever in middle school. *Roeper Review, 4*(4), 23–25.

Cross, T. L., Coleman, L. J., & Terhaar-Yonkers, M. (1991). The social cognition of gifted adolescents in schools: Managing the stigma of giftedness. *Journal for the Education of the Gifted, 15,* 44–55.

Dauber, S. L., & Benbow, C. P. (1990). Aspects of personality and peer relations of extremely talented adolescents. *Gifted Child Quarterly, 34,* 10–15.

Deiulio, J. M. (1984). Attitudes of school counselors and psychologists toward gifted children. *Journal for the Education of the Gifted, 7,* 164–169.

Dettman, D. F., & Colangelo, N. (1980). A functional model for counseling parents of gifted students. *Gifted Child Quarterly, 24,* 158–161.

Dowdall, C. B., & Colangelo, N. (1982). Underachieving gifted students: Review and implications. *Gifted Child Quarterly 26,* 179–180.

Falk, C. R. (1987, September). Children's perceptions of the effects of divorce on school life. Paper presented at the annual convention of the American Psychological Association, New York.

Feldhusen, J. F. (1995). *Talent identification and development in education, 2nd ed.* Sarasota, FL: Center for Creative Learning.

Feldhusen, J. F. & Baska, L. K. (1989). Identification and assessment; of the gifted. In J. F. Feldhusen, J. Van Tassel-Baska, & K. Seeley (Eds.), *Excellence in educating the gifted* (pp. 84–101). Denver: Love.

Feldhusen, J. F., & Jarwan, F. A. (1993). Identification of gifted and talented youth for educational programs. In K. A. Heller, F. J. Monks, & A. H. Passow (Eds.), *International Handbook of Research and Development of Giftedness and Talent* (pp. 233–251). Oxford, England: Pergamon.

Feldhusen, J. F., & Moon, S. M. (1995). The educational continuum and delivery of services. In J. L. Genshaft, M. Birely, & C. L. Hollinger (Eds.), *Serving gifted and talented students: A resource for school personnel* (pp. 103–121). Austin, TX: PRO-ED.

Feldhusen, J. F., Hoover, S. M., & Sayler, M. F. (1990). *Identifying and educating gifted students at the secondary level.* Monroe, NY: Trillium Press.

Fine, M. J., & Pitts, R. (1980). Intervention with underachieving gifted children: Rationale and strategies. *Gifted Child Quarterly, 24,* 51–55.

Ford, D. Y. (1995). *Counseling gifted African American students: Promoting achievement, identity, and social and emotional well-being.* Storrs, CT: National Research Center for the Gifted and Talented.

Ford, D. Y., & Harris, J. (1995). Exploring university counselors' perceptions of distinctions between gifted black and gifted white students. *Journal of Counseling and Development, 73,* 443–450.

Ford, M. (1989). Students' perceptions of affective issues impacting their social emotional development and school performance of gifted/talented youngsters. *Roeper Review, 11*(3), 131–134.

Fox, L. H. (1983). Gifted students with reading problems: An empirical study. In L. H. Fox (Ed.), *Learning-disabled gifted children* (pp. 117–139). Baltimore: University Park Press.

Frederickson, R. H. (1986). Preparing gifted and talented students for the world of work. *Journal of Counseling and Development, 64,* 556–557.

Gardner, H. (1983). *Frames of mind: The theory of multiple intelligences.* New York: Basic Books.

Gelbrich, J. A., & Hare, E. K. (1989). The effects of single parenthood on school achievement in a gifted population. *Gifted Child Quarterly; 33,* 115–117.

Genshaft, J. L., Greenbaum, S., & Borovsky, S. (1995). Stress and the gifted. In J. L. Genshaft, M. Birely, & C. L. Hollinger (Eds.). *Serving gifted and talented students: A resource for school personnel* (pp. 257–268). Austin, TX: PRO-ED.

Goetz, J. R., & LeCompte, M. D. (1984). *Ethnography and qualitative design in educational research.* San Diego, CA: Academic Press.

Gross, U. M. (1989). The pursuit of excellence or the search for intimacy? The forced-choice dilemma of gifted youth. *Roeper Review, 11,* 189–194.

Hackney, H. (1981). The gifted child, the family, and the school. *Gifted Child Quarterly, 25,* 51–54.

Hafenstein, N. L. (1985, September). Pyschological intensities in your gifted children. Paper presented at the Esther Katz Rosen Symposium on the Psychological Development of Gifted Children, Lawrence, KS.

Hoge, R. D., & Renzulli, J. S. (1991). *Self-concept and the gifted child.* Storrs, CT: National Research Center on the Gifted and Talented.

Hoge, R. D., & Renzulli, J. S. (1993). Exploring the link between giftedness and self-concept. *Review of Educational Research, 63,* 449–465.

Hollinger, C. L. (1995). Counseling gifted young women about educational and career choices. In J. L. Genshaft, M. Bireley, & C. L. Hollinger (Eds.). *Serving gifted and talented students: A resource for school personnel* (pp. 337–350). Austin, TX: PRO-ED.

Hollingworth, L. S. (1926). *Gifted children: Their nature and nurture.* New York: Macmillan.

Janos, P. M., & Robinson, N. M. (1985). Psychosocial development in intellectually gifted children. In F. D. Horowitz, & M. O'Brien (Eds.), *The gifted and talented: Developmental perspectives* (pp. 149–195). Washington, DC: American Psychological Association.

Keirouz, K. S. (1990). Concerns of parents of gifted children: A research review. *Gifted Child Quarterly, 34,* 56–63.

Kelly, K. R. (1992). Career maturity of young gifted adolescents: A replication study. *Journal for the Education of the Gifted, 16,* 36–45.

Kelly, K. R. (1994). Career planning and counseling for highly able students. In J. B. Hansen and S. M. Hoover (Eds.), *Talent development theories and practice* (pp. 281–296). Dubuque, IA: Kendall/Hunt Publishing Company.

Kelly, K. R., & Cobb, S. J. (1991). A profile of the career development characteristics of young gifted adolescents: Examining gender and multicultural differences. *Roeper Review, 13*, 168–175.

Kelly, K. R., & Colangelo, N. (1990). Effects of academic ability and gender on career development. *Journal for the Education of the Gifted, 13*, 168–175.

Kerr, B. (1991). *Handbook for counseling the gifted and talented.* Alexandria, VA: AACD.

Kerr, B. A. (1986). Career counseling for the gifted: Assessments and interventions. *Journal of Counseling and Development, 64*, 602–604.

Kerr, B. A. (1988). The college plans of academically talented students. *Journal of Counseling and Development, 67*, 42–49.

Kerr, B., & Colangelo, N. (1988). The college plans of academically talented students. *Journal of Counseling and Development, 67*, 42–49.

King, J. P., & Lonquist, M. D. (1995, April). A review of writing on action research. Paper presented at the American Educational Research Association, San Francisco.

Kitano, M. K. (1990). Intellectual abilities and psychological intensities in young children: Implications for the gifted. *Roeper Review, 13*(1), 5–10.

Kolb, L., & Jussim, K. J. (1993). Teacher expectations and underachieving gifted children. *Roeper Review, 17*(1), 26–30.

Lewis, R. B., Kitano, M. K., & Lynch, E. M. (1992). Psychological intensities in gifted adults. *Roeper Review, 15*(1), 25–31.

Lovecky, D. V. (1992). Exploring social and emotional aspects of giftedness in children. *Roeper Review, 15*(1), 18–25.

Madaus, G. F., Scriven, M., & Stufflebeam, D. L. (1983). *Evaluation models: Viewpoints on educational and human services evaluation* (pp. 23–43). Boston: Kluwer-Nijhoff.

Maker, J. (1996). Identification of gifted minority students: A national problem, needed changes, and a promising solution. *Gifted Child Quarterly, 40*, 41–50.

McMann, M., & Oliver, R. (1988). Problems in families with gifted children: Implications for counselors. *Journal of Counseling and Development, 66*, 275–278.

Meckstroth, E. A. (1991). Guiding parents of gifted children: The role of counselors and teachers. In R. M. Milgram (Ed.), *Counseling gifted and talented children: A guide for teachers, counselors, and parents* (pp. 95–120). Norwood, NJ: Ablex.

Mendaglio, S. (1993). Counseling gifted learning disabled: Individual and group counseling techniques. In L. K. Silverman (Ed.), *Counseling the gifted and talented* (pp. 131–150). Denver: Love.

Milgram, R. M. (1991). *Counseling gifted and talented children: A guide for teachers, counselors, and parents.* Norwood, NJ: Ablex.

Montgomery, J. L., & Benbow, C. P. (1992). Factors that influence the career aspirations of mathematically precocious females. In N. Colangelo, S. G. Assouline, & D. L. Ambroson (Eds.), *Talent development: Proceedings from the 1991 Henry B. and Jocelyn Wallace National Research Symposium on Talent Develoment* (pp. 384–386). Unionville, NY: Trillium Press.

Moon, S. M., & Dillon, D. R. (1995). Multiple exceptionalities: A case study. *Journal for the Education of the Gifted, 18*, 111–130.

Moon, S. M., Jurich, J. A., & Feldhusen, J. F. (in press). Families of gifted children: Cradles of development. In R. Friedman (Ed.), *Talent in context: Historical and social perspectives.* Washington, DC: APA.

Moon, S. M., Nelson, R. S., & Piercy, F. P. (1993). Family therapy with a highly gifted adolescent. *Journal of Family Psychotherapy, 4*, 1–16.

Myers, R. S., & Pace, T. M. (1986). Counseling gifted and talented students: Historical perspectives and contemporary issues. *Journal of Counseling and Development, 64,* 548–550.

Nielsen, M. E., Hammond, A. E., Higgins, L. D., & Williams, R. A. (1994). Gifted children with disabilities. *Gifted Child Today, 16*(5), 29–36.

Olszewski, R., Kulieke, M., & Buescher, T. (1987). The influence of the family environment on the development of talent: A literature review. *Journal for the Education of the Gifted, 11,* 6–28.

Passow, A. H. (1991). A neglected component of nurturing giftedness: Affective development. *European Journal for High Ability, 2,* 5–11.

Peterson, J. S., & Colangelo, N. (1996). Gifted achievers and underachievers: A comparison of patterns found in school files. *Journal of Counseling and Development, 74,* 399–407.

Pirozzo, R. (1982). Gifted underachievers. *Roeper Review, 4*(4), 18–21.

Plucker, J. A. (1996). Gifted Asian-American students: Identification, curricular, and counseling concerns. *Journal for the Education of the Gifted, 19,* 315–443.

Porter, G., & Meyers, J. (1995). Family consultation as an approach to providing psychoeducational services to gifted children. In J. L. Genshaft, M. Bireley, & C. L. Hollinger (Eds.). *Serving gifted and talented students: A resource for school personnel* (pp. 303–322). Austin, TX: PRO-ED.

Post-Kammer, P., & Perrone, P. (1983). Career perceptions of talented individuals: A follow-up study. *The Vocational Guidance Quarterly, 31,* 203–211.

Proctor, T. B., Feldhusen, J. E., & Black, K. N. (1988). Guidelines for early admission to elementary school. *Psychology in the Schools, 25,* 41–43.

Renzulli, J. S., & Reis, S. M. (1985). *The schoolwide enrichment model: A plan for comprehensive educational excellence.* Mansfield Center, CT: Creative Learning Press.

Rimm, S. B. (1995a). Impact of family patterns upon the development of giftedness. In J. L. Genshaft, M. Bireley, & C. L. Hollinger (Eds.). *Serving gifted and talented students: A resource for school personnel* (pp. 243–256). Austin, TX: PRO-ED.

Rimm, S. B. (1995b). Underachievement syndrome in gifted students. In J. L. Genshaft, M. Birely, & C. L. Hollinger (Eds.). *Serving gifted and talented students: A resource for school personnel* (pp. 173–200). Austin, TX: PRO-ED.

Rimm, S. B. (1995c). *Why bright kids get poor grades and what you can do about it.* New York: Crown.

Rimm, S. B., & Lowe, B. (1988). Family environments of underachieving gifted children. *Gifted Child Quarterly, 32,* 353–359.

Roberts, S. M., & Lovett, S. B. (1994). Examining the "F" in gifted: Academically gifted adolescents' physiological and affective responses to scholastic failure. *Journal for the Education of the Gifted, 17,* 241–259.

Robinson, A. (1986). The identification of gifted children. What does research tell us? In K. A. Heller & J. F. Feldhusen (Eds.), *Identifying and nurturing the gifted: An international perspective* (pp. 103–109). Toronto: Hans Huber.

Robinson, N. M., & Noble, K. D. (1991). Social-emotional development and adjustment of gifted children. In M. C. Wang, M. C. Reynolds, & H. J. Walberg (Eds.), *Handbook of special education: Research and practice* (Vol. 2, pp. 57–76). New York: Pergamon Press.

Schiff, M. M., Kaufman, A. S., & Kaufman, N. L. (1981). Scatter analysis of WISC-R profiles for learning disabled children with superior intelligence. *Journal of Learning Disabilities, 14,* 400–403.

Schroer, A. C. P., & Dorn, F. J. (1986). Enhancing the career and personal development of gifted college students. *Journal of Counseling and Development, 64,* 567–571.

Shore, B. M., Cornell, D. G., Robinson, A., & Ward, S. (1991). *Recommended practices in gifted education.* New York: Teachers College Press.

Silverman, L. K. (1989). The highly gifted. In J. F. Feldhusen, J. Van Tassel-Baska, & K. Seeley (Eds.), *Excellence in educating the gifted* (pp. 71–83). Denver: Love.

Silverman, L. K. (1991). Preventive counseling for the gifted. *Understanding Our Gifted,* 3(4), 1, 11–13.

Silverman, L. K. (Ed.) (1993a). *Counseling the gifted and talented.* Denver: Love Publishing Co.

Silverman, L. K. (1993b). Counseling Families. In L. K. Silverman (Ed.), *Counseling the gifted and talented* (pp. 151–178). Denver: Love.

Silverman, L. K. (1993c). Social development, leadership, & gender issues. In L. K. Silverman (Ed.), *Counseling the gifted and talented* (pp. 291–328). Denver: Love.

Silverman, L. K. (1995). Highly gifted children. In J. L. Genshaft, M. Bireley, & C. L. Hollinger (Eds.). *Serving gifted and talented students: A resource for school personnel* (pp. 217–240). Austin, TX: PRO-ED.

Silverman, L. K. (1994). The moral sensitivity of gifted children and the evolution of society. *Roeper Review, 17*(2), 110–116.

Silverman, L. K., & Kearney, K. (1989). Parents of the extraordinarily gifted. *Advanced Development, 1,* 41–56.

Sowa, C. J., McIntire, J., May, K., & Bland, L. (1994). Social and emotional adjustment themes across gifted children. *Roeper Review, 17*(2), 95–98.

Suter, D. P., & Wolf, J. S. (1987). Issues in the identification and programming of the gifted/learning disabled child. *Journal for the Education of the Gifted, 10,* 227–237.

Swiatek, M. A. (1995). An empirical investigation of the social coping strategies used by gifted adolescents. *Gifted Child Quarterly, 39,* 154–161.

Tannenbaum, A. J. (1983). *Gifted children: Psychological and educational perspective.* New York: Macmillan.

Van Tassel-Baska, J. (1990). *A practical guide to counseling the gifted in a school setting.* Reston, VA: Council for Exceptional Children.

Waldroo, P. B. (1990). A structure for affective education for young gifted children. *Early Child Development and Care, 63,* 119–129.

Webb, J. T., & DeVries, A. R. (1993). *Training manual for facilitators of SENG model group discussions.* Dayton, OH: Ohio Psychology Press.

Webb, J. T., Meckstroth, E. A., & Tolan, S. S. (1982). *Guiding the gifted child.* Columbus, OH: Ohio Psychology.

Wieczerkowski, W., & Prado, T. M. (1991). Parental fears and expectations from the point of view of a counseling center for the gifted. *European Journal of High Ability;* 2, 56–72.

Wiener, J. L. (1968). Attitudes of psychologists and pscyhometrists toward gifted children and programs for the gifted. *Exceptional Children, 34,* 354.

Zuccone, C. F., & Amerikaner, M. (1986). Counseling gifted underachievers: A family systems approach. *Journal of Counseling and Development, 64,* 590–592.

Index

Note: References to tables or figures are indicated by *italic type* and the addition of *"t"* or *"f,"* respectively.

CORWIN PRESS

The Corwin Press logo—a raven striding across an open book—represents the union of courage and learning. Corwin Press is committed to improving education for all learners by publishing books and other professional development resources for those serving the field of K–12 education. By providing practical, hands-on materials, Corwin Press continues to carry out the promise of its motto: **"Helping Educators Do Their Work Better."**